WOMEN

IN THE MAZE

Questions & Answers on Biblical Equality

Ruth A. Tucker

INTERVARSITY PRESS
DOWNERS GROVE, ILLINOIS 60515

InterVarsity Press is the book-publishing division of InterVarsity Christian Fellowship, a student movement active on campus at hundreds of universities, colleges and schools of nursing in the United States of America, and a member movement of the International Fellowship of Evangelical Students. For information about local and regional activities, write Public Relations Dept., InterVarsity Christian Fellowship, 6400 Schroeder Rd., P.O. Box 7895, Madison, WI 53707-7895.

All Scripture quotations, unless otherwise indicated, are from the New Revised Standard Version Bible, copyright 1989, by the Division of Christian Education of the National Council of the Churches of Christ in the USA and used by permission.

Cover illustration: Roberta Polfus

ISBN 0-8308-1307-1

Printed in the United States of America ∞

Library of Congress Cataloging-in-Publication Data

Tucker, Ruth 1945-
    Women in the maze: questions and answers on biblical equality/
  by Ruth A. Tucker.
      p.   cm.
    Includes bibliographical references and index.
    ISBN 0-8308-1307-1
    1. Women in the Bible. 2. Women in Christianity. 3. Patriarchy—
Religious aspects—Christianity. I. Title.
BS575.T83 1992
261.8'344—dc20
                                  91-41728
                                     CIP

17	16	15	14	13	12	11	10	9	8	7	6	5	4	3	2	1
06	05	04	03	02	01	00	99	98	97	96	95	94	93	92		

Introduction

*"Dear God,
Are boys better than girls?
I know you are one,
but try to be fair."[1]*

This simple fifteen-word inquiry, written by a young girl, sums up the whole "women's issue" set before us as Christians.

Are boys better than girls? Is there a difference of position and worth between boys and girls—or men and women? Should men rule or have headship over women? Should they enjoy privileges women are denied? Does the fact that man was created first give him superiority in the scheme of things?

I know you are one. Who is God? Is God a *boy,* as this little girl had been led to believe? We smile at her naiveté, but have we advanced so far beyond it? Don't we adults often think of God very much in masculine terms? Perhaps it is our conception of God that causes us difficulties in regard to women's issues.

Try to be fair. The fairness issue is where the rubber meets the road. How do we apply Scripture? How do biblical injunctions of the first century fit into our contemporary context? What is fair and right and biblical when it comes to male and female relationships and roles?

This book will seek to address these large questions by asking and answering scores of more specific questions—questions that span the ages from the beginning of time to the present day. This is by no means an exhaustive investigation of the topic. Rather, it is a handbook—an easy and accessible guide. The questions are relevant and practical; they bear directly on the debate dividing Christians today. They prompt the reader to think through the issues and challenge the inconsistencies that are prevalent in many of our evangelical churches.

In some instances the questions relate to basic, underlying issues. Why, for example, is it presumed commendable for a man to reverse the effects of the curse in Genesis 3 (toiling amid thorns and thistles by the sweat of his brow), but not commendable for a woman to reverse the part of the curse that declares her husband will rule over her?

In other instances, the questions relate to practices that we tend to take for granted. Why can a woman prepare the Communion bread and fill the cups but, in many churches, not serve them to the people? Does a "literal" rendering of the Bible dictate this practice, or have Christians inadvertently latched onto traditions that discriminate against women?

It is my hope that this book will shed light on the women's issue in the church today and that it will foster harmony and reconciliation between the sexes. With so many challenges facing the church as it moves into the twenty-first century, we must strive to move beyond the acrimonious "in-house" conflicts that denigrate the cause of Christ. We need more people—of both sexes—reaching out with the gospel, not fewer. And we need more partnership and cooperation, not less.

The women's issue is very real and personal to me, and I admit I am unable to approach it in an entirely objective and disinterested manner.

It is an issue that confronts me daily, and one that had a profound impact on my little corner of the world even before I was born.

The setting was a rural community in northern Wisconsin in the 1930s. Enter two "lady preachers"—Miss Salthammer and Miss Cowan—convinced that they were called by God to plant a church where there was no gospel ministry. In the years that followed they did just that. First they opened a Sunday school, and then they initiated church services. They evangelized, visited the sick, taught classes and preached sermons. Finally, when the little church was on solid footing, they moved on to plant other churches, and a succession of male pastors took over the work.

Miss Salthammer and Miss Cowan occasionally returned to my community to teach vacation Bible school, and it was through this ministry that I became acquainted with them. I thought they were rather odd characters, and it has not been until recent years that I have begun to appreciate them for who they were and for the incredible sacrifice they made. Their pay was rarely in cash—it was more often a trunkload of potatoes or turnips—and they lived and died in poverty. Indeed, when Miss Cowan died, she was buried in a pauper's grave. The county paid for her burial because no one else—not even the people of my little country church—came forward with the money.

Today I often wonder if I would be a follower of Christ had it not been for their sacrificial service. Yet there are many Christians who would censure their ministry. Women, they argue, are not supposed to preach or teach. They are not supposed to be the leaders in the church.

Was it wrong for Miss Salthammer and Miss Cowan to plant that little church in northern Wisconsin? Was it wrong for them to preach and teach? And what about other forms of ministry? Is it wrong for a woman to baptize a convert, but praiseworthy if she leads someone to faith in Christ—an activity that involves far more teaching and preaching than does baptizing? Is it wrong for a woman to teach men because, like Eve, she is prone to be deceived, yet not at all objectionable for her to teach little children, whose minds are impressionable?

When I was growing up in that little country church in the 1950s, long after Miss Salthammer and Miss Cowan had moved on, I never heard the voice of a woman preacher. Women were urged to be foreign missionaries, but they could not be preachers. Why the inconsistency? Why is it right for women to preach in Africa, a Kenyan student once asked me, but wrong for them to preach in North America? Was it racism? he wondered.

These are serious questions that we can no longer dismiss. From the standpoint of the church *universal,* and as *world* Christians, we must seriously address the women's issue.

Indeed, this is one of the most critical issues that confront the church today. It touches every member of the Christian community—not just women—and it profoundly affects the image and the very mission of the church worldwide. The evangelical church is at a crossroads. Which way will it go?

The answers to the questions posed in this book will serve as a guide through the maze of inconsistencies and difficulties that have developed over the centuries. Once we have wound our way through that maze, the path to the future will emerge, I hope, in unmistakable clarity.

With this purpose in mind, let's seek to work our way thoughtfully through the questions and answers that lie before us, looking to the guidance of Scripture and to God's leading among his people throughout history and during this present time.*

---

*The terms *traditionalist* and *feminist* (or *egalitarian*) are used throughout the book as they are generally used by contemporary Christians. For amplification of definitions, see chapter 26.

PART 1

God the Father, Son and Holy Spirit

1

Is
God
Masculine?

If the question were worded, "Is God the Father *male*?" many Christians would immediately answer with a resounding no. Yet the impression that God is indeed male may be indelibly imprinted in our subconscious minds, as was seen in the little girl's letter to God. She wrote, "I know you are one"—a boy, that is.

We laugh at the innocence of a child, but in our own minds we struggle with the concept. Though we're sure that God is not *male,* we're less sure when the term *masculine* is used. God is spirit, it is reasoned, so it is impossible for God to be anatomically male, but God could have masculine characteristics—and, indeed, a predominance of masculine or male characteristics.

But what is masculinity apart from physical maleness? Are certain of God's *attributes* more masculine than feminine? That is a difficult issue to tackle without falling into unfounded stereotypes of what actually constitutes masculinity and femininity—distinctions that are often defined much more by cultural norms than by any absolute standard. A man dressed in a Scottish kilt might appear effeminate to an American cowboy, but not to other Scots. In Kenya, adult male friends often hold hands as they are walking down the street—hardly the masculine thing to do in our Western culture. Given the difficulty of absolutely determining real masculinity or femininity, we might turn to Scripture. But Scripture is not clear in describing God as mainly masculine or mainly feminine. Much clearer is a notion that arises out of the first chapter of Genesis, where we find the most striking self-revelation of God in the whole Old Testament: "So God created humankind in his image, in the image of God he created them; male and female he created them" (v. 27).

This offers us a glimpse of the essence of God—one whose image cannot be fully reflected in one sex—who created male and female together to reflect that image equally.

"God is neither masculine nor feminine," writes Susan Foh. "He created the two sexes, he created gender. God existed before such distinctions."[1]

Why does the Bible use only masculine pronouns for God?

If someone were to take issue with the assertion that God is not masculine, the most obvious question would be, "Why, then, is God a *he*?"

"In all languages persons can only be referred to by masculine or feminine pronouns," write Letha Scanzoni and Nancy Hardesty. "Usually in referring to members of a group or a person whose sex is unknown, we use the masculine. It is generic, whereas the feminine is used in reference only to individuals known to be female. God is neither and both. He contains all personhood; we are all made in his image, male and female. In thinking of God we should use neither 'he' nor 'she' but 'Thou' in whose presence we stand at all times."[2]

Paul Jewett enlarges on this theme, emphasizing that the personal pronouns used for God "are to be understood *generically, not specifically.*" He argues that "*personal* pronouns are necessary because God is not the philosophic Absolute or Ground of Being (Tillich) but the God who reveals himself as personal Subject (*I* am who *I* am, Ex. 3:14)."³

Is God's image reflected as fully in woman as in man?

If God were masculine, could a woman, who is feminine by nature, reflect the image of God to the same extent that men do? Many Bible teachers and theologians have argued that the female is not made in the image of God to the same degree that the male is. This argument is tersely summed up by John R. Rice, writing in 1941: "Man is made in the image of God. God is a masculine God. The masculine pronoun is used of God everywhere in the Bible. . . . God is not effeminate. God is not feminine, but masculine. And man is made in the image of God. On the other hand, a woman is not made so much in the image of God, but in the image and as a mate to man."⁴

We cannot simply dismiss such statements as those of a barnstorming fundamentalist of half a century ago. The same kinds of arguments are made today. Indeed, I recently heard an argument like Rice's in an adult Sunday-school class in a mainline Protestant church. When the teacher stated that God is neither male nor female, a man countered with a number of contentions, the most novel of which was that God comes *into* our hearts as the male comes *into* the female in sexual intercourse. He went on to argue that women cannot possibly be made in the image of God to the extent that men are.

The well-known Christian counselor Jay Adams is bold enough to make such statements in print. In his book *Christian Living in the Home,* he insists that "when a husband fails he mars the image of our Lord in a peculiar way in which the wife cannot."⁵

It is impossible for humans to comprehend God fully. We can recite God's attributes—omnipotence, omniscience, omnipresence and so on—but can we really *know* God? God is "wholly other," Karl Barth declared, and that settles the matter for some people. But Barth was wrong. God is not *wholly* other. Genesis 1:27 powerfully captures the essence of God—one whose very image is reflected in humanity, male and female. God is spirit—neither a male nor a female—yet God is a person who can somehow be comprehended through male and female humanity. To suggest that a woman is somehow less reflective of the image of God than a man is not consistent with Genesis 1:27, and it presents an unfortunate distortion of God's nature.

Does God the Father have feminine characteristics?

If God is not primarily masculine, then surely God is not primarily feminine either. But God is a "person"—and in portraying that "personality" the Bible often describes God in human terms with human qualities. These qualities are both masculine and feminine in nature. The fatherly image of God is the most common masculine expression of who God is, and other masculine expressions abound in Scripture. But there are feminine expressions as well—especially ones that portray God as a mother.

Such expressions go all the way back to Moses, who perceived God in motherly images. Frustrated with the people of Israel and with God at the same time, Moses cried out, "Why have you treated your servant so badly? Why have I not found favor in your sight, that you lay the burden of all this people on me? Did I conceive all this people? Did I give birth to them, that you should say to me, 'Carry them in your bosom, as a nurse carries a sucking child' . . . ?" (Num 11:11-12). The answer to his rhetorical questions is obviously, "No, Lord, you did." God's self-revelations are also expressed in motherly images, as is seen in the following passages:

Deuteronomy 32:18: "You were unmindful of the Rock that bore you; you forgot the God who gave you birth."

Isaiah 42:14: "For a long time I have held my peace, I have kept still and restrained myself; now I will cry out like a woman in labor, I will gasp and pant."

Isaiah 46:3-4: "Listen to me, O house of Jacob, all the remnant of the house of Israel, who have been borne by me from your birth, carried from the womb. . . ."

Isaiah 49:15: "Can a woman forget her nursing child, or show no compassion for the child of her womb? Even these may forget, yet I will not forget you."

Isaiah 66:13: "As a mother comforts her child, so I will comfort you."

Matthew 23:37: "Jerusalem, Jerusalem . . . ! How often have I desired to gather your children together as a hen gathers her brood under her wings, and you were not willing!"

It is interesting that God's self-revelation is figuratively portrayed through anatomy that is exclusively female—the womb and the breasts. Nowhere, however, does Scripture portray God through anatomy that is exclusively male. When I pointed that fact out to my teenage son, his immediate reply was that it would be too embarrassing for God to do that. While I am not suggesting that there is any profound significance in this discrepancy, I am not sure I can concur with my son. The Bible is filled with explicit references to the male anatomy, but not in connection with the image of God. Could it be that God knew well that any such imagery could tempt us into making God the Father a male god, as the Mormons have done?

2

Is the Term
Father for
God Figurative
or Literal?

The term *Father* is used repeatedly throughout Scripture in reference to God. There is no debate on that issue. But how should the term be understood?

The term is used in the Old Testament to refer to God's relationship with the children of Israel, as in Jeremiah 3:19 (NIV), when the Lord says, "I thought you would call me 'Father' and not turn away from following me." Here it seems evident that God wants people to use the term *Father* to designate a very special relationship, not because in any sense God is literally a father. The passage continues in this same type of figurative language, "But like a woman unfaithful to her husband, so you have been unfaithful to me." So God is not only *father,* figuratively, but also *husband*—a point that is made even more directly in verse 14 of this same passage, when God declares, "Return, faithless people . . . for I am your husband."

Jesus used the term *Father*, but again the meaning was not literal, as if God were a biological father. As in the Old Testament, the term suggested a unique relationship—so much so that Jesus could charge his followers to "call no one your father on earth, for you have one Father—the one in heaven" (Mt 23:9). And so intimate and personal was this relationship that he used the term *Abba*, or "Daddy" in modern English.

The term *Father* when used of God does not imply a literal male parent's relationship with a child. It is a figure of speech, a metaphor. My *Random House Collegiate Dictionary* defines a metaphor of "the application of a word or phrase to an object or concept it does not literally denote, in order to suggest comparison with another object or concept, as in 'A mighty fortress is our God.' " God is a mighty fortress, but not literally. God is Father, but not literally a male parent.

This is much more than a trivial debate over semantics. In affirming the fatherhood of God, it is very important that we do not go to an extreme that would border on Mormon heresy. Mormons believe that God is a male "personage of flesh and bone" who "sits off in yonder heaven"; they hold that he is the actual parent of living human beings—in the pre-existent world—and that Jesus was conceived through sexual intercourse between God and Mary.[1]

This portrayal of God seems utterly preposterous to orthodox Christians, but it is a natural consequence of viewing God as a literal father. We ourselves often have very fuzzy notions of God. God is a person with personality, as Scripture tells us, but God is also spirit—one who is understood and known and grasped best through figurative concepts.

God is husband, as in Jeremiah 3:14. God is comforting mother, as in Isaiah 66:13. But above all, God is Father. Again and again, Scripture portrays God as the all-knowing and all-loving heavenly Father who watches over us and cares for us. We dare not dismiss this lightly and simply substitute Mother for Father. The stakes are too high. As Christians we worship a triune God, and the trinitarian formula is Father, Son and Holy Spirit. That will never change. Mother is no substitute. We worship Three in One, and the primary relationship we have to the first person of the Godhead, as expressed in the Bible, is one of children to a father. We ought to revel in that relationship, while at the same time not discarding other biblical images of God.

Is God both Father and Mother?

One does not have to travel far in ecumenical circles today to hear someone pray to "God, our Father and Mother." The first time I heard the phrase used in a public prayer was several years ago at the Unification Seminary in Barrytown, New York. In order to prepare for a cults class I was to teach, I was attending a weekend seminar hosted by Sun Myung Moon's Unification Church, and it was in that setting that a "Moonie" gave thanks for our noon meal, addressing God as Father and Mother. My reaction was negative: "Just another cult heresy."

To most evangelical Christians, the phrase "God, our Father and Mother" is objectionable. We have become so used to referring to God as father that any other relational term seems almost sacrilegious. But we freely use other kinds of figurative language to address God, so is it it inconsistent for us to absolutely reject the term *Mother*?

We must remember that while the Bible refers to God in motherly images, it never says that God is our mother or that we ought to pray to "Our Mother in heaven," even as Jesus taught us to pray to "Our Father in heaven." Yet the Bible never strictly limits our terminology for God, and to say that it would be wrong or sinful to refer to God as mother may be going beyond biblical standards.

Would it be wrong to refer to God in prayer as husband? In Jeremiah 3 God is self-described as a husband, and some women pray to God in that relationship in their most private moments. Is it wrong to address God as "bright heaven's Sun" or "my Treasure," as we do when we sing a well-known hymn, "Be Thou My Vision"? For some, the idea of referring to God as mother is blasphemous, but the Bible itself uses the metaphor of mother for God—even as it speaks of God as a shepherd. "Shepherd" is a lowly analogy for God, but it pictures God as caring deeply for each one of us. We sing the words of John W. Petersen in worshipful praise, "Shepherd of love, You knew I had lost my way; Shepherd of love, You cared that I'd gone astray." Would it be worse, or blasphemous, to sing something like "Mother of love . . ."? Both are figures of speech. But because of our fear of taking on the trappings of radical feminism or goddess worship, we dare not sing those words—except perhaps in our closets of prayer.

What are the emotional benefits of perceiving God as mother?

We cannot judge the validity of perceiving God as mother based on emotional or psychological benefits, but assuming it is not improper to perceive God in female images, there can be real value on an experiential level.

The story of Evelyn Brand provides an example. During the early years of her missionary work in India, she and her husband returned home on furlough for a year with their children. "The year was blessing," writes her biographer, "and it was torture." The torture was the constant dread of parting once more from her young school-age children—leaving them in England to be properly educated.

The night before that painful parting, Evelyn gave each child a hand-painted plaque. For Connie: "As one whom a mother comforteth, so will I comfort you." For Paul: "I will be a father unto you." The next day the children left for school, and Evelyn knew that she would not see them again for several years. "Evie stood by the gate looking after them, eyes so blurred with tears she could scarcely see the waving of their hands before they ran around the corner." It was anguish she had never felt before: "As I stood watching them, something just died in me."[2]

The pain in that moment and in the days and months and years that followed was soothed by the realization that God could be mother to Evelyn's children in a way that she could not be in her absence. And her children surely must have taken comfort in knowing that God was not only a father but also a mother who, as Isaiah says, comforts us.

And the motherly love of God is not just for young children, according to Herbert Lockyer, who was known for his long association with Moody Bible Institute. He challenges his readers to think in terms of "turning to God as our Mother" and calls attention to Isaiah 66:13:

And mark, the prophet is not thinking of a little child, but of a grown man heartsore and broken, fleeing back for the comfort of his mother's presence. . . . Many a man weary and broken by a pitiless world, with things against him, and fortunes ruined, or with dear ones gone, or faith almost giving way, or entangled in the net of sin, has retreated in such dark, lone hours to the mother who gave him being.[3]

For some, the desire to perceive God in motherly or feminine images comes from painful experience with men—and perhaps more specifically with a father. If one's father was sexually or physically abusive or if he was distant and uncaring, perceiving God only in fatherly images may conjure up feelings of anger and resentment. Indeed, this has been the testimony of many people. Actually, God's fatherliness can become all the more meaningful to those whose earthly father has been inadequate. God, unlike an earthly father, never fails—never turns his back on us. He meets all the needs we have for a loving father.

How do "earth goddess" feminists distort the image of God?

While Mormons view God in male imagery, goddess worshipers go to the opposite extreme in emphasizing female images. Unlike the Mormon heresy, which describes God in very physical terms as a man of flesh and bone who has a wife and was biologically the father of Jesus, the goddess heresy pictures God in pantheistic terms. God is Mother Earth, the sustainer and nurturer of the universe. This theme is illustrated in a Jewish feminist doxology: "Blessed is She who in the beginning gave birth. . . . Blessed is she whose womb covers the earth."[4]

Goddess worship is just one facet of the neo-pagan or New Age belief, the basic philosophy of which is that all is one and all is god—a view that denies the biblical depiction of a personal God who exists outside the world. The New Age belief is articulated by Miriam Starhawk, a self-described witch and the president of a church known as the Covenant of the Goddess: "Mother Goddess is reawakening and we can begin to recover our primal birthright, the sheer intoxicating joy of being alive. We can open our eyes and see that there is nothing to be saved from . . . no god outside the world to be feared and obeyed."[5]

"Finding the 'Goddess' in God has become increasingly important to many American and Western European women, who no longer feel comfortable with male-dominated religious institutions," writes Jim Spencer of the *Chicago Tribune*. "Although there is no way to quantify the movement, feminist interpretations of faith are rampant and pushing for changes within and outside of traditional power structures."[6]

Goddess worshipers, like members of other aberrant movements, profess to be restoring the true religion. They claim that in ancient times religion was matriarchal and that it remained so until the late medieval period, when patriarchal religion began to dominate. But historians of religion challenge that thesis. According to Wendy O'Flaherty, an expert on goddess worship who teaches at the University of Chicago, "These women are trying to revive a religion that may not have existed in the first place. . . . Christianity has been unfair to women, Judaism more so, but these people [goddess worshipers] are jumping to conclusions that aren't historically founded."[7]

Is God a chauvinist?

The normal reaction to a question like "Is God a chauvinist?" is one of disgust. How could I be so irreverent as to pose such a question? It is patently absurd even to contemplate the idea. Yet though the question sounds ludicrous, in some respects it is the most basic question in the debate among Christians on the women's issue.

In contemporary usage, a *chauvinist* is someone who champions male supremacy and female subservience. The term, though often used to describe a mean-spirited bigot, does not necessarily carry that connotation. A chauvinist is analogous to a racist. A racist need not be a raving fanatic. In fact, many racists are calm, methodical, "decent" people who simply believe that their race is superior to others. The natural consequence of that belief is race discrimination.

So also with chauvinism. Its natural outcome is sex discrimination. On the basis of gender alone, women are not accorded the rights and privileges that are available to men. The rationale behind this practice in the Christian context is that God has predetermined that the male is the "head" of the female. Though "equal" to her male counterpart, the female is to function in a secondary role—particularly in the church and in the home.

So, *is* God a chauvinist? The question is really no more outrageous than asking a Mormon whether God is a racist—albeit a benign one. It was allegedly God, after all, who barred Blacks from the Mormon priesthood—a ban that was rescinded by a new revelation in 1978, only after church leaders prayed earnestly for God to change his mind. In the understanding of the Mormons, God was the author of race discrimination, and only God could reverse that pattern.

Is God, likewise, the author of sex discrimination? Has the triune God, through biblical revelation and personal guidance, mandated that the female sex be subordinate to the male sex? Is it God, rather than man, who has given women a subservient or secondary role solely on the basis of gender?

God is not a chauvinist—not even a benign chauvinist. God is not the author of either race discrimination or sex discrimination. We can confidently affirm with the apostle Peter that God is no respecter of persons (1 Pet 1:17). God created both woman and man in his image. It is true that sin has disfigured humanity, but in Christ we are beyond the curse, for "there is no longer Jew or Greek . . . slave or free . . . male and female" (Gal 3:28).

3

Do Jesus
and the Holy Spirit
Have Feminine
Characteristics?

If God the Father is not male or exclusively masculine in nature, what about the other persons of the Trinity?

There ought to be no question as to Jesus' physical maleness. The first chapter of Matthew records that Mary gave birth to a son. On that issue, no further proof is necessary—even to those who would figuratively suggest otherwise. Indeed, a female thorn-crowned Jesus hanging on the cross, as sculptor Edwina Sandys portrayed him, is no more representative of the man Jesus than a female image of Abraham Lincoln would represent the man Abraham Lincoln. Her work was "art," and it was symbolic of her perception of Jesus—nothing more.

Regarding a gender identity of the Holy Spirit, the Bible is silent—unless one argues that the masculine pronoun used for the third person of the Trinity is denoting gender, which I believe it clearly is not. It is perhaps worth noting that in John 14:17 the Spirit is twice referred to with the neuter pronoun *auto* (it), though the word is translated in the King James and New International versions as "him." It is enough to say that like the Father, the Spirit is *spirit*. To suggest that the Spirit is male or masculine is to step beyond the bounds of Scripture. Nevertheless, it has been tempting for some Christians to see in the Holy Spirit the feminine side of the Godhead.

What is the significance of Jesus' maleness?

The significance of Jesus' maleness is equivalent to the significance of any individual's gender. As a human, Jesus was male. That is important. It was his *gender* identity, just as being a Jew was his *cultural* identity, and being a carpenter's son from Nazareth was part of his *social* identity.

Could Jesus have conducted his ministry on earth in a female body? Would his ministry have had the same power and effectiveness if he had been a woman rather than a man? Such questions are too hypothetical to entertain seriously, but the argument could be made that Jesus' maleness was essential to his human agenda on this earth. Jesus offered the gospel of the kingdom to the Jews in the person of a rabbi. He was a teacher, like other teachers of his day, who traveled the countryside with disciples. There was no such role for women.

Jesus, likewise, was the promised messiah of Old Testament prophecies. As such, his maleness was essential—though it could be argued that had God foreordained Jesus to become flesh through a female, the Old Testament prophecies would correspond to that form of incarnation.

Jesus' maleness has no particular theological significance, according to Paul Jewett. "Since the trinitarian fellowship of the Godhead knows no distinction of male and female," he writes, "and since the human fellowship of male and female knows no discrimination against the female as less in the divine image than the male, therefore the Incarnation in the form of male humanity, though historically and culturally necessary, was not *theologically* necessary."[1]

Was it necessary that Jesus be a man to atone for our sins?

This question raised some controversy a few years ago when a student innocently (or perhaps not so innocently) brought it up in a seminary class I was teaching with a colleague. In response to the question, my colleague suggested that it would be pure speculation to assume that it was *necessary* for Jesus to be anatomically male in order to atone for our sins. He could not think of any Scripture passage that would indicate that male anatomy had any necessary connection with the atonement. But certain students did not see it that way, and soon rumors spread that erroneous teaching about Jesus was being promulgated in one of the seminary courses—to the point that other professors inquired about the matter. It was hardly an issue for a heresy trial, but the fact that the issue was controversial enough to spread beyond the class surprised me. It had not dawned on me that my colleague's indefinite, noncommittal answer would create controversy.

I have learned since, however, that some students of Scripture take the theology of Christ's maleness very seriously. Susan Foh argues from Romans 5:19 that it was necessary that Jesus be male to atone for our sins: "For just as by the one man's disobedience the many were made sinners, so by the one man's obedience the many will be made righteous." She asserts that "by creating the man first, God established him as the head of the human race." The male represents all humanity, and "since God has given this representative ability to the male, Christ, as the head, source, and representative of the church, had to become incarnate as a man."[2]

The primary purpose of the Incarnation was so that Christ might atone for our sins. It was necessary that Jesus become "flesh"—that he be human as we are—but to argue that it was necessary that he be male adds something to Scripture that simply is not there. Romans 5:19 is, indeed, a key passage of Scripture, but not in defending the "maleness" of Christ. The Greek word for man—in reference to both Adam and Jesus—is *anthropos,* meaning human. Jesus was a man. There is no doubt about that, but, as Aida Spencer points out, "the New Testament writers are always careful to describe Jesus with the generic Greek term 'human' or *anthropos* rather than the term 'male' or *aner*. Although God became a male, God primarily became a human; otherwise, in some way males would be more saved than females."[3]

What can we learn from feminine portrayals of Jesus?

If Jesus' maleness is established beyond a doubt, why would anyone, aside from a feminist artist, seek to portray him in feminine imagery? Such portrayals are not as common today as they were in earlier times. The church fathers—including Clement, Origen, Irenaeus, Chrysostom, Ambrose and Augustine—all, at one time or another, described Jesus as mother. Later, Anselm, an eleventh-century theologian and archbishop of Canterbury, wrote a prayer that spoke of Jesus as mother: "But you, Jesus, good Lord, are you not also a mother? Are you not the mother who, like a hen, collects her chickens under her wings? Truly, master, you are a mother. . . . It is then you, above all, Lord God, who are mother."[4]

Bernard of Clairvaux, a celebrated twelfth-century monastic reformer and mystic, was even more graphic and personal in his portrayal of Jesus as mother. To a young follower he wrote: "Do not let the roughness of our life frighten your tender years. If you feel the stings of temptation . . . suck not so much the wounds as the breasts of the Crucified. . . . He will be your mother, and you will be his son."[5]

Some critics have argued that celibacy contributed to the medieval monks' need to relate to Jesus as a female, and perhaps there is some truth in that, but women also looked to Jesus as mother. Julian of Norwich, a fourteenth-century mystic, is an example: "God rejoices that he is our Father; and God rejoices that he is our Mother. . . . God almighty is our kindly Father; and God all-wisdom is our kindly Mother. . . . The second person of the Trinity is our Mother. . . . Jesus Christ, who does good against evil, is our very Mother."[6]

Is there any harm in perceiving Jesus as mother? Jesus is the incarnation of God, and if God can be perceived metaphorically as mother, perhaps the same images cannot be used for Jesus. It seems to me, though, that the medieval Christians' motivation for perceiving Jesus as mother was that it was only through such an image that Jesus' love and nurture could be fully comprehended. For some people this motherly image is helpful. Most of us, however, are more comfortable perceiving Jesus as the perfect *man* that he was, one whose love and nurture far surpass those of a human mother (or father).

Does the Holy Spirit represent the feminine side of God?

Some feminists have sought to make the Holy Spirit the feminine person of the Godhead, reasoning that it would be a difficult claim to deny since a "spirit" could certainly not be automatically deemed masculine. Other feminists, however, have been quick to reject the model, recognizing that such a construction of the Godhead (assuming the Father and Son are masculine) still leaves a 2:1 ratio of masculine to feminine.

But the idea of a feminine Holy Spirit is not simply an assertion of feminists. Cultic movements have made such claims, most notably Christian Science, founded by Mary Baker Eddy, and more recently the Unification Church, founded by Sun Myung Moon.

The conviction that the Holy Spirit is feminine, however, is not confined to feminists or cultists. A. B. Simpson, a noted evangelical churchman and the founder of the Christian and Missionary Alliance, made the claim. In a book entitled *When the Comforter Came,* published in 1911, Simpson cited Isaiah 66:13 ("As a mother comforts her child, so I will comfort you") as a reference to the Holy Spirit and proceeded to build his case for a feminine Holy Spirit: "And this aspect of His blessed character finds its perfect manifestation in the Holy Ghost, our Mother God. So that we have in the divine Trinity not only a Father, and a Brother and a Husband but also One who meets all the heart's longing for motherhood. . . . As our heavenly Mother, the Comforter assumes our nurture, training, teaching, and the whole direction of our life."[7]

Is Simpson's line of reasoning valid? As with the first person of the Godhead, there are feminine images of the Spirit—most prominently the references in John 3 to being "born of the Spirit." But, in my mind, Simpson is stretching the biblical text to make it fit his model. He rightly points out, however, that in the Godhead we have all that meets the heart's longings—both masculine and feminine.

PART 2

Creation
and Fall

4

Does the Creation Account Support Male Headship?

hose who argue that the Bible teaches man's authority over woman contend that God instituted male headship when he created male and female. The fact that this design was *creational* makes it particularly significant, because it cannot then be viewed as a temporary provision that might at some point be rescinded.

James Hurley seeks to apply his belief in creational headship to today's church: "Christian worship involves re-establishing the creational pattern with men faithfully teaching God's truth and women receptively listening."[1] Even if it were true that male headship was instituted at the time of creation, it would not necessarily follow that it must remain in force throughout all history. The seventh-day sabbath is a case in point. We read in Genesis 2:2-3: "And on the seventh day God finished the work that he had done, and he rested on the seventh day. . . . So God blessed the seventh day and hallowed it." Seventh-day Adventists and others who continue to worship on Saturday argue that sabbath-keeping is apart of the law that is *creational* and thus cannot be rescinded. If the appeal to creation is used regarding male headship, then, it should also be used regarding the sabbath.

But what do the Scriptures actually say about male headship prior to the Fall? The fact of the matter is, there is no reference to headship in the creation account. "The whole created universe—from the stars in space to the fish in the sea—is carefully organized in a hierarchy or order that is meticulously defined in Genesis 1. And yet, there is not the slightest indication that such a hierarchy existed between Adam and Eve," points out Gilbert Bilezikian. If such an organizational structure had been established between Adam and Eve, it would be hard to imagine that it would not have been mentioned. "Man and woman were not negligible or incidental happenings in the story of creation. They constitute the climactic creative achievement of God. Consequently, the definition of authority structures between man and woman would be at least as important as the definition of their authority over birds, fish, and cattle." But such authority structures are simply not there. "Nowhere is it stated that man was intended to rule over woman within God's creation design."2

What is the significance of the two different creation stories?
I have known the creation story since I was a little girl, but it was not until a few years ago that I realized that there are two accounts of the creation of humans—one favored by traditionalists and one favored by feminists. According to Evelyn and Frank Stagg, "There are at least two creation narratives in Genesis, woman having equality with man in one (1:24-30) but subordinated to man in the other (2:7-25)."3 The only one I had ever heard preached on was the account emphasized by those who affirm male headship—the account in Genesis 2 of Adam's creation from the dust of the earth and Eve's creation from Adam's rib. The first chapter of Genesis, which gives a more general account of God's creation and seems to underscore the equality of male and female, was overlooked in the churches I attended.

As different as they might appear on the surface, however, the two accounts ought not to be pitted against each other. They are not contradictory, nor are they focused on opposite sides of the issue. They are complementary and are equally important in shedding light on the subject of male and female roles and relationships.

Were woman and man *equally* created in the image of God?

The question is not whether woman is created in the image of God. There is little debate on this today, though in generations past even this doctrine was challenged. St. Augustine believed that "the woman together with her husband is the image of God," but that she alone is not. "When she is assigned as helpmate, a function that pertains to her alone, then she is not the image of God; but as far as the man is concerned, he is by himself the image of God."[4]

More recently, John R. Rice, a well-known radio preacher of a generation ago, insisted that "a woman is not made so much in the image of God, but in the image and as a mate to man."[5] Some have likewise suggested that the woman is created in the image of God, but that this is only a "reflected" image—because she is primarily created in the image of man.[6] John Calvin held that woman was created in the image of God, "though in the second degree."[7]

Most contemporary traditionalists who restrict women's roles would be very careful to emphasize that women are created in the image of God. "Who, I wonder," writes Raymond Ortlund, "is teaching that men only bear God's image? No contributor to *this* volume will be found saying that."[8] But are women and men *equally* created in the image of God? That is a different issue. The volume to which Ortlund refers is a product of the Council on Biblical Manhood and Womanhood, which also produced the Danvers Statement, a two-page document that was printed as an advertisement in several issues of *Christianity Today* in 1989. The first "affirmation" of that statement is as follows: "Both Adam and Eve were created in God's image, equal before God as persons and distinct in their manhood and womanhood." This sounds like a straightforward egalitarian statement, but it is very significant that there is no affirmation that

Adam and Eve were *equally* created in the image of God. Instead, it affirms that they were "equal before God as persons."

James Hurley, who helped draft the Danvers Statement, offers an explanation for this distinction: "Man, in his authority relation to creation and to his wife, images the dominion of God over the creation. . . . The woman is not called to image God or Christ *in the relation which she sustains to her husband.* She images instead the response of the church to God and Christ by willing, loving self-subjection. . . . In *this particular sense* of authority relationships, . . . it is absolutely appropriate to say that the man images God and that the woman does not."[9]

According to this line of reasoning, woman and man are not equally created in the image of God. But a straightforward reading of Genesis 1:27 does not allow for man and woman to be differentiated in this manner—they are too closely connected for that: "So God created humankind in his image, in the image of God he created them; male and female he created them."

Is it significant that Adam was created before Eve?

Genesis 2 clearly points out that Adam was created first and Eve was created later. In the minds of some, this creation order is very significant and gives Adam some sort of primary status in relation to Eve because she was created second. Such logic, however, is not universally accepted—especially considering the fact that the animals were created before Adam.

Indeed, some have argued the opposite—that creation order was a factor in female superiority. Agrippa of Nettesheim of Geneva, a contemporary of Martin Luther, made this very case. It has been summed up as follows:

Women are even superior in some ways . . . having been made directly by God in paradise with the angels whereas Adam was created outside paradise in a field with the animals. Eve's superiority is shown by her name which means life, whereas the name Adam means earth. As the last of all that God created, Eve is the crowning achievement of God, the most perfect work of God. Original sin is to be traced to Adam, not Eve; and Christ, to save sinful humanity, was made human by means of a woman, not a man, in the more lowly male sex from which sin came forth.[10]

In 1 Timothy 2:13, "For Adam was formed first, then Eve," it might appear that Paul is appealing to creation order in his restrictions on women's teaching or having authority. A closer look at that passage, however, would indicate otherwise. See question 15.

What does the term *helper* or *helpmeet* mean in Genesis 2?
"Then the LORD God said, 'It is not good that the man should be alone; I will make him a helper as his partner' " (Gen 2:18). In reflecting on this verse, Ortlund writes, "So, was Eve Adam's equal? Yes and No. She was his spiritual equal and, unlike the animals, 'suitable for him,' but she was not his equal in that she was his 'helper.' . . . A man, just by virtue of his manhood, is called to lead for God. A woman, just by virtue of her womanhood, is called to help for God. . . . It is the word 'helper' that suggests the woman's supportive role."[11]

The depiction of a wife as the *helpmate* or *helpmeet* of her husband has reinforced the notion of female inferiority. "The man was not created to help the woman," writes Ortlund, "but the reverse. Doesn't this striking fact suggest that manhood and womanhood are distinct and non-reversible?"[12] It is hard to imagine that Ortlund is actually suggesting that a husband is not supposed to "help" his wife. The day-to-day routine of any good marriage finds the husband helping the wife and the wife helping the husband. Helping is, indeed, reversible.

The term rendered *helper* in Genesis 2:18 is the Hebrew word *'ēzer*. It is a word used elsewhere in Scripture—most often in reference to God. An example of this is when Jethro named his son Eliezer because "the God of my father was my help [*'ēzer*], and delivered me from the sword of Pharaoh" (Ex 18:4).

To argue that the word *helper* connotes subordination is neither biblical nor consistent with contemporary usage. A parent is a helper when a toddler is learning to walk. A doctor is a helper to a patient. A rich nation is a helper to refugees. Indeed, it seems more consistent to suggest that "helper" connotes strength than that it connotes weakness. The one who helps is the one who has something to offer the one who is helpless or needs help. Adam needed help. He had no partner. God created a partner—a helper. In this case there is no hint of either superiority or subordination.

5

What Was the Relationship between Adam and Eve before the Fall?

T he Bible tells us very little about Adam and Eve while they were in the garden together. We might wish that we had just a few more facts to fill out the story—at least to know how long their time in Eden lasted. Was it merely a honeymoon in which they romped together in the lush garden, or was it a long-term marriage—a true partnership that, unlike any other since, was not marred by bickering or resentment or sin of any kind?

The information we have on Adam and Eve together in the garden, prior to their encounter with Satan, is given in three short verses. After God fashioned Eve from one of Adam's ribs, he brought her to Adam.

Then the man said, "This at last is bone of my bones and flesh of my flesh; this one shall be called Woman, for out of Man this one was taken." Therefore a man leaves his father and his mother and clings to his wife, and they become one flesh. And the man and his wife were both naked, and were not ashamed. (Gen 2:23-25)

Although this passage is very short, it is packed full of meaning—sentences and phrases that give us a glimpse of the relationship between Adam and Eve and that define male-female relationships for all time.

What is the significance of "bone of my bones and flesh of my flesh"?

From the biblical account in Genesis 2, it is apparent that Adam had no knowledge of, or any part in, the creation of Eve. He was put to sleep for the surgical removal of a rib, and the next glimpse we have of him is when he is dazzled by this creature that has been fashioned out of his rib.

What is most remarkable about this episode is that there is no evidence that he knows she came from his rib, which apparently came with some flesh attached, yet he instantly recognizes her as "bone of my bones and flesh of my flesh." They are alike, and it is this likeness—not their differences—that he finds so striking.

This point has been emphasized by Letha Scanzoni and Nancy Hardesty in *All We're Meant to Be*:

Adam's response upon awakening assures us that he realized woman's complementary nature at once. He saw her not as different but as one like himself. Hebrew scholars tell us that the grammar at this point is chaotic—Adam's response was much like ours when we are surprised and delighted. The repetition of the word "this" indicates that he was at a loss for words to describe his joy and could only point:

"*This* at last is bone from my bones."[1]

According to Bilezikian, Adam identified Eve "as his alter ego, much like his female twin. . . . The identity indicated by this phrase is so complete that common usage has adopted it to describe bonds of consanguinity that exist between parent and child rather than marital ties."[2]

Is there significance in a man's leaving his father and mother?

It is interesting that *because* woman was created out of man, "a man leaves his father and his mother and clings to his wife." Why does one follow the other, and why should the man, rather than the woman, leave his family home? This is certainly not the patriarchal pattern that developed after the Fall. "It is interesting to note," writes Mary Evans, "that far from supporting patriarchalism, Genesis 2:24 sees the man, rather than the woman, leaving home to 'cleave' to his wife. The verb 'cleave' here is used almost universally for a weaker cleaving to a stronger. It is used of Israel, cleaving to God (e.g., Joshua 23:8; Psalm 91:14), but never the other way around."[3]

A woman, in light of this model, is "a free agent, in command of her own life." Her parents—particularly her father—are not mentioned. Here, "the woman represents the stable point of reference. It is the man who moves toward her after leaving his parents. He attaches himself to the woman. She is not appended to his life. He is the one who adds his life to her as he 'cleaves' to her."[4]

What significance does "one flesh" have for male-female relationships?

When a man and woman marry, they become "one." That concept is often symbolized in the marriage ceremony with candles. The bride and groom together light a solitary candle from the flame of their own individual candles. Sometimes they blow their own candles out—a practice that, in my mind, flaws the symbolism. Marriage doesn't mean extinguishing the individual self. The two individuals remain separate even as they become one. But worse than blowing out both candles is a version that I have never seen—only heard about. In this little candle ritual, only the bride blows her candle out.

The "one flesh" concept of Genesis 2 does not suggest a loss of individual personhood. Rather, it is a confirmation of mutuality in the marriage relationship. Only husband and wife are described as "one flesh"— not parent and child, though they actually share a blood relationship. Why is this? In marriage the woman and man establish a relationship that is higher in the eyes of God than the blood ties between parents and child. It is a "one-flesh" mutuality that goes far beyond sexual intimacy. This relationship of interdependence and mutuality is like no other.

Did Adam give Eve her name prior to the Fall?

To someone who is not well versed in the debate over male headship, this question may seem extraneous. Who cares? But for those who insist that Adam was created to rule over Eve, even before the Fall, this business of naming is critically important. Adam, they argue, *named* Eve when he saw her, saying that she "shall be called Woman." But did Adam actually name her "woman," or did he merely *recognize* her as woman, "for out of man this one was taken"? Here lies the crux of the issue. Those who contend that Adam *named* Eve insist that this proves Adam's authority over her, even as his naming of the animals meant that they were brought under his dominion.

Mary Evans, however, challenges this position. She concedes that in some instances in the Old Testament "an exercise of authority of the namer over the named is involved," but she argues that this is by no means universal. She also points out that in the "standard naming formula we find both the verb 'to call' and the noun 'name'; as for example in Genesis 4:25 'she bore a son and called his name Seth.' " These words are together in Genesis 2, when Adam is naming the animals. But in verse 23, where Adam is recognizing Eve as woman, the word for "name" does not appear. "Similarly it must be noted that the word 'woman' is never used as a proper name, it is simply a common noun designating gender. Thus verse 23 can be seen as something other than an official naming."[5]

After the Fall, Adam did *name* his wife Eve, and in this instance, both terms are used. If authority is involved here, it probably reflects one of the effects of the curse on Eve—that her husband would rule over her.

6

Was Eve Responsible for the Fall into Sin?

Blaming Eve for bringing sin into the world began with Adam's excuse, "The woman whom you gave to be with me, she gave me fruit from the tree, and I ate," and has continued ever since—though typically with harsher rhetoric. The church fathers were adept at blaming Eve, most notably Tertullian, who insisted that all women had been tainted by Eve: "You are the devil's gateway; you are the unsealer of that [forbidden] tree; you are the first deserter of the divine law; you are she who persuaded him whom the devil was not valiant enough to attack. You destroyed so easily God's image, man. On account of your desert [punishment], that is, death—even the Son of God had to die."[1]

Down through church history Eve has been made the scapegoat for sins that were particularly identified with women. In the sixteenth century, Argula von Stauffer, one of Martin Luther's strongest defenders, was accused by a Catholic official of being "an insolent daughter of Eve, a heretical bitch and a confounded rogue." (Luther described her as "a singular instrument of Christ.")[2]

In the seventeenth century, Anne Hutchinson was banished from Boston by church officials because she had allegedly contaminated the minds of many of the parishioners. According to the Reverend Thomas Weld, Anne's sin was similar to that of Eve. She had deceived the women, "the weaker to resist," who were "more flexible, tender, and ready to yield"; that was tragic enough, but worse yet was that "as by an Eve" they might "catch their husbands also, which often proved too true amongst us."[3]

Did Eve "catch" her husband and cause him to sin? Whose fault was the Fall? Satan, of course, was the instigator of sin. He tempted Eve, and Adam succumbed to his wife's deception. But to blame Eve almost exclusively as so many churchmen have done through the ages is to distort Scripture and discriminate against the woman. Eve was responsible for the Fall into sin, but only as a partner in crime with Adam.

Why might Eve have been more vulnerable to Satan than Adam was?
The standard explanation for Eve's vulnerability has been that Eve was somehow less competent than Adam, and thus a more likely target. Luther offered a version of this scenario: "The subtlety of Satan showed itself also when he attacked human nature where it was weakest, namely in Eve, and not in Adam. I believe that had Satan first tempted the man, Adam would have gained the victory."[4]

A far less common explanation of Satan's attack on Eve rather than Adam—one that presents Eve in a favorable light—is that she was the perfecting element in the male-female duo. Satan knew that if she succumbed to temptation, the man would follow, but if the situation were reversed, and Adam was led astray, Eve would be far more likely to stand firm in her obedience to God.[5]

When considering why Satan might have perceived Eve to be an easier target for his temptation than Adam, it's worth noting that it was Adam who had been directly informed by God that the fruit of the tree of the knowledge of good and evil was forbidden. Eve had not been created until some time later. We assume that Adam told her of the prohibition, because she was aware of it when Satan approached her. Because her knowledge was secondhand, however, it is not unreasonable to presume that it was not as indelibly impressed on her mind as it should have been on Adam's. We have no evidence that Eve was contacted directly by God regarding the forbidden fruit, but she was contacted directly by Satan— the angel of light—when he lured her with the forbidden fruit. No doubt Satan plotted out his tactics very well. Is it at all surprising that she was deceived?

Where was Adam when Satan tempted Eve?
Those who would blame only Eve for succumbing to Satan's temptation often find it very difficult to explain Adam's role during the encounter. When God initially speaks to Adam and forbids him to eat of the fruit (Gen 2:16-17), the singular form of "you" is employed. Not so when Satan tempts Eve (Gen 3:1-5). Here the plural form of "you" is employed, suggesting that Satan is speaking in the presence of both Eve and Adam. This possibility is further supported in verse 6, where we read that Eve "took of its fruit and ate; and she also gave some to her husband, *who was with her.*"

That statement is followed by the terse three-word clause "and he ate." There is no evidence whatsoever that Adam protested—that he reminded Eve of his personal and direct command from God not to eat of the fruit. We can only surmise that he stood by in silence while Eve was having her conversation with Satan, and then accepted the fruit without any outward objection. Surely any remonstrations on his part would have been worthy of including in the account.

How do we size up Adam as a person—God's first created human being? "Some scholars compare the feisty, brainy, confrontational involvement of Eve to the lethargic presence of Adam," pointing out that "his sole activity consisted of grasping the fruit offered to him and eating it without raising a question, as if he were in a state of moronic stupor, like a zoo baboon that catches a banana."[6]

Surely Adam ought not be compared to a zoo baboon. Such a depiction is a greater insult to God who created him than to Adam himself.

But Adam does not come away with high marks from his encounter with temptation. His passivity in the face of temptation and sin ought to be a reminder to all of us just how insidious our bent to sin is—even when we are not actively seeking it.

Did Adam fail to exercise his headship when Eve offered him fruit?

Although there is nothing in the account of temptation and Fall that refers to male headship, many who emphasize the concept of male headship view it as a fundamental focus of the story. Raymond Ortlund makes a major point of emphasizing that the text does not say that Eve took and ate the fruit and that Adam did likewise. Instead, he says, "Eve usurped Adam's headship and led the way into sin. And Adam, who (it seems) had stood by passively, allowing the deception to progress without decisive intervention—Adam, for his part, abandoned his post as head. Eve was deceived; Adam forsook his responsibility. Both were wrong and together they pulled the human race down into sin and death."[7]

Eve was deceived. There is no debate over that issue. But that Adam's sin was abandoning his post as head is surely a less than obvious inference. A plain reading of the text is that Adam disobeyed God's command, and that is precisely the sin for which God held him accountable. When God confronts him, the question is, "Have you eaten from the tree of which I commanded you not to eat?" The question is not, "Have you allowed your wife to usurp your authority?"

Authority and headship have nothing to do with this episode. The issues are deception and disobedience—nothing more, nothing less.

Did the Fall involve gender-role reversal?

This question is closely related to that of headship. "Isn't it striking," writes Ortlund, "that we fell upon an occasion of sex role reversal? Are we to repeat this confusion forever? Are we to institutionalize it in evangelicalism in the name of God who condemned it in the beginning?"[8]

Elisabeth Elliot echoes this same theme: "Eve, in her refusal to accept the will of God, refused her femininity. Adam, in his capitulation to her suggestion, abdicated his masculine responsibility for her. It was the first instance of what we would recognize now as 'role reversal.' This defiant disobedience ruined the original pattern and things have been in an awful mess ever since."[9]

Elliot goes on to imply that Eve was masculine (in contrast to Mary, who reflected the essence of femininity). But the text itself does not suggest that Eve sinned because she "refused her femininity" and engaged in "role reversal." It suggests simply that she was deceived—entrapped—as all Christians are prone to be. Paul writes in 2 Corinthians 11:3 (NIV), "Just as Eve was deceived by the serpent's cunning, your minds may somehow be led astray from your sincere and pure devotion to Christ." Eve does not appear to be guilty of "defiant disobedience" so much as led astray from her sincere and pure devotion.

By whom did sin enter the world?

For all the blame that Eve has endured over time for being the first sinner, the Bible clearly states, in Romans 5:12-14, that by one man— Adam—sin entered the world.

If Eve was the first to eat the fruit, as Genesis 2:6 reports, why then did Paul emphasize in Romans that sin entered the world through Adam? And does that not seem to contradict 1 Timothy 2:14, which states that "Adam was not deceived, but the woman was deceived and became a transgressor" (or a "sinner," as the NIV renders the term)? In reference to this passage Hurley writes: "Paul seems to be saying that Eve was *not* at fault; she was deceived. Adam, on the other hand, was not deceived but, deliberately and with understanding, chose to sin."[10]

Adam had been given clear and direct instructions from God not to eat the fruit. Satan, crafty as he was, deliberately used his wiles on Eve. She was led astray, but Adam knowingly and deliberately sinned. So Paul can say that through Adam sin entered the world—though surely that does not let Eve off the hook.

7

What Is the Significance of the "Curse" on Adam and Eve?

A close reading of the biblical text reveals that neither Adam nor Eve was "cursed," as is often assumed. Satan was cursed and the ground was cursed; the latter had a very real effect on Adam, but neither he nor Eve was the direct object of a curse. In many respects the curse and its effects reversed the conditions of the Garden. The serpent, which "was more crafty than any other wild animal," became more "cursed," sentenced to a life of eating dust. And the very woman Satan deceived would one day prevail, in that her offspring (Jesus) would strike the serpent's head, and it would strike his heel (Gen 3:14-15).

The effects of the curse on the woman were straightforward: "I will greatly increase your pangs in childbearing; in pain you shall bring forth children, yet your desire shall be for your husband, and he shall rule over you" (Gen 3:16).

The portion of the curse relating directly to Adam is the longest, and again, it reversed the conditions in Eden. The ground out of which he came and the trees from which he ate would no longer be a natural source of plenty. Rather, he would be required to toil by the sweat of his brow amid thorns and thistles, and in the end he would return to the dust from which he came. There was more than a little irony in God's great reversal known as the curse: "Adam became subject to the soil from which he had been taken. Eve became subject to Adam from whom she had been taken. . . . As a result of Satan's work, man was now master over woman, just as the mother-ground was now master over man. For these reasons it is proper to regard both male dominance and death as being antithetical to God's original intent in creation."[1]

What are the lasting effects of the "curse" on the world today?

The serpent and the ground were cursed, and for all practical purposes that curse is irreversible. The serpent is doomed forever to slither on its belly and eat the dust. And the ground will never return to Eden's splendor. Despite the best efforts of modern agriculture, the ground naturally produces thorns and thistles and weeds.

Men and women also suffer from the continuing effects of the curse. Male rule and domination over women and female dependence on men have continued through the centuries and can be seen throughout the world today. This is true even in Christian circles, though it is not nearly as pervasive as it was in Judaism (and surrounding cultures) before the time of Christ.

Indeed, these tendencies not only remain but are sometimes championed by those who advance the concept of male headship. The husband finds justification in "ruling over" the wife; the woman, too, often finds encouragement to be overly dependent. This was seen a couple of decades ago with the popularity of Marabel Morgan's *The Total Woman* and Helen Andelin's *Fascinating Womanhood*. Andelin's theme was to "revere your husband and his right to rule you," yet she encouraged women to "acquire a childlike manner"—to stomp the foot and pout—in order to get their own way. In her view, the curse was a commandment: "The first commandment which God gave unto woman was, '*thy desire shall*

50 ☐ WOMEN IN THE MAZE

be unto thy husband, and he shall rule over thee.' " About the man, she says, "We must understand *his desire to be superior in his role as man.* It is only in his role as man that he longs for supremacy over woman. ... Nothing gives him a more enjoyable sense of power and manliness than does his supremacy. Therefore, if he does not feel superior now, woman must make him feel so."[2]

What did God mean when he told Eve that her "desire" would be for her husband?

A straightforward reading of the text would seem to indicate that despite the terrible pain of childbearing, a woman's desire—sexual desire, that is—will still be for her husband, even though she knows full well that such intimacy may lead to another pregnancy. It could also be interpreted to mean that she will desire his rule, since the phrase "and he shall rule over you" immediately follows. This could well imply an unhealthy dependence on him. Or, as John Calvin seemed to suggest, it could imply a *healthy* dependence on her husband—that a woman will desire only what her husband wishes.

Susan Foh takes issue with Calvin, and rightly so, pointing out that "if the wife so loses her will that she does not disagree with her husband, the hardship of his rule, which is the punishment for sin, is lost." This passage, Foh says, "is God's judgment against sin; therefore, the desire of the woman in no way contributes to the rule of the husband."

So what, according to Foh, does *desire* mean in this passage? "The woman's desire is to control her husband (to usurp his divinely appointed headship), and he must master her, if he can." Foh argues that "the 'curse' here describes the beginning of the battle of the sexes."[3]

The major problem with this interpretation is that the woman's "desire" is part of the effect of the curse on the woman—not the man. By Foh's definition, the woman's "desire" would most adversely affect the man. But the effects of the curse on him do not begin until the following verses. If the woman here is only seeking to reclaim her rightful position alongside the man, it makes no sense to include this as having a negative effect on her. On the other hand, if the "desire" means an unhealthy dependence on the man, then truly it can be seen as a judgment of God against the woman.

Is this overdependence an inherent characteristic of woman's fallen nature? Gini Andrews believes it is:

> I'm wondering if this immense, clinging, psychological dependence on man which is part of us as women is not something we should face as part of our fallenness. . . . We'll jettison any plans, rearrange our lives or our hair-dos; we'll work our fingers to the first joint, throw up a promising career, and too often even undercut our best friend— all for some man we find compellingly attractive.[4]

Was the husband's "rule over" the wife prescriptive?

Those who emphasize male headship often use the "curse" as a strong argument for their case. They contend that the Bible says the husband "shall rule over" the wife. That phrase is about as straightforward and blunt as it is possible to be in the English language.

The issue here, however, is not the meaning of the phrase itself, but the intent behind the statement. Is the husband's rule a statement of fact—the inevitable result of the Fall—or is it a statement of what *ought* to be? Is it descriptive or prescriptive? This is a crucial question, one that is basic to the issue of male headship. If, indeed, the husband has a proper and irreversible function of "ruling over" his wife, the case for male headship is greatly strengthened. If, however, the husband's rule over the wife is a sinful result of the Fall, then the argument for male headship is seriously undermined.

Phyllis Trible contends that the "curse" on woman *describes* rather than *prescribes*. It in no way condones the man's rule over the woman.[5]

In seeking to determine the correct interpretation and application of this passage, it is only reasonable to look at the context. How do we understand the other effects of the curse? One of them is that the woman's pain in childbearing will be greatly increased. Is it imperative to preserve that pain, just as some would suggest the husband's rule ought to be preserved? Is it a violation of God's will for a woman to seek to relieve her pain in childbirth? Today that question sounds preposterous, but not so in generations past. In sixteenth-century Scotland, Eufame MacLayne took a pain-killing herb to sustain her through the birth of twins. She and the babies survived.

> However, someone found out what she had done. Painkillers were forbidden to women in childbirth. It was against God's law. He wanted women to suffer in labor. The Bible said so, their punishment for Eve's sin.
>
> So Eufame was brought before those who decided punishment. . . . Her babies were taken from her arms and given to someone else's care. Eufame was tied to a stake. Bundles of wood were laid at her feet. The new mother Eufame was burned alive.[6]

I am not aware of any Christian leader today who would argue that it is wrong for a woman to relieve the pain of childbirth. Nor do I know of any Christian leader who would suggest that it is wrong for a man to overcome the effects of the curse. Most men do not toil for their food by the sweat of their brow amid thorns and thistles; many work at computers in air-conditioned office buildings, never imagining that they could be defying God's purpose in the curse.

Should the husband's rule over the wife be seen in a different light from the other effects of the curse? If it is appropriate for a woman to relieve pain in childbirth and for a man to gain his livelihood by operating a computer, does it not follow that it is also appropriate for a woman to seek an egalitarian marriage, one in which her husband does not rule over her and she does not develop an unhealthy dependence on him?

Was the curse meant to reinforce gender roles?

Those who make a strong distinction between male and female roles often speak of the curse as God's strategy to reinforce the gender differences that had already been introduced at creation. They argue that the "curses" are very appropriately suited to each gender. "The woman's punishment revolves around husband and children," writes Foh, "and the man's around his work. In other words, the woman feels the effects of sin in her roles as mother and wife and the man in his role as provider. Does this sound like sexual stereotypes? Does this support 'the woman's place in the home"?"[7]

Trible has countered that argument by suggesting that the terms of the curse are culturally defined. The woman is associated with her husband and her work—childbearing—and the man is linked with his work of tilling the soil. But even as the man has progressed beyond subsistence farming, so has the woman progressed beyond a life devoted exclusively to childbearing and the home.[8]

In Christ is it possible to go beyond the curse?
The effects of the curse on man and woman are not irreversible. Aida Besançon Spencer captures that truth in the title of her book *Beyond the Curse*. Biblical history is marked by three decisive events: creation, Fall and redemption. Never before Christ's return will the earth return to its original perfection and splendor; but, as a result of Christ's redemption, we are "beyond the curse." Christ died to redeem fallen humanity—so fallen that even the law was ineffectual. Indeed, anyone who relies on works is under the "curse" of the law, as Paul writes in Galatians 3:10: "For all who rely on the works of the law are under a curse; for it is written, 'Cursed is everyone who does not observe and obey all the things written in the book of the law.'" Paul goes on to say in verse 13 that "Christ redeemed us from the curse of the law by becoming a curse for us—for it is written, 'Cursed is everyone who hangs on a tree.' "

Until we reach the point of perfection in the life hereafter, we are all saddled with a fallen nature, but that fallenness—that proclivity to sin—can be harnessed through redemption in Christ. As we grow in our Christian faith, relationships are healed, and the carnal tendencies toward domination and dependence resulting from the curse are subdued by a spirit of oneness in Christ. Yes, we can move *beyond the curse*.

Isaac Watts's most famous hymn captures this concept. The hymn was written as a reflection on Psalm 98, but it has since become one of our most beloved Christmas carols—"Joy to the World." The third verse speaks of going beyond the curse:

No more let sins and sorrows grow,
Nor thorns infest the ground;

He comes to make His blessings flow
Far as the curse is found. . . .

The second line, of course, refers to the portion of the curse that most affected Adam. It occurred to me recently, while singing that lovely carol, that the verse would be just as appropriate—perhaps more so—if, instead of "Nor thorns infest the ground," the second line read, "Nor rule by man abound." Maybe that phrase will one day become the alternate rendition and challenge us to go *beyond the curse* and "let sins and sorrows grow" no more.

PART 3

The
Old Testament
and
Jewish Culture

8

Is the Old Testament a Patriarchal Book?

Following the Fall into sin in Genesis 3, a new patriarchal order began, with the husband ruling over not only his wife but also the rest of his family. A man's leaving his father and mother and cleaving to his wife was no longer the standard. Power belonged to the oldest living male in the family and was passed on to the sons at his death.

"In the patriarchy the power of the male over females was direct, personal, and absolute," writes Faith Martin. "In each stage of her life, a woman was under the civil authority of a specific man—first her father, then her husband, and, if she was widowed, her son. . . . All males were permanent family members; they had rights, privileges, and a future power within the family. . . . Women passed from one family to another, never owning property."[1]

Israelite women did have status as mothers, but virtually none in the arenas of religion and politics. "They were at best spectators," writes

Denise Carmody. "It is clear that when the push came, many women were consigned to harsh treatment. The law did command honor for both father and mother, yet it kept women dependent from cradle to grave."[2]

Yes, in many respects the Old Testament is a patriarchal book. It is true that on many occasions the rigid gender barriers were broken, but at every turn women confronted sex discrimination, many instances of which are included in Scripture with no disclaimer. Patriarchalisn developed after the Fall and should be seen in light of our fallen natures.

How do we regard the patriarchy of the Old Testament? Because it is there—in holy Scripture—ought it be seen in any way as a standard for today? I think not. Many aspects of the Old Testament have been superseded by the teachings of Jesus. Indeed, one of his common expressions was, "You have heard that it was said . . . But I say to you. . . ." The New Testament overturns some of the most basic tenets of patriarchy, such as polygamy and the double standard regarding adultery and divorce, even as it overturns other practices, such as animal sacrifice and avenging one's enemies. These changes ought not to trouble us, but rather prompt us to rejoice in the freedom we have in Christ.

How were men of God infected by the evils of patriarchy?

A blatant example of sexual exploitation of women is seen in the life of Abraham, the "father of the faithful." The most notorious incident, recorded in Genesis 12, involves his wife, Sarah. Abraham tells Sarah to say that she is his sister because her beauty might so entice the Egyptians that they will kill him in order to add her to Pharaoh's harem.

"For Abraham the worst scenario was 'they will kill me but let you live,' " writes Gretchen Hull. "That Sarah might become 'fair game' (as indeed happened when she was taken into Pharaoh's palace) did not figure in Abraham's reasoning. The fact that Abraham repeated this cowardly and expedient deception in Genesis 10:1-7, and that his son Isaac copied it with his wife in Genesis 26:1-11, shows the expendability of women."[3]

Even righteous Job seems to have been tainted by the patriarchalism of his society. In his defense of his upright life in Job 31:9-10, he says,

"If my heart has been enticed by a woman, and I have lain in wait at my neighbor's door; then let my wife grind for another, and let other men kneel over her"—have sex with her, that is. Such a statement reflects an utter disregard for a woman—that she should be used as property and abused as a sex object because of her husband's sin.

What incident in the Old Testament depicts patriarchalism at its worst?
While Job may have *thought* of women as sex objects, others acted their thoughts out in vivid scenes of infamy. One despicable example is found in Judges 19:22-26—a story that is similar in many ways to the one recorded in Genesis 19, involving Lot and the men of Sodom. The story in Judges opens with a demonstration of hospitality that was common in ancient Hebrew culture. An old man from Gibeah, of the tribe of Benjamin, saw some strangers in town (a man accompanied by his concubine and a male servant) and invited them to spend the night at his home. As the evening progressed, some men of the town—"a perverse lot"—began pounding at the door and demanding that the guest be sent out so that they could rape him.

The host was adamant that his guest not be treated in such a fashion, but his solution to the problem demonstrates the potential evil of the patriarchal system: "Since this man is my guest, do not do this vile thing," the old man pled. "Here are my virgin daughter and his [the guest's] concubine; let me bring them out now. Ravish them and do whatever you want to them; but against this man do not do such a vile thing." The men outside would have none of this reasoning, but finally the guest "seized his concubine, and put her out to them. They wantonly raped her, abusing her "all through the night until the morning."

The bizarre plot of this story does not end here. In the morning the guest found his concubine dead on the doorstep. He returned home with her dead body and cut it into twelve pieces, sending the pieces throughout Israel with the message, "Has such a thing ever happened since the day that the Israelites came up from the land of Egypt until this day? Consider it, take counsel, and speak out."

The reaction was one of outrage, and the tribe of Benjamin was duly punished. Indeed, what the men of Gibeah had done was deemed a heinous crime. But there was no outrage shown toward the old man or his guest for their misuse of women by offering both women and then giving one of them to appease the crazed mob. And in the end, after the tribe of Benjamin was so demolished that there were not enough wives for the men, once again women were misused—this time in a gesture of good will toward the enemy. The leaders in Israel "instructed the Benjaminites" to "go and lie in wait in the vineyards, and watch; when the young women of Shiloh come out to dance in the dances, then come out of the vineyards and each of you carry off a wife for himself from the young women of Shiloh" (Judg 21:20-21).

How have discriminatory purification rites affected women?

The Old Testament law is often viewed as being discriminatory toward women. While it is true that all bodily discharges—male or female—were considered unclean, it was the woman who, by her very nature, was the most restricted by "uncleanness."

This is evident in Leviticus 15. The whole chapter is devoted to the matter of bodily discharges, which made both men and women ceremonially unclean. The man was generally able to control a discharge of semen simply by abstaining from sex, but even then he was unclean only until the evening of the same day, assuming he washed properly.

A woman, however, was not able to control her monthly menstrual flow, and her uncleanness extended over a longer period of time. In verse 19, we read: "When a woman has a discharge of blood that is her regular discharge from her body, she shall be in her impurity for seven days." By her very anatomy, a woman was at a disadvantage. "Women could not exercise control over menstruation or childbirth," writes Martin, "and so could not be commanded to appear before God. This might be one reason why women were not to serve as priests. Childbirth, menstruation, and intercourse would render them ceremonially unclean and unable to serve with regularity in the temple."[4]

Many of these restrictions of the ceremonial law were carried over into the Christian era. This was evident in 601, when Augustine of Canterbury wrote to Pope Gregory I, inquiring about ceremonial restrictions on women's involvement in the church. Pope Gregory responded with the explanation that it would make no sense to deny a pregnant woman baptism, for that would negate grace to one whose very condition was evidence of God's gift of fertility. As to whether an "unclean" woman ought to be permitted to partake of the Eucharist, Gregory reminded Augustine of the "unclean" woman who touched the hem of Jesus' garment and was healed. In these instances, then, the Old Testament law was no longer determinative—at least while Gregory was on the papal throne. Several decades later Augustine's successor reinstituted rules that denied women the sacrament during pregnancy or menstruation.[5]

What effect did polygamous marriage have on Old Testament women?

Polygamy was an accepted practice in ancient Hebrew culture. Abraham had, in addition to Sarah, a number of wives and concubines—the most noted of whom was Hagar. His grandson Jacob had twelve sons, born of four different women. The great hero Gideon also practiced polygamy. How else would he have fathered seventy sons? He had many wives, and at least one concubine, according to Judges 8:30-31.

Polygamy did not work well for David, who was ever troubled over the women in his life, but he nevertheless "took more concubines and wives" (2 Sam 5:13). His attitude toward them was not necessarily characterized by love—or even lust. In 2 Samuel 20:3 we read: "David came to his house at Jerusalem; and the king took the ten concubines whom he had left to look after the house, and put them in a house under guard, and provided for them, but did not go in to them. So they were shut up until the day of their death, living as if in widowhood." Such were the effects of patriarchalism. What is worse, we may ask, having to share a man with many other women or being held under guard with no contact whatsoever with the so-called partner?

But David, of course, does not take the prize for polygamy. His celebrated son Solomon made a game out of the custom, with his seven hundred wives and three hundred concubines (1 Kings 11:3).

Like other aspects of patriarchalism, polygamy had a very negative effect on women. Indeed, it often brought out the worst in them, as was true of Sarah, who gave her slave-girl Hagar to her husband, Abraham, when she herself was unable to conceive. When Hagar realized that she had conceived, "she looked with contempt on her mistress. . . . Then Sarai dealt harshly with her, and she ran away from her" (Gen 16:4-6). In this instance, Sarah "succumbed to the patriarchal system with her manipulative use of Hagar and lived to regret it."[6]

Another contentious polygamous situation involved Hannah and Peninnah, the wives of Elkannah. In 1 Samuel 1:4-6, we read that when Elkannah went to the temple to sacrifice, he gave a portion to his wife Peninnah, "but to Hannah he gave a double portion, because he loved her, though the Lord had closed her womb." This favoritism rankled Peninnah, who "used to provoke [Hannah] severely, to irritate her, because the Lord had closed her womb."

Yet these were perhaps among the least of the devastating effects on women of the patriarchal system and polygamy. The case of Michal, one of David's many wives, illustrates the utter degradation of the system. Michal was initially married to David as a political pawn, at the insistence of her father, Saul. Later, however, when Michal aided David in escaping Saul, Saul abruptly married her to another man—a man who, amazing as it may seem, truly loved and cared for her. But the story does not end with a "happily ever after." David later decided that he needed Michal's political connections, and he demanded that she return to him as his wife. "Ishbaal sent and took her from her husband Paltiel the son of Laish. But her husband went with her, weeping as he walked behind her all the way to Bahurim. Then Abner said to him, 'Go back home!' So he went back" (2 Sam 3:15-16). Hull confesses, "I have always had a soft spot for Paltiel, the only man who cared for Michal and who was loyal and open enough to show it." Hull reflects further on Michal:

> What of Michal? We can imagine her dismay, not only at being wrenched from a loving husband (to whom she had now been married for about ten years) but upon finding herself back in David's household, part of an evergrowing list of wives and concubines (2 Samuel 5:13-16). Is it any wonder that when Michal saw David exuberantly

dancing in a religious celebration, she despised him? Was she thinking: *You, who care so much for your God, don't care much for human beings He made.* Is it surprising that she greeted him with sarcasm when he returned? There was no relationship between these two, no "one flesh" union. The story of this unfortunate woman's life concludes on a bitter note. Michal's punishment for her lack of respect for the man who treated her as a possession was to be deprived of the ancient world's female status symbol: "And Michal daughter of Saul had no children to the day of her death."[7]

How did the life of Hebrew women compare to those in other cultures?
There is no agreement among scholars as to how the lot of Hebrew women compared to that of women in other cultures. Herbert Lockyer dogmatically asserts that it was far better:

While the ancient world was predominantly a man's world, women enjoyed a status in Israel not generally experienced in the East. The Jews, holding to the revelation given to Moses of woman's endowments, worth and right position, were outstanding among other oriental nations in holding women in high esteem, honor and affection. . . .

The position of women in Israel was in marked contrast with her status in surrounding heathen nations. Israelite law was designed to protect woman's weakness, safeguard her rights, and preserve her freedom (Deuteronomy 21:10-14; 22:13; 22:28). Under divine law her liberties were greater, her tasks more varied and important, and her social standing more respectful and commanding than that of her heathen sister. . . . Womanly virtues were foreign to pagan cultures under which women became subject to inferior and degrading conditions. Decline of woman in Israel was always due to the invasion of heathen influences.[8]

All cultures in the ancient world in one way or another discriminated against women; despite this fact, however, in some cultures women played very significant roles in religion. "There is not a trace of a priestess in Israel," write Evelyn and Frank Stagg, but "there were priestesses alongside priests in the ancient pagan world."[9]

9

How Did God Work through Women in the Old Testament?

lthough women did not serve as priests in ancient Judaism, they did function in other capacities that at times gave them authority in both religious and secular matters. Indeed, for all the patriarchy manifested throughout the pages of the Old Testament, women are remarkably prominent. They take part in the biblical drama with no apologies, and they often outmaneuver their male counterparts, with no censorship from God. "Any prominence woman attained," writes Herbert Lockyer, "was obtained by force of character."[1]

"We have a double sided picture of the leadership of women in the Old Testament," writes Mary Evans. "Women leaders were few and far between. . . . Women were not eligible for the priesthood. But on the other hand, there is no indication that women were ineligible for or incapable of leadership or authority. That women leaders did exist in a society where women were generally considered inferior is significant," and there is "no indication in the Old Testament that the leadership of women over men is somehow alien to their created nature."[2]

Does Sarah fit the role of an obedient wife?
The wives of the patriarchs were strong women—sometimes portrayed in Scripture as stronger than their husbands—and they played very important roles within the family structure.

The first of these great women was Sarah, a figure who has been batted around a lot in the feminist-traditionalist controversy. This is largely because of Peter's reference to her in his first epistle: "It was in this way long ago that the holy women who hoped in God used to adorn themselves by accepting the authority of their husbands. Thus Sarah obeyed Abraham and called him lord (3:5-6)." Peter goes on to enjoin "husbands, *in the same way*," to "show consideration for your wives . . . , paying honor to the woman," but it is *Sarah's* obedience that is often made the issue. Traditionalists argue that all women should, like Sarah, obey their husbands, though they hedge on the issue of calling them "lord," or "master," as it is sometimes rendered. "It is unthinkable to modern wives to call their husbands 'master' and would seem impersonal to most husbands," writes Hurley. "We would consider the term appropriate to a slave/master relation. This is one of those cases in which the cultural context is very important."[3] One might ask whether "cultural context is very important" in understanding the issue of obedience as well.

Bilezikian has pointed out that "in Genesis, Abraham is shown as obeying Sarah as often as Sarah obeyed Abraham—once at God's behest as he was told, 'Whatever Sarah says to you, do as she tells you' (Gen. 16:2; 21:11-12)." As for her addressing him as "lord," it was "in a monologue to herself, when he was out of earshot (18:12)."[4]

What is the significance of two books being named for women?
The books of Ruth and Esther are both named for women, indicating that women did play a very important role in ancient Jewish patriarchal society. But in each instance it is the woman's acquiescence to the pa-

triarchal structure that makes her a role model for the Jewish people.

Ruth was actually not Jewish. She married into a Jewish family who had come to Moab fleeing famine. Eventually her father-in-law, brother-in-law and husband died, and after the famine had subsided she went with her mother-in-law, Naomi, to Bethlehem.

By the end of the first chapter of the book, Naomi and Ruth are back in Bethlehem. The remaining three chapters offer an interesting account of what might be considered scheming on the part of Naomi and Ruth to secure a husband for Ruth and scheming on the part of Boaz to negotiate the marriage.

For her part, Ruth sent the right signals to Boaz. She was a hard worker—"on her feet from early this morning until now, without resting even for a moment" (2:7); and she was duly submissive, referring to Boaz as "my lord" and to herself as "your servant" (2:13). But Ruth was not entirely passive in the developing relationship. Indeed, at the prompting of Naomi, she lay down at the feet of Boaz while he was sleeping at the threshing floor. He responded according to Naomi's plan and agreed to arrange for Ruth's marriage—though not necessarily to himself. Custom dictated that the next-of-kin had the right to her. In the end, through clever negotiating, Boaz acquired a field and Ruth in one transaction; both were treated as the inheritance—the property—of the deceased son of Naomi.

Ruth's ultimate significance (and no doubt the reason her story is included in the canon of Scripture) is derived from her role as mother—the highest calling for a woman in ancient Jewish culture. She gave birth to Obed, who became the father of Jesse, the father of David. As the great-grandmother of David, she is found in the genealogy of Jesus through Joseph, recorded in Matthew 1:5.

Esther found fame not through motherhood, but rather by becoming a savior to her people. Yet her life, too, was largely circumscribed by patriarchal culture. On the decision of her guardian, Mordecai, she became one of the "beautiful young virgins" in the Persian king's harem. She was chosen to be queen based on her beauty, to replace the deposed queen Vashti, who had refused to display herself at a great all-male party hosted by the king (Esther 1:10). Apparently Esther was quite willing to do this, for after she was chosen queen "the king gave a great banquet to all his officials and ministers—'Esther's banquet' " (2:18).

Esther was a Jew, a matter she had kept secret from the gentile king and his officials at the insistence of her guardian, Mordecai, "for Esther obeyed Mordecai just as when she was brought up by him" (2:20). In the end, with the help of her guardian and the favor of the king, Esther saved her people, and the feast of Purim was inaugurated to commemorate what she had done. She was a role model for Jewish women.

Did women write any Old Testament books?

To suggest that a woman wrote any portion of the Old Testament would be tantamount to heresy in the minds of some, but to suggest that a woman was a major contributor to the Pentateuch—the first five books of the Bible—would be unthinkable. Yet that is exactly what one scholar has suggested.

The debate over who actually wrote the Pentateuch is not new. According to Jewish tradition, the author was Moses, and his authorship is accepted virtually without question in evangelical circles. Yet in *The Book of J,* Harold Bloom, a recognized literary critic from Yale University, conjectures that "the most memorable sections of *Genesis* and *Exodus,* plus bits of *Numbers* and *Deuteronomy,* were the work of an anonymous woman." Bloom's case is based on circumstantial evidence at best. "Among his arguments: *Genesis* contains the only known account from the ancient Middle East of the creation of woman—six times as long as the story of Adam's advent from a 'mud pie.' Furthermore, the women of the Pentateuch (Eve, Sarah, Rebecca, Rachel, Tamar, Zipporah) are strong."[5]

A more likely example of female authorship in the Old Testament is the Song of Songs. Although its authorship has usually been ascribed to Solomon, there remain serious questions in the minds of many scholars. It may have been a song that he compiled—as is true of Proverbs 31.

"The Song of Songs is a candid celebration of human love," writes Martin. "Of interest to us is its understanding of female sexuality and the fact that it is written from a woman's point of view." Martin further points out that "women singers were common in the literary history of the Hebrews. The Bible contains other songs written by women: Hannah, Deborah, and Mary. Miriam led the women in a song of victory after the defeat of the Egyptians. Women singers are specifically mentioned in 2 Samuel 19:35, 2 Chronicles 35:25, and Ecclesiastes 2:8."[6]

What role did women play as prophets in the Old Testament?

The role of the prophet is a very significant one in the Bible, and the fact that women filled that role is surely worth noting. Indeed, in ancient Israel, for all its patriarchalism, women were actually permitted to represent God to the people.

> The prophet whom the Lord would raise was to be like Moses; just as Moses was a mediator between God and the nation, so that prophet would serve as a mediator. At Horeb, when God appeared to the nation, the people trembled and asked that Moses alone should speak to them. God commended Israel for their request and announced that there would be a mediator, even the prophets. The prophets, then, served as mediators between God and the nation. Just as the priests represented the people before God, so the prophets represented God to the people.[7]

There are at least five women in the Old Testament who represented God as prophetesses at one time or another. The best known are Miriam, the sister of Moses (Ex 15:20), Deborah, the judge (Judg 4:4), and Huldah (2 Kings 22:14). Lesser-known prophetesses are Noadiah (Neh 6:14) and the unnamed mother of Isaiah's children (Is 8:3). None of these women wrote books of prophecy, as did many of their male counterparts, and their numbers were few in comparison to the host of male prophets referred to in the Old Testament. Yet they played crucial roles in the life of the ancient Hebrew people.

Many Bible commentators, not least among them Calvin, have sought to denigrate the role of the female prophet. In Calvin's view, the prophetess was called upon "whenever God wishes to brand man with a mark of ignomy." He believed this to be true of Deborah and Huldah: "God doubtless wished to raise them on high to shame the men." Miriam, he maintained, "never ceased to be a reproach to her brother."[8]

There is no evidence whatsoever that women were *used* in this manner—that their ministry only served the purpose of disgracing men. And these women were not tokens or merely last-minute substitutes to fit contingency plans. They were women who were recognized for their unique communication with God Almighty.

Huldah is an example. One of the great prophets of the Old Testament, she was sought out by King Josiah—who, we remember from our Sunday-school days, was one of the *good* kings. What is perhaps most significant about her role in Israel at this time is that there were others well known for their prophecy—including Jeremiah and Zephaniah—but King Josiah sent an official delegation of five men, including the high priest, to seek out Huldah. And the issue here was not who would win a battle or whether there would be a famine, but the very Word of God. "Only Huldah could interpret the significance of Deuteronomy to the devout King Josiah, to Hilkiah the high priest, and to Josiah's cabinet, Shaphan, Ahikam, Achbor, and Asaiah."[9]

Huldah delivered to these eminent men "a scathing denunciation of the religious corruption of the nation and a powerful prediction of doom that motivated the king to effect profound changes in the religious life of the people (2 Kings 22:11-23:25). Thus, the spiritual leadership of a woman . . . affected the history of the whole nation."[10]

What is the significance of Deborah's authority as a leader?

Deborah was a prophetess, but she is known more for her role as a judge and leader of an army than for her prophecies. She is almost universally held in high esteem by modern-day writers—though there are a few detractors who would seek to minimize her achievements. God's revelation to Deborah that he would "sell Sisera into the hand of a woman" (Judg 4:9), according to John R. Rice, "shows that Barak's insistence on taking Deborah with him displeased the Lord. Deborah was not a preacher, not a leader. God did not want her leading the army. She did not have any authority over men and did not teach men."[11]

Hurley takes issue with this analysis. "It has sometimes been suggested that Deborah's calling as a judge and prophetess constituted a shaming of Israel," he writes. "The evidence for such a view is simply lacking in the text. Barak is shamed by the fact that he, the warrior who would not go forth at God's command, will not have glory for his victory but that it will go to a non-combatant woman, Jael. There is no shame implied in the fact that he received direction from Deborah."[12]

The significance of Deborah's story lies in the fact that she was a devout woman who submitted herself to God as a prophetess and took command as a judge and army leader as she served the people. In patriarchal Israel, men followed the lead of this remarkable woman.

10

What Glimpses of the Modern Woman Can Be Found in the Old Testament?

For some people the Old Testament is an ancient relic that does not seem particularly relevant to contemporary life. So strange is biblical culture that sometimes the characters almost appear to be living on a different planet.

Yet the Old Testament offers fascinating examples of very modern personalities—women as well as men. While the settings and props have changed dramatically from their day to ours, the issues and inner struggles have changed very little. Indeed, Old Testament women met with challenges and frustrations in their roles and relationships that were similar to those modern women encounter.

In some instances, Old Testament women seem to have been ahead of their time or to have swum against the current of prevailing thought. Despite the restrictions of Jewish patriarchal culture, they did not always follow prescribed rules. Some of them struggled with problems and weaknesses that are all too common among women today. These women might have profited by a good dose of modern therapy. They all show us that, for better or for worse, womanhood is not so different today from what it was in ancient times.

Was there any feminist protest in the Old Testament?

The Old Testament contains an amazing account of feminist protest that is often overlooked because it is only a short scene in the drama of a historic adventure in which Esther plays the lead role. Vashti, though a queen, is the minor character who takes a stand for women's rights in a very patriarchal society.

Vashti, born a Persian princess, married the powerful King Xerxes (Ahasuerus in the Hebrew); according to Esther 1:1, Xerxes "ruled over one hundred twenty-seven provinces from India to Ethiopia." He was a wealthy and ostentatious monarch who threw a 180-day celebration in the third year of his reign. As queen, Vashti carried out her required duties. She is first shown giving a banquet for the women, while her husband was entertaining the men. In their Eastern culture, men were separated from women at social functions.

The name Vashti means "beautiful woman," and she lived up to her name. She was indeed beautiful and "fair to behold" (Esther 1:11), and it was this beauty that led to her downfall. "On the seventh day, when the king was merry with wine, he commanded . . . the seven eunuchs who attended him, to bring Queen Vashti before the king . . . in order to show the people and the officials her beauty."

Here was the dilemma. Should she go against her upbringing and culture and obey the king by displaying her body to hundreds of drunken military and political officials? Or should she be true to her conscience and insist that such a setting was not a proper place for a lady? If her inebriated husband wanted to bring in dancers or female entertainers of some other sort, she could not prevent it. But to lower herself, the queen, to his inappropriate demand was something she simply could not accept. There is no reason to believe that she had defied patriarchal authority before, but in this instance "Queen Vashti refused to come at the king's command."

The king was furious, and after he had consulted with his advisers, Queen Vashti was shown the door. It was decreed that she was "never again to come before King Ahasuerus" and that the king would "give her royal position to another who is better than she" (Esther 1:19).

The rationale behind the decree was simple—to offset the "feminist" protest of the queen: "For this deed of the queen will be made known to all women, causing them to look with contempt on their husbands." But with the decree in force, "all women will give honor to their husbands, high and low alike" (Esther 1:17, 20). We do not know if that actually was the case, but we do know that Vashti was humiliated by her pompous husband, and Esther filled her place. How should we regard Vashti? "Her self-respect and her high character meant more to her than her husband's vast realm," writes Lockyer. "Rather than cater to the vanity and sensuality of the drunkards she courageously sacrificed a kingdom." Lockyer further suggests that "the only true ruler in that drunken court was the woman who refused to exhibit herself, even at the king's command."[1]

Vashti was a "feminist" of her day. She refused to be used or controlled by the opposite sex, and her protest was regarded as dangerous—so dangerous that it could potentially infect the whole female population and result in the loss of male authority. And that would, indeed, have been a devastating turn of events in such a patriarchal society.

What Old Testament woman fits the label "Smart Woman, Foolish Choices"?

Much has been written in recent years about women who are paralyzed by codependency and women who make foolish choices regarding the men in their lives. The books *Women Who Love Too Much* and *Smart Women, Foolish Choices* are addressed to women who tend to become involved with men who are very self-centered, physically abusive or alcoholic—or perhaps all three. The woman facilitates her partner's inappropriate behavior or lifestyle and as such is classified as codependent. She covers up for him, makes excuses when he is found out, and expends considerable energy in the attempt to show that everything is all right.

Abigail, the wife of Nabal and later David, fits the profile for "smart women, foolish choices" and to a large degree the profile for a codependent. She recognized the depravity of her husband and was not afraid to formulate plans of her own, but she was unable to let him face the consequences of his behavior. A second marriage promised little more in the way of personal fulfillment for this attractive and intelligent woman.

Abigail's story is told in 1 Samuel 25, where we learn that Nabal "was very rich; he had three thousand sheep and a thousand goats." If wealth could be considered a redeeming quality, though, it was the only one Nabal apparently possessed. The Bible goes on to describe this couple in clearly contrasting terms: "The woman was clever and beautiful, but the man was surly and mean."

We would probably never know the story of Abigail had David not entered the picture. He and King Saul were at odds, and David and his armies were out in the countryside in the vicinity of Nabal's vast estate. David had protected Nabal's property and herds, so it seemed only natural that he could expect some provisions of food from this wealthy man. His request, however, was rudely rebuffed, so David and his men prepared for a fight.

When Abigail learned of the situation, she secretly brought large provisions of food to David and his men. On seeing David, she got off her donkey and fell on her face before him, begging him not to attack. "Upon me alone, my lord, be the guilt," she pleaded. "My lord, do not take seriously this ill-natured fellow, Nabal." David agreed to grant her petition. She returned home to find her husband drunk. In the morning when he was sober, she told him what she had done. At the news, he collapsed, and he died several days later.

Abigail was not what we would envision as a grieving widow. Soon after her husband's death, she married David. Her relationship with him has been interpreted by some as a romantic love story—and it may have been, but she had to share him with other wives and viewed herself as his virtual slave, as her response to his marriage proposal indicates: "She rose and bowed down, with her face to the ground, and said, 'Your servant is a slave to wash the feet of the servants of my lord' " (1 Sam

25:41). "Here a beautiful love story," Bilezikian says, "is sullied by male dominance and its nefarious effects."[2]

What does Proverbs 31 have to say to the modern woman?

To some women, the figure described in Proverbs 31 is a superwoman who is more than any human can be expected to emulate. Truly, she is just that. She is an ideal and ought not to be seen as the norm for women. Given that she is an ideal, though, it is very significant that she is not a mother and housewife only; she is not exclusively confined to the home.

For those who insist that a woman's place is in the home, Proverbs 31 can be a difficult passage to deal with. Here is a woman who is very clearly a loyal wife and a caring mother. There is no indication that she is domineering or self-centered, but there is every indication that she is independent and self-sufficient. She has her husband's trust, and "she does him good, and not harm." She is an effective administrator in her busy household, but in addition to that she is skilled in crafts such as sewing and weaving. Besides her home activities, she is involved in business transactions—selling her crafts to merchants and buying and selling real estate. And on the side, she does a little farming. In all this, humanitarian endeavors are not forgotten: "She opens her hand to the poor, and reaches out her hands to the needy."

Perhaps as important as anything else, "her children rise up and call her happy; her husband too, and he praises her." As involved in life as she is, she has not forgotten to care for herself. She is happy, and her husband and children recognize that. Surely this is the ideal woman, as verse 29 suggests: "Many women have done excellently, but you surpass them all." We know virtually nothing about the real woman on whom this description is based, except for what is revealed in the first verse of the chapter: "The words of King Lemuel. An oracle that his mother taught him." The heading in the text is simply "The Teaching of King Lemuel's Mother."

Was this king's mother some kind of ancient Palestinian feminist? No. She was simply a woman with varied interests and large horizons, and her ideals became the very Word of God.

What light does the Song of Songs shed on women?

If many of the incidents, pronouncements and writings of the Old Testament appear to be influenced by the patriarchal structure of Hebrew culture, the Song of Songs (or Song of Solomon) certainly does not. Here "the woman is independent, fully the equal of the man," and there is "no male dominance." This poem shows "that in Old Testament thought the concept of mutuality and equality between the sexes could be envisaged as possible and even perhaps as desirable, although it must be stressed that the concept is rarely found worked out in practice within the Israelite society."[3]

"We believe that the Song of Solomon was included in the canon of Scripture because it celebrates conjugal love in its generic state," writes Bilezikian. "It miraculously catches a glimpse of the divine intent for the ways of man and woman together, above and beyond their fateful separation as ruler and subject. As such it may be considered a poetico-dramatic commentary on the original charter of God's definition of male/female relations found in Genesis 2:23-24."[4]

PART 4

The
New Testament
and Women

11
Was Jesus
a Feminist?

In his article "Jesus Was a Feminist," Leonard Swidler offers a definition of feminism by showing how the concept was personified by Jesus. He contends that "Jesus neither said nor did anything which would indicate that he advocated treating women as intrinsically inferior to men, but that on the contrary he said and did things which indicated that he thought of women as equals of men, and that in the process he willingly violated pertinent social mores."[1]

In presenting his case, it is this last point that Swidler makes most powerfully. By today's standards, Jesus' attitude toward women may not appear unusual, but by the standards of first-century Palestine, he was nothing less than revolutionary. Women were regarded as inferior, and such was the pronounced teaching of some of the Jewish rabbis. Eliezer, a first-century rabbi, did not mince words: "Rather should the words of the Torah be burned than entrusted to a woman. . . . Whoever teaches his daughter the Torah is like one who teaches her lasciviousness." The Talmud warned men of dire consequences if women were involved in spiritual matters, including prayer: "Let a curse come upon the man who [must needs have] his wife or children say grace for him." A common daily prayer of thanksgiving spoke of women in derogatory terms: "Praised be God that he has not created me a gentile; praised be God that he has not created me a woman; praised be God that he has not created me an ignorant person."[2]

Whether or not Jesus ought to be labeled a "feminist" is debatable. It is also worth noting that Stephen Clark and other scholars take issue with Swidler, claiming that Jesus was not overtly bucking Jewish custom in his association with women, and that his opponents did not challenge him on that count as they did regarding his association with sinners.[3] Yet however Jesus' attitude toward women is characterized, it is safe to say that he had an unusual sensitivity to women and their needs—remarkably so for a man of first-century Palestine. Dorothy Sayers captures this sensitivity in her oft-quoted description of Jesus:

> They had never known a man like this Man—there never had been such another. A prophet and teacher who never nagged at them, never flattered or coaxed or patronized; who never made arch jokes about them, never treated them as "The women, God help us!" or "The ladies, God bless them"; who rebuked without querulousness and praised without condescension; who took their questions and arguments seriously; who never mapped out their sphere for them, never urged them to be feminine or jeered at them for being female; who had no axe to grind and no uneasy male dignity to defend; who took them as he found them and was completely unselfconscious. There is no act, no sermon, no parable in the whole Gospel that borrows its pungency from female perversity; nobody could possibly guess from the words and deeds of Jesus that there was anything "funny" about woman's nature.[4]

What can we learn about Jesus from the story of the Samaritan woman? Many stories in the Gospels illustrate the respect that Jesus showed women on a personal level. Indeed, time and again he had interchanges with them that reveal not even the slightest hint of male superiority—that women were in any way less capable of understanding or assimilating the truths that he was seeking to communicate.

The story that perhaps best illustrates this takes place in Sychar and involves the Samaritan woman who was drawing water from the well. John 4:7-26 is an account of one of the most intense conversations between Jesus and a woman recorded in the Bible. John devotes as much space to this interaction as he does to the very significant conversation Jesus had with Nicodemus in the previous chapter (which includes the most memorized verse in the whole Bible, John 3:16). The conversation with the woman, however, involves twice as much interaction as does the conversation with Nicodemus. At six points, John records that "the woman said to him" (or "answered him"); Nicodemus, on the other hand, comes into the conversation only three times, and even then his questions seem less weighty than hers. Nicodemus asks whether a person can return to the womb and be born again—his only specific inquiry—while the woman delves into significant matters, asking Jesus about his status in comparison to the patriarch Jacob, about the geography of worship, and whether the Messiah will be all-knowing. Her questions are both personal and spiritually perceptive, and Jesus appears not to be at all offended by her ability to hold her own. Jesus treats her with as much or more respect as he did the educated Pharisee Nicodemus. Nothing in his manner singles her out as a woman.

When we reflect on Jesus' interaction with the woman of Sychar and compare his attitude toward her with the attitude of biblical commentators, we find Jesus all the more remarkable. Abraham Kuyper, a theologian and Bible teacher in the Calvinist tradition, characterizes the Samaritan woman as "positively uncouth," "superficial, mundane, and gullible."[5] When I read his comments, I almost have to wonder if we are reading the same biblical account. There is nothing that would indicate she could be characterized by any of those adjectives—least of all "gullible." Indeed, she was no pushover when it came to theological matters. Jesus told her pointblank that he was the Messiah, but when she returned to the town to share the news, her claim to his identity was less certain: "Come and see a man who told me everything I have ever done! He cannot be the Messiah, can he?" (Jn 4:29). "It is not that she was a doubter, for it is remarkable that any Samaritan would on the basis of one conversation even entertain the possibility that the speaker was the Jewish Messiah! She had ventured into the area of faith, willing to break with her own tradition but not rushing headlong and wide-eyed into something she did not understand."[6]

The Samaritan woman found Jesus to be a man like none she had ever encountered—one who did not view her as a sex object (as many other men apparently did) and one she could introduce to her neighbors, knowing that they could never accuse him of being just another man in her life.

Why did Jesus not show more honor and respect for his mother?

Jesus' treatment of his mother has much to say to us regarding his attitude toward women. Mary was the ultimate mother. She above all other mothers deserved honor and respect. Yet from the time of Jesus' childhood, when he was found by his parents in the temple, to the end of his life, he did not single out his mother for special honor. It would have been normal for him to do so. While Jewish culture often showed very little respect for women per se, great honor was paid to mothers and the ideal of motherhood. In the case of Jesus, however, the Gospels almost seem to present the very opposite.

Although Mary herself recognized that she was *blessed*—from Elizabeth's words in Luke 1:42 ("Blessed are you among women") and from her own words in Luke 1:48 ("Surely, from now on all generations will call me blessed")—Jesus did not speak of her in that way. In fact, when a woman called out from the crowd, "Blessed is the womb that bore you and the breasts that nursed you!" he responded, "Blessed rather are those who hear the word of God and obey it" (Lk 11:27-28). Jesus had made the same point clear on an earlier occasion. When he was told that Mary and his brothers were waiting on the outskirts of the crowd to see him, he used the interruption to emphasize the primacy of spiritual relationships: "My mother and my brothers are those who hear the word of God and do it" (Lk 8:21).

It was important to Jesus that his disciples understand that motherhood was secondary to discipleship—even in the patriarchal culture of first-century Palestine. He personally did not make exceptions to the rule, even in his attitude toward his own mother. Mary was first and foremost a disciple.

There were hints of this relationship when Mary found the twelve-year-old Jesus in the temple and said, "Child, why have you treated us like this?" His response was, "Did you not know that I must be in my Father's house?" (Lk 2:48-49). At the wedding of Cana, Jesus responded in a similar manner when Mary showed concern that the guests had run out of wine: "Woman, what concern is that to you and me? My hour has not yet come" (Jn 2:4).

Jesus was not being rude to his mother, but he was demonstrating that he was above human relationships—above blood ties—and that all his followers, whether male or female, unrelated or kin, had equal status in his sight. In his response to the woman who wanted him to affirm her blessing on Mary, with one sentence he "catapulted women along with men, both shoulder to shoulder, to the cutting edge of God's program for the redemption of the world."[7]

Is it possible that Jesus was married?

Most Christians' immediate response to this inquiry is, *How dare you even ask the question?* But the issue does relate to how the man Jesus identified with women, and it has been seriously posed by at least one Bible scholar. In a book titled *Was Jesus Married?* William E. Phipps argues that it is only logical to assume that he was. He contends that Jesus, being a good Jew, would naturally have gotten married, as all good Jews of his day did. The belief that he remained celibate has been fostered by a tradition of sexual asceticism developed in the early church and adopted by Roman Catholicism; Phipps calls this tradition a "virus," a "malignancy" that has "eaten like a cancer into the body of Christ, causing sick attitudes and practices."[8]

From a human perspective, Phipps's arguments appear well reasoned. In the early church a perverted view of women did indeed lead to the belief that sexual intercourse was sinful—even within marriage. Thus celibacy became the ultimate standard for holiness. Is it possible, then, that we shun the idea of Jesus' being married only because of our wrong notions about women and about sex? Surely we would agree today that there is no sin involved in marriage and sexual intercourse within the bonds of marriage.

Might Jesus have been married? Paul Jewett has responded to this question very perceptively: "If Jesus was only and essentially a first-century Palestinian Jew, then in all likelihood he was married. But if he was the Word made flesh who dwelt among us (Jo. 1:14), then in his person the kingdom of heaven is present, the kingdom in which 'they neither marry nor are given in marriage' (Lu. 20:34-36)." Jewett goes on to say that "to believe that he was unmarried is not to deny *his* humanity, but to affirm that the sexual congress of husband and wife is not an essential part of *our* humanity."[9]

Assuming that Jesus was not married, did he experience normal feelings toward women? The Bible is silent on this issue, except to say that Jesus was in every way tempted as we are and yet was without sin (Heb 4:15). Did Jesus then have sexual fantasies? Marjorie Holmes, a gifted writer and committed Christian, has speculated that he did. In her novel *Three from Galilee,* she deals with this in a sensitive way. In one scene in the book, Jesus is dreaming of finding "a woman whom he could love," a "wife who would bear him children to nurse at her breast." Then suddenly he awakes in a cold sweat out of his restless sleep and realizes that he has been face to face with temptation.[10] But this was not the first time, Holmes speculates in her novel: "The girls at the grape treadings, young and lovely, sometimes unsteady from the very smell of wine. The girls who came into the shop on pretext of some tool to be mended for their fathers—their flirting eyes and sometimes casually touching hands."[11]

Yes, Jesus was a human being who faced all the temptations to sin that anyone might face, *yet without sin*. With certainty we can say that he was never married and never lusted after women, but it is obvious from the Gospel accounts that he loved and he loved deeply—not in the romantic or familial sense that we are accustomed to, but in a spiritual sense. "Here are my mother and brothers!" he exclaimed, pointing to his followers. "Whoever does the will of God is my brother and sister and mother" (Mk 3:34-35).

What do the parables show us about Jesus' view of women?
Teaching truths through parables was common in Jesus' day. Other rabbis taught in that manner. "But Jesus' parables are notably different from theirs in that he enriches them with materials drawn from the everyday world of a woman's cares and joys."[12] Jesus did not make an issue of this deviation from rabbinic custom; "he simply accepts women as whole and worth-while persons."[13] The parables were used to illustrate deep truths of the kingdom, and it was in that sense that his teaching was meaningful to both women and men who followed him.

The parables portray women in natural activities which illustrate various points which Jesus wished to make. Thus, a woman kneading yeast into flour illustrates the hidden but pervasive work of the kingdom (Mt. 13:33). A woman looking for a lost coin (from her dowry?) illustrates the concern of God for lost sinners (Lk. 15:8-10). Prepared and unprepared bridesmaids are examples of readiness for the Lord's return (Mt. 25:1-13). A persistent woman confronting a lazy judge teaches about the need for faithful prayer and not losing heart (Lk. 18-1-8). And a poor widow who gives the little that she has shows that devotion is not measured by the magnitude of our gifts but the commitment of our hearts (Mk. 12:38-44).[14]

How did Jesus nullify the double standard for women?
Jesus' abrogation of the double standard that differentiated between men and women is seen most powerfully in relation to the issue of marital infidelity. Then, even more than in modern Western society, it was taken for granted that men were not required to live up to the same standards of purity that women were. But Jesus made it clear that purity had

nothing to do with gender. When he was called upon to condemn a woman who was guilty of adultery, he took a powerful stand against custom and placed men on an equal par with women in the area of sin. Rachel Wahlberg refers to this story (recorded in Jn 8:3-11) not as "Jesus and the Woman Caught in Adultery," as it is usually identified, but as "Jesus and the Adulterous Men." "Ostensibly it is about a woman," she writes, "but basically it is about men and their double standard of morality."[15]

The scribes and Pharisees reminded Jesus that the penalty for a woman's adultery, according to Deuteronomy 22, was stoning. Although men were also to be stoned for committing adultery, the law was enforced more rigorously for women than for men. The scribes and Pharisees were testing Jesus and thought they had him trapped. After writing something with his finger on the ground, Jesus responded, "Let anyone among you who is without sin be the first to throw a stone at her." At that, the men left, leaving the woman with Jesus. He turned to her and said, "Woman, where are they? Has no one condemned you?" She responded, "No one, sir." And he said, "Neither do I condemn you. Go your way, and from now on do not sin again."

In nullifying the double standard, Jesus did not suggest that there are no gender distinctions in the tendency toward sexual sins. Indeed, in the Sermon of the Mount he singled men out in condemning the sin of lust: "You have heard that it was said, 'You shall not commit adultery.' But I say to you that everyone who looks at a woman with lust has already committed adultery with her in his heart" (Mt 5:27-28).

Unlike other Jewish rabbis, Jesus did not believe that the only way to prevent lust was to keep men and women separated. He was convinced that men and women should have social interaction, but that they should live on a higher standard than had previously been taught. "It is not the presence of a woman, but the sinful thoughts of a man, which makes the situation dangerous. Jesus, therefore, called upon his [male] disciples to discipline their thoughts rather than to avoid women."[16]

12

Did Jesus Offer Public Ministry to Women?

N o serious biblical scholar would deny that Jesus' message was for women as well as men, but there is debate regarding the role he gave women in ministry. Jesus called people to forsake the world and follow him and be his disciples. We know from the Gospels that women were among those who followed him, but what was their role in his public ministry? Hurley argues that "it stretches the text unwarrantably to suggest that they should be considered female apostles." Rather, they should be viewed as "parallel to the twelve as travelling companions rather than as apostles. . . . The only positive information which we have from Luke about their contribution to the ministry has to do with financial affairs."[1]

To view the women who followed Jesus as merely "companions" or financial supporters is to minimize their role. It is important to keep in mind that Jesus, unlike other Jewish rabbis, had women disciples—women who believed in him and followed with him when he traveled, no doubt at considerable cost to their home life. This is evident from a number of passages in the Gospels, though most notably in Luke 8:1-3. Concerning these verses, Grant Osborne writes:

> The basic scene is antithetical to Jewish mores; women never accompanied a rabbi and his band of disciples. While many rabbis . . . allowed women to study Torah to an extent, their becoming part of the inner circle of disciples was unheard of. Equally startling is the make-up of the central trio. Mary of Magdala came from a small unimportant town and had been exorcised of "seven demons"; yet she is mentioned before Joanna, the wife of Herod's steward. The prominence of the former (she is always first in Luke's lists) further demonstrates the reversal of status in Jesus' new order. The three named are merely representative of the "many other" women (v 3) who accompanied Jesus and "supported him with their own money." It was not unusual for women to support rabbis . . . but unheard of to participate also in the mission. Jesus broke several barriers in his acceptance and use of women.[2]

Why were there no women among Jesus' twelve disciples?

"If Jesus had been a revolutionary feminist," Grant Osborne contends, "he would have included a woman among his inner circle of twelve disciples. . . . Jesus clearly accepted the basic patriarchal matrix of his time; the roles of women were redefined within rather than outside that structure, and Jesus never abrogated the social order."[3] I could quibble with my friend Grant on this point. It seems to me that if Jesus had been a revolutionary feminist, he would have included six women among his inner circle of disciples—or maybe twelve. But he did not—not even one.

Why did Jesus choose only males? Did he have less confidence in women? In reading through the Gospels it is preposterous to imagine that Jesus regarded women as less qualified to serve than men. He related to women on the basis of equality, and women were among his most faithful followers.

Indeed, there is nothing in Jesus' teaching to indicate that gender would prevent anyone from fully carrying out the ministry of an apostle and being in Jesus' innermost circle of followers. There were no "male-only" mysteries or rituals to preserve or conceal. The women were in on all the "secrets" of the kingdom message—and often seemed to understand better than the men did. It is true, however, that the twelve disciples were perhaps seen as representative of the twelve tribes of Israel, and only males could symbolically fill these roles.

The most compelling explanation for Jesus' failure to call women to be among the twelve has to do with decorum. The potential for scandal was too great. Jesus was not afraid of opposition. It was an inevitable response to his startling new teachings. But that the gospel message might be slandered because of rumors of sex scandals was a risk he could not justify. So women were not to be numbered among the twelve disciples.

Does that fact have any application for the church today? It does in the minds of many people who use it as a primary reason for not allowing women to have positions of authority in the church. But we must remember that Jesus did not have any gentile disciples either. If being Jewish and being male are prerequisites for leadership in the church, the vast majority of today's leaders are not qualified.

How did women, as disciples, respond to Jesus?

To suggest that women were merely "companions" or menial servants of Jesus is to fail to recognize that Jesus had confidence in women on all levels, including matters of faith and doctrine. We often think of Peter as the apostle with authority who made the powerful Christological confession in Matthew 16:16: "Thou art the Christ, the Son of the living God"—as I memorized it in the King James Version. But we forget (or simply did not know in the first place) that Martha of Bethany made an almost identical confession, recorded in John 11:27: "You are the Messiah, the Son of God."

Even though Peter had made that great confession of who Jesus was, he and the other male disciples did not "understand that the Cross had to precede the crown" until after the resurrection. "But one disciple did seem to understand."[4] In John 12:3, it is recorded that "Mary took a pound of costly perfume made of pure nard, anointed Jesus' feet, and

wiped them with her hair." Judas complained that she could have sold
the perfume and given the money to the poor instead of "wasting" it. But
Jesus rebuked him, recognizing that Mary, "by pouring this ointment on
my body . . . has prepared me for burial." His next statement shows the
significance of her act: "Truly I tell you, wherever this good news is
proclaimed in the whole world, what she has done will be told in remem-
brance of her" (Mt 26:12-13). "It is hard to escape the conclusion that
this woman had a deeper understanding of the impending cross than did
Jesus' male disciples."5

How did Jesus' view of ministry restrict male or female authority?

The debate over women in ministry is really a debate over women and
authority. No one argues that women should not have ministry. Women
can perform works of charity, teach young children, and be prayer war-
riors. They may not, however, perform ministry that entails authority—
so argue the traditionalists.

But ministry, in the teaching of Jesus, was not to be associated with
authority. That truth is most evident in Matthew 20:20-28. Here the
mother of James and John requested that Jesus give her sons places of
special honor in his kingdom. The rest of the disciples became angry with
the two brothers for trying to put themselves above the rest, but Jesus
knew that this appetite for position and authority was not unique to
James and John. He called all the disciples together and said: "You know
that the rulers of the Gentiles lord it over them, and their great ones are
tyrants over them. It will not be so among you; but whoever wishes to
be great among you must be your slave, and whoever wishes to be first
among you must be your slave" (vv. 25-27). That passage ends with the
familiar self-revelation of Jesus: "just as the Son of man came not to be
served but to serve, and to give his life a ransom for many" (or as it is
rendered in the King James Version, "even as the Son of man came not
to be *ministered* unto, but to *minister* and to give his life a ransom for
many").

On another occasion, Jesus asked his disciples what they were arguing
about. They fell silent and did not answer him, but he knew. He brought

them together and said, "Whoever wants to be first must be last of all and servant of all." Then he drew a child into their midst and said, "Whoever welcomes one such child in my name welcomes me" (Mk 9:35-37). The disciples were all too conscious of position and making the right connections. A little child was the perfect illustration of someone who could offer no status. Jesus' message recorded in Matthew 18:3-4 is very similar: "Truly I tell you, unless you change and become like children, you will never enter the kingdom of heaven. Whoever becomes humble like this child is the greatest in the kingdom of heaven."

Jesus demonstrated his teaching on servanthood when he washed his disciples' feet. After he was finished he said, "For I have set you an example, that you also should do as I have done to you" (Jn 13:15).

Ministry is servanthood, and when that model is first and foremost in our minds, we focus on reaching out with the love of Jesus rather than on authority and position for ourselves.

What role did women play at the time of Jesus' death and resurrection?
We are very familiar with the stories of the faithful women who followed Jesus, especially between the time of his death and resurrection. In reference to the Gospel of Mark, Osborne writes that "the presence of the women in 15:40-41 as witnesses to the passion is important because they form the link between Jesus' death and his resurrection. Only they are present as witnesses to the death, burial, and resurrection. . . . In a sense the women are almost replacing the other disciples who 'all left [Jesus] and fled' (14:50)." Indeed, according to Mark, only the women followed Jesus to the end.[6]

Why were women chosen to announce the resurrection of Jesus—the most remarkable news bulletin ever dispatched? Would it not have made more sense if Jesus' chief spokesman, Peter, or one of his other disciples had confirmed that the prophecies he made of himself were indeed true? That issue has been much debated, with some Bible commentators suggesting that the resurrection story sheds light on a woman's proper place—not as a herald of the risen Christ but as one involved in menial household duties: "The correct answer to the question of why God chose women to receive the news first has often been missed because it is so obvious," according to Charles Ryrie. "Women were honored with the news of the resurrection first simply because they were being faithful to womanly duties. . . . They were at the tomb . . . because they were bringing spices for the body. This was a woman's work. God so honored them because of their faithful performance of their sex."[7]

The argument that "bringing spices for the body . . . was a woman's work" is certainly not a conclusion that we could draw from Scripture, as Dorothy Pape has pointed out. "Nicodemus and Joseph of Arimathea had already brought and applied nearly one hundred pounds of spices. . . . Even if spicing dead bodies was a woman's duty, the reward seems out of all proportion to the duty."[8]

Why was it that Jesus appeared to women first? We can only speculate that they were so honored because of their faithfulness. "Whereas John the Baptist's disciples buried him (Mk. 6:29), Jesus' male disciples fled, leaving the burial to others. Women, however, had some role in the burial of Jesus. They affirmed him in his darkest hour. Did Jesus have his reasons for choosing thus to affirm them?"[9]

Concerning the resurrection, Osborne writes that "God's choice of women as the first witnesses is one of the bedrock truths of the resurrection narratives." This is no minor detail. In the minds of many Bible scholars it is one of the key arguments for the historicity of the resurrection, for "it is very unlikely that any Jew would have created such a story as fiction, since women were not allowed to serve as legal witnesses."[10]

Were the Great Commission and Jesus' charge in Acts 1:8 for women?

> Go therefore and make disciples of all nations, baptizing them in the name of the Father and of the Son and of the Holy Spirit, and teaching them to obey everything that I have commanded you.

The Great Commission recorded in Matthew 28:19-20 was given specifically to Jesus' core disciples—minus Judas—though even among those eleven, "some doubted" (28:16-17). According to tradition, the apostles carried out this commission. They spread out with the gospel, with Peter,

James and John going separately to various locations in Europe, Philip and Andrew going to points north toward present-day Russia, Mark going south into Egypt, Bartholomew and Simon the Zealot to Persia, and Thomas to India.

Did they then fulfill the Great Commission—a directive limited to them alone? This view has not been uncommon throughout church history. In fact, it was the argument that William Carey, the "father of modern missions," faced when he began making the appeal to reach out with the gospel to the ends of the earth. Many, if not most, eighteenth-century churchmen believed that the Great Commission was given only to the apostles, and therefore converting the "heathen" was not their concern.

Today that position is almost universally rejected in the church. The Great Commission is for all Christians. But is it really? Are women left out—at least partially? Yes, women are strongly encouraged to "make disciples of all nations" (and as missionaries they far outnumber their male counterparts), but can they officiate in "baptizing them" and be fully involved in "teaching them"? The Great Commission sums up the mission of the church—a mission in which women do not participate equally.

Jesus restated the Great Commission just before his ascension, as recorded in Acts 1:8: "But you will receive power when the Holy Spirit has come upon you; and you will be my witnesses in Jerusalem, in all Judea and Samaria, and to the ends of the earth." Here again this charge would seem to be to all Jesus' followers who would be empowered by the Holy Spirit. But is the text applied equally today to women and men? Women are encouraged to be witnesses "to the ends of the earth" as foreign missionaries, but are they welcome as "witnesses in Jerusalem"—as preachers in their home country?

13

What Ministry Roles Did Women Fill in the Infant Church?

W omen were actively involved in ministry as Jesus' disciples, and that pattern continued after his death and resurrection. We see in the book of Acts that "great numbers of both men and women" were added to the church in Jerusalem (Acts 5:14). In Samaria, where Philip was preaching, "both men and women" were baptized (Acts 8:12). Dorcas is spoken of as a disciple in Acts 9:36: "Now in Joppa there was a disciple whose name was Tabitha, which in Greek is Dorcas. She was devoted to good works and acts of charity." In the verses that follow we learn that there were other women disciples who mourned her death. Lydia, a dye merchant from Philippi, is also spoken of as an early church leader (Acts 16:13-15, 40). Among the multitude of believers in Thessalonica there were "not a few of the leading women" (Acts 17:4). The same was true in Berea, where "not a few Greek women . . . of high standing" believed (Acts 17:12). In Athens, Damaris was among the believers (Acts 17:34).

These women were not merely listeners and believers in the gospel; they were baptized into full membership. Under the Old Testament order only men could partake of circumcision, the outward sign that they were God's people. Some of the Jewish believers from Judea had actually gone and told the new Christians at Antioch, "Except ye be circumcised after the manner of Moses, ye cannot be saved" (15:11), showing how vital a part of Jewish thinking it was. But Acts clearly indicates women's equal place as members of the body of Christ. . . . Thus women who only recently had been recognized as and included in Christ's company, now were able to enjoy full membership in his body, the church.[1]

What significance did the Day of Pentecost have for women?

Pentecost was a hallmark day for the infant church. With the crucifixion, resurrection and ascension past history, there was some uncertainty as to what would happen next. The eleven disciples "together with certain women" devoted themselves to prayer, and the matter of a replacement for Judas among the twelve was settled when "the lot fell on Mathias" (Acts 1:26). Jesus had promised that the Holy Spirit would come upon them, but all they could do was wait. Then, on the Day of Pentecost, things suddenly began to happen.

The Holy Spirit descended in vivid sights and sounds—tongues of fire and a multiplicity of languages—all so astonishing that a crowd gathered to find out what was taking place. Some of the people sensed that this was truly a spiritual happening, but to others it seemed like madness. Were these believers drunk or insane?

Peter, the spokesman for the disciples, stood up to interpret the events to those who had crowded around. He displayed no uncertainty that "this is what was spoken through the prophet Joel":

In the last days it will be, God declares, that I will pour out my Spirit upon all flesh, and your sons and your daughters shall prophesy, and your young men shall see visions, and your old men shall dream dreams. Even upon my slaves, both men and women, in those days I will pour out my Spirit; and they shall prophesy. (Acts 2:16-18)

The Jews had understood in theory the prophecy of Joel, which spoke of the Holy Spirit's being poured out on "all flesh," but they had never experienced such a phenomenon. In the Old Testament, the Holy Spirit had come only on certain occasions to selected individuals, but now a new age of the Spirit had dawned. It would be difficult to exaggerate the significance of this event. It involves far more than tongues-speaking. The world would never be the same. God's people were now equipped for ministry in a most extraordinary way—through personal empowerment of the third person of the Trinity, the Holy Spirit.

This was the very Spirit Jesus had promised, and consistent with the style of his ministry, all people were welcomed on an equal plane—old and young, slave and free, women and men. Not only would they all receive the Spirit on equal terms, but they would also go forth to minister with no distinction. Both sons *and* daughters would prophesy. Both men and women had prophesied in Old Testament times, but not side by side on equal terms, as Joel's prophecy quoted by Peter emphasizes.

As a youth and young adult actively involved in fundamentalist dispensational churches, I learned that Pentecost was the beginning of the church age. The dispensation of the church began on that momentous day. But Peter's explanation for what was happening and the leveling effect it would have on all Christians was somehow lost in the dispensational shuffle of times and dates. Peter's quoted prophecy from Joel was not seen as primarily for the "church age," but rather for the "last days" that would precede the final dispensation, the "kingdom age." Then, and only then, would both sons and daughters prophesy. So, while the Holy Spirit had been given, only part of the prophecy was operative for Christians in the church age. The portion that establishes women alongside men in ministry would not be fulfilled until sometime in the future.

The only problem with that interpretation is that it is not Peter's interpretation. He is the one who, under the inspiration of the Holy Spirit, applied Joel's prophecy of the "last days" to the Day of Pentecost.

What role did women play as prophets in the New Testament?
Even before the Day of Pentecost, the New Testament speaks of Anna

and her important function as a prophet. Along with Simeon, she confirmed God's blessing on the baby Jesus when his parents brought him to the temple in Jerusalem "to present him to the Lord" (Lk 2:22). Anna's response to Jesus is recorded in Luke 2:36-38:

> There was also a prophet, Anna the daughter of Phanuel, of the tribe of Asher. She was of a great age, having lived with her husband seven years after her marriage, then as a widow to the age of eighty-four. She never left the temple but worshiped there with fasting and prayer night and day. At that moment she came, and began to praise God and to speak about the child to all who were looking for the redemption of Jerusalem.

We know nothing about Anna beyond what is recorded in these three verses. But that an eighty-four-year-old widow should be given such an honor should not surprise us. In Scripture, it is not the great and mighty who receive the most tribute. It would seem that she was being rewarded for her faithfulness to God.

Yet that explanation is too simple for some. Abraham Kuyper suggests that she just happened to be at the right place at the right time. In Kuyper's scenario, Anna was a "feminine aide" to Simeon; she was his assistant and thus had a secondary role. But the text (Lk 2:25-28) clearly indicates otherwise. Anna was a "prophet" who lived in the temple, while Simeon was a "man in Jerusalem" who was "righteous and devout," who, "guided by the Spirit," "came into the temple." There is no evidence that he lived there or even served there as Anna did.

There were other female prophets in the New Testament. In the book of Acts, we read that Philip the evangelist, one of the seven chosen to serve as deacons, had four unmarried daughters who were prophets (21:9). This fact is mentioned in passing, with no indication that this was necessarily unusual or that their ministry was censured in the early church.

Indeed, from 1 Corinthians 11:5 we learn that Paul instructed women to *prophesy* and pray with their heads covered. So there is no reason to believe that prophesying was not considered just as appropriate for women as for men.

What do Euodia and Syntyche tell us about women in ministry?

Women of the early church were involved in active ministries—so much so that Paul often refers to them as "fellow-workers" or "co-workers," the same terminology that he uses for Timothy and Titus, his closest male associates. An example is found in his letter to the Philippians, in his appeal to Euodia and Syntyche "to be of the same mind." He continues: "Yes, and I ask you also, my loyal companion, help these women, for they have struggled beside me in the work of the gospel, together with Clement and the rest of my co-workers, whose names are in the book of life" (4:2-3).

Apparently the dissension between these two women was so great that Paul feared it might have serious negative consequences on the ongoing work of the gospel. What that difference of opinion was we do not know, but there is no reason to assume that it was trivial. Some years ago, the teacher in an adult Sunday-school class that I was attending gave a little personal commentary on this matter as he was teaching through the book of Philippians. In his opinion, the women were probably "bickering about the color of tile for the remodeled ladies' restroom." I asked why he would suppose that it was so trivial, and his response was something to the effect that it is the nature of women to bicker over trivial things. I suggested that it may instead have been a very serious matter having to do with their work in the ministry—perhaps similar to Paul's dispute with Barnabas over the reliability of John Mark, recorded in Acts 15:38-39.

It is important to note that in this matter of Euodia and Syntyche Paul does not suggest that the church "elders" or "authorities" take the matter in hand. Nor are these women told to be "submissive" or "silent." They are admonished to handle the problem themselves.

What was Priscilla's role in teaching Apollos?

Priscilla's role in the early church has been widely debated. Some see her simply as a woman who worked alongside her husband, Aquila, in ministry and in tent-making—"a most energetic and wise helpmeet," as Kuyper says.[2] But the biblical record suggests that she, rather than Aquila, was the prominent one in this marriage partnership. In the ancient world it was rare for a woman's name to be listed before her husband's. When that happens, as it does repeatedly with Priscilla and Aquila, it indicates an unusual relationship—one in which the wife had greater status or importance than the husband.

But more significant than Priscilla's prominence is the effectiveness of this wife-husband team. Women are often cited as Paul's co-workers, but here we have a partnership—the husband being a Christian and actively participating in gospel outreach, but with Priscilla taking the lead. They were friends of Paul, who spent eighteen months in their home in Corinth, and he considered them among his closest associates. Together, Priscilla and Aquila taught Apollos "the Way of God . . . more accurately" (Acts 18:24-26), and he later became a powerful leader in the church. They also had the oversight of a church that met in their home (Rom 16:3-5).

What was Priscilla's precise role in all of this? Was she an elder or teacher? "Of this nothing is said," Hurley points out. "The only evidence which we have is that she taught Apollos together with her husband in her home (Acts 18:24-28). It would be a mistake to say that she was theologically ignorant! It would also be a mistake to suppose that Luke intended us to infer from his comment that she was acting as an elder or teacher in a formal sense."[3]

It is true that the Bible does not state that Priscilla was a teacher or elder "in the formal sense," but her teaching Apollos ought not be diminished because it took place in her home. Probably all the earliest churches spoken of in the New Testament were house churches.

As in the cases of Anna and the women at the tomb, Bible commentators have sometimes sought to minimize Priscilla's role. That she was a "key leader in the apostolic church has not always been easy to accept," writes Gilbert Bilezikian. "In order to avoid divulging such a scandal, the translators of the King James Version followed a variant that inverted the names of Priscilla and Aquila in Acts 18:26, thus preferring to commit violence on the text of Scripture rather than face the fact that God calls qualified women to be teachers."[4]

What was Phoebe's position in the church?

As with Priscilla, there is debate regarding Phoebe's actual role in the church. According to James Hurley, she "is the most controversial female figure in Paul's letters." Phoebe is known to us through a brief reference to her by Paul in Romans 16:1-2: "I commend to you our sister Phoebe, a deacon of the church at Cenchreae, so that you may welcome her in the Lord as is fitting for the saints, and help her in whatever she may require from you, for she has been a benefactor of many and of myself as well."

What was Phoebe's role in the church? From Paul's opening statement, we know that she was the bearer of Paul's great epistle to the church at Rome, and that he commends her to the church there. His description of her as a "deacon," as the Greek word *diakonos* is rendered in the New Revised Standard Version, is controversial. In the King James and the NIV, *diakonos* is rendered "servant." Both renderings are consistent with the Greek term, but which is more appropriate, when applied to Phoebe? Is the term rendered "servant" simply because she is a woman? Hurley concedes that "if the name in the text were Timothy or Judas, ninety-nine per cent of the scholars would presume that *diakonos* meant 'deacon' and a few footnotes would remark that it could mean 'servant.' "[5]

When referring to a male, the noun *diakonos* is typically rendered "minister" in Bible translations, and that would be an appropriate designation for Phoebe. "Phoebe is not only a minister," says Spencer, "she is also a minister who should be welcomed as worthy by the saints at Rome and assisted *(paristemi)* in anything she requires, for Paul explains 'she herself has been a *prostatis* over many and even of myself.' " *Prostatis* has generally been rendered "help," but according to Spencer it carries the connotation of "help by ruling." Thus, Phoebe is "a woman set over others." She is the only one in the New Testament called by this term. "The Romans are to be at Phoebe's disposal because she has been a leader over many and even over Paul!"[6]

What is the significance of Romans 16 for women's ministry?

Romans 16 is a virtual hall of fame for women in the early church at

Rome. Phoebe and Prisca (or Priscilla) are the best known and the first two mentioned in the chapter. Next comes Mary, "who has worked very hard among you." Also listed are Narcissus, who apparently is the head of her family; Tryphaena and Tryphosa, "workers in the Lord" ("a cute sounding couple whose names mean 'Dainty' and 'Delicate,' who may have been twins"[7]); Persis, "who has worked hard in the Lord," whom Paul also describes as "beloved"; Julia; and two unnamed women, the mother of Rufus, "a mother to me also," and the sister of Nereus. The most debated of the women on the list is Junia. Paul writes, "Greet Andronicus and Junia, my relatives who were in prison with me; they are prominent among the apostles, and they were in Christ before I was" (v. 7). The controversy over Junia has to do with whether she is actually a male or a female. The issue would not be so serious if Junia were not termed an apostle, but because of that fact, it has been typical for commentators in recent centuries to assume that she was actually a man and that her name was Junias. "Junia is a common Latin woman's name," Spencer writes, while "Junias is the male counterpart. . . . What some scholars have done is to posit that Junias . . . was the shortened form of Junianus. However, Latin diminutives were formed by lengthening, not shortening a name, as, for example, Priscilla which is the diminutive of Prisca. Understandably, then the form 'Junias' has yet to be found in extrabiblical sources."[8]

Early biblical commentators, including Jerome and John Chrysostom, referred to Junia as a woman. Chrysostom is most interesting along these lines, because he often had very negative things to say about women in general, but in reference to Junia he wrote: "Oh! how great is the devotion of this woman, that she should be even counted worthy of the appellation of apostle.[9] It was around the turn of the fourteenth century that Junia seems to have gotten a sex change. Aegidus of Rome referred to Andronicus and Junia as "men," as have many commentators since.[10]

What book of the New Testament might have been written by a woman?
A number of biblical scholars have conjectured that a woman might have written the epistle to the Hebrews, and at least one book has been written

to defend that position: *Priscilla: Author of the Epistle to the Hebrews* by Ruth Hoppin. Hebrews is a major work that, unlike most other ancient books, bears no author identification, leading to the speculation that its author may, in fact, have been female.

Is such a belief tenable? The answer to that question is left to the reader, in light of Pape's summary of the evidence:

(1) The letter is anonymous. The name of a woman might have prejudiced its acceptance. (2) [Priscilla] was known to be an illustrious teacher. Much of what is said in Hebrews might well have been said to Apollos. (3) She had close associations with Paul and Timothy, as the author of Hebrews obviously had. (4) At the time of its writing Paul seems to be dead, and in his last known letter he had specifically mentioned Timothy, Priscilla and Aquila. (5) The author seems closely identified with the readers of the letter (Ephesians seeming to fit best) and hopes to return to them. (6) In the list of heroes of the faith several women are mentioned. (7) There are a number of practical references to both childhood and parenthood. (8) The letter contains the theme of pilgrimage ("Here have we no continuing city," 13:14) as if the writer had personal experience of this. Four nautical terms are mentioned in the Greek, although these are not all apparent in the English translation, and Prisca made at least four sea voyages. (9) Hebrews shows a great interest in the tabernacle, natural if the author and her husband were tent and leather makers. (10) Sometimes the author's voice is in plural form, which might indicate the inclusion of Aquila.[11]

Who was the "elect lady" in 2 John?

The elder to the elect lady and her children, whom I love in the truth, and not only I but also all who know the truth, because of the truth that abides in us and will be with us forever. (2 Jn 1-2)

I did not know that the elect lady of 2 John was actually a "lady" until several years ago. I had been taught that the elect lady was a church. Why I did not question the teaching I do not know, but it took someone else's writing on the matter to jog my thinking. Had I been more astute, I would have quickly noticed that 3 John opens in a similar manner: "The elder to the beloved Gaius, whom I love in truth." No one would suggest that Gaius was a church, but the unnamed lady has been deemed by some commentators to be just that.

Lockyer asks,

Did [John] write to a particular, prominent woman in the local church or was his precious letter addressed to the church itself that John represented as a lady? As the Bible was written by plain men for plain people that they might understand it in the most common-sense way, the explicit language John uses implies that the woman he addressed was prominent in the vicinity of Ephesus, and being of a most worthy Christian character, she was worthy to receive an exhortatory epistle from him.[12]

Spencer offers additional insights:

John addresses his second letter to the "elect lady and her children" (v. 1). Today a "lady" can refer to a woman with manners, although usually it is simply a more polite version of "woman." *Kuria* is the feminine of *kurios,* "lord" or "master." . . . The noun *kuria* simply means "authority" or "power." . . .

This woman addressed in 2 John was not only an authority. She also is chosen. . . .

All the data is best understood if John were writing the letter to a woman who was the person in authority over a congregation. He uses for her the singular metaphor *kuria* and for the congregation the plural metaphor "children." Consequently, the children are "hers," just as the children of 1 John are "his" (John's).[13]

If the "elect lady" is taken to be a church, who then are her children? It would be logical to assume that the children are the members of the congregation, as John himself directs his first epistle to his "children," his "little children" (2:1, 12, 18, 28).

The simplest explanation of the mystery "elect lady" of 2 John is that she was a leader of a house church that met in her home, that her "elect sister" (v. 13) served in a similar role, and that their children were their congregations.

14

Was Paul
a Chauvinist?

This has been a serious question for many women—and men, too, especially since the advent of the modern feminist movement. Joan Berends posed a slightly different form of the question in 1971, in an article entitled "Was St. Paul a Woman-Hater?" In that article, which is written in the form of a conversation between her and Paul, she asks him whether it is true that he dislikes women. His answer is emphatic: "Dislike women! Perish the thought! Why, some of my most loyal and treasured friends have been women. Priscilla, Lydia, and Phoebe are just a few who worked diligently with me to further the Gospel."[1]

Not all women, however, have been as positive in assessing Paul's views. Indeed, many people have declared just the opposite. Paul, they insist, was a blatant chauvinist. Pearl Buck, the Pulitzer Prize-winning novelist, took that stance. In her book about her mother, Carie Sydenstricker, a missionary to China, she wrote: "Since those days when I saw all her nature dimmed I have hated Saint Paul with all my heart and so must all true women hate him, I think, because of what he has done in the past to women like Carie, proud free-born women, yet damned by their very womanhood."[2]

A milder version of Buck's perspective confronted me in the 1970s when I was serving as a pastor's wife in a small fundamentalist church. One of the more outspoken women in the congregation commented to me on one occasion that she "never got along with Paul." She just couldn't accept his views on women. But Jesus, in her mind, was entirely different; she never had any problems with what *he* said.

Jewett has argued that Paul's attitudes toward women were two-sided. On the one hand, Paul was influenced by his environment and training. Having been "steeped in rabbinic learning," he "thought of the woman as subordinate to the man for whose sake she was created (1 Cor. 11:9)." But, on the other hand, Paul was "an ardent disciple of Jesus Christ," and through this powerful influence he could affirm "the woman as the equal to the man in all things, the two having been made one in Christ in whom there is neither male nor female."[3]

Was Paul a chauvinist? Was he a typical man of his day? Did he view women as inferior to men? He indeed was a chauvinist, if certain of his admonitions to women are taken out of the larger context. Understood in the light of his culture and in light of his missionary principle, however, his teachings were, and are, not chauvinistic.

Did Paul and Jesus have different positions on women's roles?
"Jesus was a feminist," according to Leonard Swidler, in his article by that title. It is an attention-getting statement, and one that does not seem altogether absurd to someone who has studied Jesus' attitude toward and interactions with women. But it would seem altogether absurd to assert that Paul was a feminist. It is the view of many people that Jesus and Paul were, if not on opposite sides, at least on different planes regarding this issue.

Claiming Jesus was a feminist and Paul was a chauvinist is an extreme position, but that view is frequently expressed in more moderate tones.

One version of the theory was summed up by President Jimmy Carter, in response to a question regarding the Equal Rights Amendment: "I think if one reads different parts of the Bible you can find a good argument either way.... I know that Paul felt very strongly that there ought to be a sharp distinction between men and women, and women's role ought to be minimal. But I have a feeling that Christ meant for all of us to be treated equally, and he demonstrated this in many ways."[4]

Even those who have done extensive study on the teachings of Jesus and Paul have come to the conclusion that they offered different perspectives on women. Evelyn and Frank Stagg argue that the difference between Jesus and Paul stems from their focus on the Genesis creation accounts: "Jesus built upon the creation narrative of ch. 1 [usually viewed as the more egalitarian of the two accounts] . . . whereas, Paul and other followers built upon the narrative in ch. 2."[5]

How do we evaluate this view? Did Paul back away from the progressive stance of Jesus? Perhaps in some respects he did. Jesus was a religious revolutionary in many ways. He overturned long-held Jewish traditions and offered radical alternatives. Paul, on the other hand, had responsibility for laying the foundation for those new ideas in an organized structure. As such he was perhaps more concerned about proper decorum for social interaction and for worship.

How were women treated in the first-century Mediterranean world?

As Paul, the missionary, sought to bring the gospel to various regions in the Mediterranean world, he confronted cultures that were very different from the Palestinian culture to which Jesus' ministry had been confined. Paul was educated and well traveled, and he recognized the necessity of respecting cultural differences—as is seen in his willingness to be "all things to all people" (1 Cor 9:22). In light of this, it is important to understand how women were treated in the first-century Greco-Roman world.

In ancient Greece, there were women who occasionally rose to heights of glory, but the role of women generally was clearly inferior to that of men. Athenian law supported and sustained this inferiority, regarding "the wife as a veritable child, having the legal status of a minor compared to her husband." Women did function as priests and prophetesses in the religious realm, but not as teachers—a factor that may have influenced Paul's restrictions in this area.[6]

In the Roman world, women generally had more freedom than their Grecian counterparts. This was especially true of the Roman matrons, women who had access to wealth and political influence by birth or by marriage. But all women, rich or poor, were inferior to their husbands in the eyes of the law, though liberalizing tendencies were being felt during the time of Paul.

It was against this backdrop and that of Palestinian Judaism that Paul made what often appear to us today to be conflicting statements regarding the role of women in the church. His recommendations were no doubt frequently influenced by circumstance. Some women who actively served with him as "co-workers" were on the level of the Roman matrons, while others he came in contact with in the congregations lived much more secluded lives, controlled by their husbands. Whatever their circumstances, Paul viewed these women as indispensable to the mission of the expanding church.

Why did Paul not credit women as witnesses of the resurrection?

For I handed on to you as of first importance what I in turn had received: that Christ died for our sins in accordance with the scriptures, and that he was buried, and that he was raised on the third day in accordance with the scriptures, and that he appeared to Cephas, then to the twelve. Then he appeared to more than five hundred brothers and sisters at one time, most of whom are still alive, though some have died. Then he appeared to James, then to all the apostles. Last of all, as to one untimely born, he appeared also to me. (1 Cor 15:3-8)

To some people it is troubling that Paul did not present his account of the appearances of the resurrected Christ in the same manner as they are recorded in the Gospel narratives. Why did he not recognize women as the first witnesses of Jesus' resurrection? Did he not know of the account of the empty tomb and of the women's heralding of the risen Christ?

Some scholars make that argument, pointing to the fact that Paul's first epistle to the Corinthians was written prior to the Gospel narratives. But surely Paul, the great apostle, was quite familiar with the eyewitness accounts of the resurrection, and he was writing under the inspiration of the Holy Spirit.

The most likely reason that Paul did not mention the women "was that, along with the rest of the church, he stressed only the appearances to men as the 'official' witness of the church. . . . The witness of a woman was not recognized in Jewish courts. Paul and the tradition he follows seem concerned with the 'official' witness of men."[7]

We have to recognize how pervasive cultural restrictions were in the ancient world, and how even a historical record of women's witnessing a great event needed to be officially verified by men. Paul was not slighting the women here, but offering a gospel that was legally corroborated.

Why did Paul insist that women pray and prophesy with heads covered?
Today it is no longer expected that women come to church with their heads covered. Some traditions, including Roman Catholics, Mennonites and Plymouth Brethren, have not yet entirely forsaken this tradition, but among most Christians the practice is viewed as archaic. But Paul clearly stated in 1 Corinthians 11:5 that "any woman who prays or prophesies with her head unveiled disgraces her head," and he goes on to say that if she does not cover her head she might as well disgrace herself to the point of cutting off her hair altogether.

Is it right to ignore Paul's admonitions concerning head-coverings in 1 Corinthians 11? It is worth noting that "the longest passage in the New Testament devoted solely to the issue of women in the church concerns the wearing of certain head-coverings."[8]

Scholars have long debated Paul's rationale for insisting that women wear a head-covering (or bind up their hair, as some interpret the injunction). In all probability, he was concerned that the women in the Corinthian congregation be in no way associated with cultic religions that were prevalent at the time. "At certain religious events," write Richard and Catherine Kroeger, "women also shaved their heads, and men assumed veils or long flowing hair and golden hairnets," practices that "were viewed as sexual inversions."[9] Some of these cults were identified with temple prostitution, homosexuality and other immoral practices, and Paul would naturally be concerned that the new "cult of Jesus" not be identified with these practices in any way.

In verses 14-15 of this passage, Paul rhetorically asks: "Does not nature itself teach you that if a man wears long hair, it is degrading to him, but if a woman has long hair, it is her glory?" These words are puzzling to us. How does "nature" teach us about hair length? Patricia Gundry has some perceptive reflections here: "But nature as we think of it does not teach us that at all. In fact, nature makes it impossible for some women to have long, flowing hair. Black African women wear elaborate braided and twisted hairdos close to their heads because their curly hair does not fall long naturally. So 'nature' here cannot mean what we think of as nature, but rather custom—what was universally considered appropriate, attractive, and respectable in Corinth."[10]

It would also seem that Paul's admonition is more of a suggestion of propriety than an absolute rule, because at the end of this section on hair and head-coverings he adds, "But if anyone is disposed to be contentious—we have no such custom, nor do the churches of God" (v. 16). Some Bible scholars maintain that the woman's wearing a head-covering indicated her submission to her husband's headship, and that this is the primary reason Paul was concerned with the matter. But if Paul were demanding that women show proper submission, it is difficult to understand why he would end the section by saying that the church has "no such custom."

Foh, a strong traditionalist on women's issues, argues that the "covering" for women has "fallen into disuse without any theological justification," and that "our response should be to look again at those exhortations that are being overlooked with an intent for further, greater obedience."[11] While most traditionalists would not agree with her contemporary application of Paul's stipulations on head-coverings, hers is a consistent position. If we do not interpret Paul's admonitions to women regarding public ministry in light of the cultural context, it is inconsistent to ignore his directives regarding head-coverings and hair length on men and women, claiming that they alone are culturally conditioned.

How did Paul's missionary principle affect women in ministry?

Paul was first and foremost a missionary. He was ever concerned that the gospel go forth in a way that would not be offensive to the recipients. His commitment is most clearly summed up in a powerful and uncompromising statement of mission in 1 Corinthians 9:19-23:

> For though I am free with respect to all, I have made myself a slave to all, so that I might win more of them. To the Jews I became as a Jew, in order to win Jews. To those under the law I became as one under the law (though I myself am not under the law) so that I might win those under the law. To those outside the law I became as one outside the law (though I am not free from God's law but am under Christ's law) so that I might win those outside the law. To the weak I became weak, so that I might win the weak. I have become all things to all people, that I might by all means save some. I do it all for the sake of the gospel, so that I may share in its blessings.

Even as Paul was willing to become "all things to all people," he exhorted believers to follow certain proprieties so the gospel would not be shamed. In Titus 2:5, for example, he admonishes young women to submit to their husbands "so that the word of God may not be discredited."

Regarding Paul's missionary principle, Walter Liefeld writes:

> Paul's principle, then, is not the wearing of veils or the silence of women, but rather conforming to Jewish and moralistic pagan norms for the sake of the gospel. . . . In biblical times even for a woman to speak publicly was considered a symbol of impropriety. . . . If a woman speaking in the first century was an offense to the people Paul sought to reach, today it is just the reverse. A society that accepts women as corporation executives and university presidents will find it difficult to listen to a church that silences them. . . . If some in Paul's day considered it shameful for women to speak publicly, or to appear without a facial veil, or to have their hair flowing down, what are the implications of the fact that it is shameful in our society today to

restrict women from full equality and opportunity? If Paul could accommodate principle without abandoning it, can we say something to those we seek to reach by the equality and opportunities given women in the church. . . ? If not, we may be perpetuating form (the silence of women) while actually abandoning Paul's principle of accommodation.[12]

Why are Paul's lengthy guidelines on widows not followed today?

The longest passage in 1 Timothy pertaining to women is in chapter 5, where Paul gives instructions regarding widows. This passage lays down regulations that are rarely followed today: "Let a widow be put on the list if she is not less than sixty years old and has been married only once. . . . But refuse to put younger widows on the list. . . . So I would have younger widows marry, bear children, and manage their households" (vv. 9, 11, 14).

While the much shorter passage in 1 Timothy 2 regarding women's teaching and having authority is viewed by most traditionalists as fully applicable today, chapter 5's lengthy instructions to widows are seen as cultural and thus functionally irrelevant. The former passage is debated in books and scholarly conferences, while the latter is virtually ignored. But Paul himself made no such distinction.

The task of determining which biblical instructions are applicable for today and which are not is no simple matter. It is all too easy to focus on one issue more than another because it seems appropriate for the times we are living in. The issue of widows is not a matter that grips us today. Welfare and social agencies are available, if a widow over the age of sixty is not gainfully employed. I do not know of any church that supports such an individual. But the matter of women teaching and having authority, which Paul discusses in considerably fewer words, is seen as very relevant today. Especially since the advent of the modern feminist movement in the 1960s, women have been perceived by many men as a threat. Thus, the verses in 1 Timothy 2 are regarded with gravity by many traditionalists and are deemed applicable for all times.

15

Did Paul, in 1 Timothy 2, Forbid Women to Teach and Have Authority?

L̲et a woman learn in silence with full submission. I permit no woman to teach or to have authority over a man; she is to keep silent. (1 Tim 2:11-12)

These two very short verses, written by Paul to Timothy in Ephesus around A.D. 64, are those on which the role of women in the church today hangs. These are the verses most often quoted to deny women ministry. Other passages of Scripture are used for support, but it is here that Paul's position is stated most succinctly.

Assuming we can take the verses at face value as they have been translated into English, a first step to applying the passage appropriately is to determine whether this was an admonition particularly aimed at the congregations in Ephesus and other churches where Paul had ministered, so that it was culturally conditioned, or whether it is one that is in force for all times. The context here is crucial. Paul is discussing proper decorum for worship. The section actually begins with verses 8-10:

> I desire, then, that in every place the men should pray, lifting up holy hands without anger or argument; also that the women should dress themselves modestly and decently in suitable clothing, not with their hair braided, or with gold, pearls, or expensive clothes, but with good works, as is proper for women who profess reverence for God.

Most evangelicals today regard the fashion directives in this passage as cultural, and they do not expect women to conform. That was not true when I was growing up in a rural fundamentalist church in the 1950s. A truly spiritual woman was not to wear jewelry—whether gold, pearls, or even costume jewelry. Braided hair was not taboo—I'm not sure why. None of the men in that little church adhered to Paul's command to lift "holy hands" in prayer. Only the Pentecostals did that, and we were not Pentecostal. Besides, it was reasoned that what Paul meant when he wrote "holy hands" was actually "holy hearts," and anyone who was lifting a "holy heart" to the Lord was properly carrying out Paul's instructions.

In the 1990s, evangelicals more freely lift their hands in worship, but we laugh at the old-fashioned rules about make-up and jewelry. It is important, however, that we do not too casually argue that Paul's directives on these issues are inconsequential, while his directives in the two short verses that immediately follow are consequential enough to deny women ministry in the church.

Understanding the background of Paul's letter to Timothy is also crucial for making application in the church today. In Ephesus, as in Corinth, there were religious cults with sexual overtones that particularly appealed to women. Paul warns Timothy of "certain people" who are teaching "different doctrine" and devoting themselves to "myths and endless genealogies" (1 Tim 1:3-4). And in his second epistle to Timothy, Paul speaks of false teachers "who make their way into households and captivate silly women, overwhelmed by their sins and swayed by all kinds of desires, who are always being instructed and can never arrive at a knowledge of the truth" (3:7-8). So there were problems at Ephesus among both women and men who were either teaching or accepting false doctrine.

In light of that, Paul's admonition to women "to learn in silence with full submission" is very appropriate. They were to take learning seriously and not be among those who could "never arrive at a knowledge of the truth." A woman told to "learn in silence" today might feel offended. Why should *she* learn in silence, when all the men can ask questions and interact? But in Paul's day, learning in silence under a rabbi was common. It was not a put-down of women, as Spencer has pointed out: "silence was . . . a positive attribute for rabbinic students. Paul's words were declaring to his Jewish friends that at this time women were to be learning in the same manner as did rabbinic students."[1]

But what is even more astonishing about this directive of Paul's is that women are instructed to learn. In Jewish culture, learning was not a priority for women, but in the Christian community we find that it was indeed a priority. They were not only to perform "good works, as is proper for women who profess reverence for God," but they also were to "learn."

What Greek terms and tenses are most significant in 1 Timothy 2:11-12? Language always loses some of its force in the process of translation, and it is no different with the Bible. In my Greek courses in college years ago, I was always being delighted by new shades of meaning that came through when I read the Bible in the original language. Sometimes it is virtually impossible to translate a Greek word into a precise English equivalent or to show the force of the verb tenses.

This is true regarding the matter of women's learning. Paul does not say that it would be well for women—if they have the time after performing good works—to make room in their schedule to learn. The verb here is in the imperative. It is a command. He is saying that they *must* learn.

In verse 12, Paul goes on to say, "I permit no woman to teach or to have authority over a man." Again the verb—in this instance, the present tense—is important. The phrase could be properly translated, "I am presently permitting no woman to teach . . . ," with the implication that this was Paul's policy for the time being. That emphasis on the present would correspond with the necessity that women learn before they teach.

It would surely make sense not to have anyone teaching or having authority who had not been properly instructed.

The Greek word Paul uses to say that women should not "teach" suggests that this is teaching by one who is competent. "The noun *didaskalos* implies a teacher who is qualified. . . . The women at Ephesus had to learn, consequently, they were not ready to teach."[2]

The word in this verse that has been debated the most is *authentein,* rendered "authority." The word is found nowhere else in Scripture and is uncommon even in secular Greek literature. Where it is used in extrabiblical literature, it usually has a negative connotation and essentially means "to thrust oneself" or to domineer.[3]

In the King James, *authentein* is rendered not "to *have* authority" but "to *usurp* authority." This would seem to be more consistent with the Greek. Had Paul intended to say that women were not to *have* authority (a good kind of authority when exercised by men), it would have been only natural for him to have used the usual Greek word for authority, *exousia,* but instead he chose a negative word that is found nowhere else in his writings.

In the English translations the concepts of "teaching" and "having authority" are connected with the conjunction "or" or "nor." The Greek word *oude,* however, might be more appropriately rendered "in a manner of," according to Philip Payne, who has done an extensive study of the word.[4]

In light of these shades of meaning in the Greek, then, this verse could appropriately be rendered: "I am not presently permitting a woman to teach in a manner of usurping authority over a man; she must be quiet."

What does creation order have to do with women's teaching?

Paul explains why women should not be teaching or usurping authority in verses 13-14: "For Adam was formed first, then Eve; and Adam was not deceived, but the woman was deceived and became a transgressor."

What does Adam's priority in formation have to do with women teaching? It does not necessarily appear to follow Paul's previous line of reasoning. Most commentators have assumed that because Adam was *created* first, Paul was suggesting that men would have authority or prominence. The animals, however, were created before Adam, and that certainly gave them no higher status. And what does Eve's deception have to do with creation order? If *creation* order is the issue here, Paul's statement makes little sense in context. Is it possible that Adam's being *formed* first does not mean the same as his being *created* first? Walter Kaiser, an Old Testament scholar, says that Adam "had the educational and spiritual advantage of being 'formed first' (v. 13). The verb is *plasso,* 'to form, mold, shape' (presumably in spiritual education), not 'created first' (which in Greek is *ktizo).* Paul's argument, then, is based on the 'orders of education,' not the orders of creation."[5]

It was before Eve was created that Adam was instructed not to eat the fruit. She perhaps lacked instruction, for she may have heard of the restriction only through Adam. It would seem natural, then, that she could be more easily deceived. So it was with the women at Ephesus. Paul commanded them to learn. Instruction was absolutely essential to teaching, and until they had been properly instructed they should not teach as if they had authority. Otherwise they might be deceived even as Eve was.

Did Paul teach that women are more easily deceived than men?

It is widely held that the apostle Paul taught that women are more prone to be deceived than men are because of the illustration he used of Eve being deceived in 1 Timothy 2:14: "Adam was not deceived, but the woman was deceived and became a transgressor." Robert Culver insists that though it *seems* as though this verse is referring to "the first human pair simply as individuals," in reality "Paul is referring to *womanhood* of the first woman, the archetypal woman." He goes on to argue that there is "something about woman's nature—something different about woman as woman from man as man" that forever makes her "more susceptible to temptation through deceit than was the man."[6]

The late Walter Martin, a renowned expert on cults, tried to show how the woman's deceivability has led to heresy throughout history. After quoting 1 Timothy 2:11-14, he made the following commentary:

It can be clearly seen from the study of non-Christian cults, ancient and modern, that the female teaching ministry has graphically fulfilled what Paul anticipated in his day by divine revelation, and brought in its wake, as history tells us, confusion, division and strife. This is true from Johanna Southcutt to Mary Baker Eddy to Helena Blavatsky and the Fox sisters, all of whom were living proof of the validity of our Lord's declaration that "if the blind lead the blind, both shall fall into the ditch" (Matthew 15:14b).[7]

Martin was wrong in his historical analysis of cults. Women have by no means been the most prominent in the founding and leading of cults.

The issue in Paul's reference to Eve's being deceived is not whether she was deceived but whether womanhood for all time is more prone to be deceived. Paul gives no hint that this is the case when he writes in 2 Corinthians 11:3: "But I am afraid that as the serpent deceived Eve by its cunning, your thoughts will be led astray from a sincere and pure devotion to Christ." The NIV words it even more strongly: "I am afraid that just as Eve was deceived . . . your minds may somehow be led astray." Paul here is writing to *both* men and women—not just to women—and he is saying that *just as* Eve was deceived, you (men and women) may be deceived or led astray. Gender is simply not a factor when it comes to deception. Both men and women are vulnerable.

In 1 Timothy 2:14, Paul is using Eve as an illlustration and simply that. There is no more reason to assume that he is referring to womanhood in general than there is to assume that he is referring to manhood in general in 2 Timothy 3:8, when he uses Jannes and Jambres as illustrations: "As Jannes and Jambres opposed Moses, so these people, of corrupt mind and counterfeit faith, also oppose the truth."

Because of Eve's deception, many traditionalists argue that women ought not teach or have authority today. This was the admonition Letha Dawson Scanzoni heard during her Bible-school days:

I remember a class at Moody Bible Institute in the 1950s where the professor told us that women are prohibited from pastoring churches or teaching doctrine in a school—although they could teach women and children. The reason? "Eve, the woman, was completely deceived, whereas Adam sinned with his eyes wide open. The man, filled with the Spirit, is therefore a safer repository of doctrine."

How it is that "sinning with one's eyes wide open" makes one a "safer repository of doctrine" makes no more sense to me now than it did then. And how a woman, who supposedly can be so readily deceived that she falls into doctrinal error, is nevertheless equipped to teach children and other women doesn't make sense either—unless women and children don't matter in the minds of those who spread such teachings.[8]

It is on this very issue of application that the traditionalist argument falls apart. If women were more prone to be deceived than men, how incredibly irresponsible it would be of church leaders to let them teach other women and little children, whose minds are impressionable. Far better to let women teach adult men, who would be better able to withstand the threat of heresy.

What did Paul mean when he said that women will be saved in childbearing?

Of all Paul's statements in 1 Timothy 2, verse 15—the last verse of the chapter—is the one that has most baffled Bible scholars. Referring to women, Paul writes: "Yet she will be saved through childbearing, provided they continue in faith and love and holiness, with modesty."

Is Paul suggesting that a woman will actually be saved by giving birth to children? Surely that would fly in the face of his impassioned assertion that salvation is not by works. If childbearing were added to faith, salvation would obviously not be by faith *alone*. Moreover, not all women are married or are able to bear children, so such an understanding of the passage is simply not tenable.

Is Paul promising that women will be kept physically safe in childbearing, if they continue in faith? It seems highly unlikely that he was making such a promise—one that has certainly not proved true. Some of the most faithful Christian women in the history of the church have died in childbirth—women such as Maria Taylor, Hudson Taylor's first wife, who was serving faithfully as a missionary with him in China.

THE NEW TESTAMENT AND WOMEN □ 119

A possible understanding of the passage is that Paul was referring to the childbearing of Mary—that the woman will be saved because of *the* childbirth, meaning the birth of Christ. This understanding of the passage corresponds with the truth of Scripture, but it is certainly not the "plain meaning" of the text, and it seems odd that *women* should be singled out as being saved by the birth of Christ. This is not a satisfactory meaning of the verse; it is viable only because it is preferable to the other two options.

This verse demonstrates the difficulty of understanding some of Paul's writings and should caution us about being too dogmatic in our claims to speak for him on women's issues.

Did Paul restrict women from holding office or being ordained?
A passage that is commonly used to deny women positions of authority in the church is 1 Timothy 3:1-4, which speaks of qualifications for bishops (rendered "overseers" in the NIV)—positions that are commonly designated as elders or presbyters in Protestant churches.

> Here is a trustworthy saying: If anyone sets his heart on being an overseer, he desires a noble task. Now the overseer must be above reproach, the husband of but one wife, temperate, self-controlled, respectable, hospitable, able to teach, not given to drunkenness, not violent but gentle, not quarrelsome, not a lover of money. He must manage his own family well and see that his children obey him with proper respect. (NIV)

The King James Version and other translations have rendered the second phrase of this passage: "If a *man* desire the office. . . ." This has given strength to the argument that this passage applies explicitly to the male gender. But the Greek pronoun *tis* "refers either to a male or a female."[9] Thus the rendering of this word as "anyone" or "whoever" is more accurate.

But if this pronoun does not restrict women, so the argument goes, surely the specification that an overseer be "the husband of but one wife" points exclusively to a male. Since a woman cannot be husband of one wife, it naturally follows that she cannot be an overseer. But the matter is not quite that simple. We must determine whether being a husband of one wife is actually a *qualification* or whether it is rather an *assumption* that Paul makes.

It would seem that Paul is assuming that the individual who desires this office is a man, that he is married, and that he has children. Assuming then that the man is married, he must be "the husband of but one wife"; and assuming he has children, they must "obey him with proper respect." It is unlikely that being a male, being married and having children are *qualifications* for leadership, since Paul himself probably could not have met two of those three. Furthermore, Paul placed high value on singleness, actually referring to it as a "gift" in 1 Corinthians 7:7.

Those who argue that being a male is a *qualification* for overseers are inconsistent if they do not also insist that marriage and parenthood be qualifications—which places them in opposition to 1 Corinthians 7. Most individuals and churches who deny women office on the basis of this passage, however, do not require that elders be married and have children, and all too frequently do not uphold the actual qualifications listed with rigor—that the candidate be temperate, self-controlled, respectable, hospitable, able to teach, and so on.

Did Paul designate gender qualifications for spiritual gifts?

> Now you are the body of Christ and individually members of it. And God has appointed in the church first apostles, second prophets, third teachers; then deeds of power, then gifts of healing, forms of assistance, forms of leadership, various kinds of tongues. Are all apostles? Are all prophets? Are all teachers? Do all work miracles? Do all possess gifts of healing? Do all speak in tongues? Do all interpret? But strive for the greater gifts. And I will show you a still more excellent way. (1 Cor 12:27-31)

There is nothing in this passage that would indicate that gifts are denied anyone on the basis of gender. In fact, the passage is clearly written to the body of Christ, which would include women and men. Gifts are ranked, and all Christians—not just men—are encouraged to "strive for the greater gifts," those of apostles, prophets and teachers. We know from other passages of Scripture that women were prophets (Philip's daughters) and teachers (Priscilla), and it would seem from Romans 16 that Junia was numbered among the apostles.

Paul makes it clear that the body of Christ is made up of many members and that it needs the giftedness of all the members to function effectively. To deny a gifted woman ministry on the basis of gender is in effect to say to one member of the body that it is not needed—that it is of no use to the body.

> The eye cannot say to the hand, "I have no need of you," nor again the head to the feet, "I have no need of you." . . . But God has so arranged the body, giving the greater honor to the inferior member, that there may be no dissension within the body, but the members may have the same care for one another. If one member suffers, all suffer together with it; if one member is honored, all rejoice together with it. (1 Cor 12:21, 24-26)

It is interesting that there is an apparent hierarchy within the body—that some within the body are referred to as "inferior." This would be the natural place for Paul to interject the issue of gender, if it were applicable. But he does not do that. He is talking to all members, and he is differentiating among them only on the basis of gifts, not gender.

Must women be silent in the church?

> Women should be silent in the churches. For they are not permitted to speak, but should be subordinate, as the law also says. If there is anything they desire to know, let them ask their husbands at home. For it is shameful for a woman to speak in church. (1 Cor 14:34-35)

I have sometimes wondered if these were the only two verses Ray had committed to memory. They were the only ones he ever quoted in my presence—sometimes with an air of lightheartedness, other times very seriously. I was the pastor's wife of a small Bible church, and he and his wife and three daughters were church members. I never preached in that church, nor did I have any inclination to do so, but if I ever spoke up at a business meeting or Bible study and said something he disagreed with, these verses were his immediate response.

I have not seen Ray for more than a dozen years, but I suppose he is still quoting these two verses (in the King James) to any woman whom he finds threatening. I am ashamed to admit it, but I have sometimes secretly wished that one of his three daughters might be called into the ministry—or better yet, all three!

These verses are difficult to understand. Only three chapters earlier, Paul insisted that women must keep their heads covered while praying and prophesying (11:5). It might be argued that a woman could pray silently, but surely nobody would suggest that prophesying can be done silently. By its very nature, to prophesy is to speak forth. Yet because of these later verses, some churchmen throughout history have demanded literal silence of women. Women were not even allowed to sing or respond in unison readings or liturgical prayers. The verse was being applied in its most literal sense.

Today, even those who most strongly affirm male headship do not insist that a woman must literally be silent in church. They would generally agree that she can sing, participate in congregational readings and even give testimonials, but they would argue that these verses prohibit her preaching. That is not, however, what Paul says.

It is important to note at the outset that these verses come in the middle of a lengthy three-chapter section on spiritual gifts. Among the spiritual gifts Paul discusses is the gift of tongues. Here he establishes guidelines for a church that had problems with this gift. Many evangelical churchmen argue that this passage is not relevant today in that tongues have ceased (13:8). Yet, while denying the passage's contemporary relevance in regard to tongue-speaking, they cite two nearby verses to exclude women from the teaching and preaching ministry of the church.

One thing that all Bible commentators can agree on is that this is a very difficult passage. For these verses D. A. Carson has identified no fewer than eight significantly different interpretations—all of which have a number of lesser variations. His own belief (one of the eight he lists) is that Paul was forbidding women to judge prophets—the prophets mentioned in the preceding verses.[10]

Carson's position is widely held by conservative biblical scholars. Those who hold to this interpretation concede that Paul permitted women to prophesy (1 Cor 11:5) but that they could not evaluate or judge the prophecies of others, because such activity was an exercise of high-level authority in the church.

This interpretation could not be readily identified as the "plain meaning" of the text, and there are other difficulties as well, as David Scholer points out:

> First, the word "speak" in 1 Corinthians 14:34 has no implication within the word itself or in its immediate context (14:34-35) to support identifying it with the concept of prophetic evaluation. Second, the idea of two levels of speech in the church—prophecy and the judgment of prophecy—with the understanding that one is higher than the other and is for men only has no clear or implied support elsewhere in Paul. In fact, Paul's own definition and defense of prophecy (1 Corinthians 14:1-25) implies directly that prophecy itself is authoritative speech of the highest level in the church.[11]

Perhaps the best way to interpret the passage is to let the text explain itself. How does Paul himself resolve this issue of women's silence? He instructs them to "ask their husbands at home." In this particular instance, there is no clear evidence that women were preaching or teaching or even judging prophets. It seems rather that they were simply asking questions. It ought to surprise no one that men of this era had access to more instruction and knowledge than women, and it is not hard to imagine that women may have had more difficulty understanding points of doctrine and wanted further explanation. Their questions were apparently disrupting the flow of the discourse, and it seemed reasonable that they should hold their questions until later.

Why is Galatians 3:27-28 seen as the Magna Charta for women?

> As many of you as were baptized into Christ have clothed yourselves with Christ. There is no longer Jew or Greek, there is no longer slave or free, there is no longer male and female; for all of you are one in Christ Jesus.

The Magna Charta was a landmark in history. Signed on June 15, 1215, this "great charter" guaranteed fundamental liberties for the English people. But more than a thousand years earlier, Paul the apostle had set forth an abbreviated "Magna Charta of Christian liberty" in the very heart of his spirited defense of justification by faith alone. The glorious message of the epistle is that "Christ redeemed us from the curse of the law" (3:13) and "Christ has set us free" (5:1), and as part of that freedom, "there is no longer Jew or Greek, . . . slave or free, . . . male and female."

This passage speaks not only to women whose freedom has been curtailed on the basis of gender but also to women and men whose freedom has been curtailed on ethnic or legal grounds. It is truly a remarkable statement—especially when considered within the context of the ancient world. It places Christians in stark contrast with the world and its arbitrary divisions in society. This is why the passage was so significant not only for women but also for all others who felt the force of discrimination in the ancient world.

For a slave, the effect was electric. Paul certainly had no power to change society, and he did not seek to do that. But "in Christ"—in one's standing before Christ and in the church—there was to be no difference between slave and free. "Slavery ate like a canker in Roman society. The slave, whether male or female, was always at the disposal of his master for the most menial tasks. And if he failed to satisfy his owner he could be discarded, even slaughtered like a worthless animal." In the early church, however, slaves were given "the same rights . . . as anyone else." They ministered with dignity, and "at least one former slave, Callistus, became bishop of Rome."[12]

In reflecting on this passage and its impact on women, the Staggs write:

> If this is taken at face value, the whole question is settled as to the dignity, worth, freedom, and responsibility of women. This text does not deny the reality of sexual difference any more than it denies the reality of distinctions that are ethnic (Jew and Greek) or legal (slaves and free persons). There are such distinctions, but "in Christ" these are transcended. Sexual difference is a fact and an important one, with

relevance in human existence; but so far as our being "in Christ" is concerned, being male or female is not a proper agenda item. The phrase "in Christ" implies one's personal relationship with Jesus Christ; but it also implies one's being in the family of Christ. To be in Christ is to be in the church, the body of Christ (1 Cor. 12:12f; Rom. 12:5). For those "in Christ" or in the church, the body of Christ, it is irrelevant to ask if one is Jew or Gentile, slave or free, male or female.[13]

The phrase "in Christ" has been a matter of controversy in regard to this passage. Those who would affirm male headship argue that this passage is referring only to one's standing in reference to salvation. Of course, they say, Gentiles, slaves and women have equal standing before God as regards salvation. If Paul is saying only this, however, the passage is certainly not proclaiming that there is anything *new* about being "in Christ." Women, slaves and Gentiles were not excluded from salvation in Old Testament times. So the fact that there is *no longer* Jew or Greek, *no longer* slave or free, *no longer* male and female would make no sense if this verse were referring just to salvation.

The fact is that Paul is not limiting this new freedom to salvation. We are not only baptized *into* Christ but also "clothed" *with* Christ. This terminology of being "clothed with Christ" indicates "not only *position* but *practice*. . . . That is to say, there are implications for social relationships, not only for spiritual standing."[14]

16

Did the Apostles Affirm Male Headship and Wifely Submission?

T his is one of the pivotal questions regarding women's roles in the family and in the church. Virtually everything else revolves around the issue of male headship, and wifely submission is a complementary issue. The Scripture passages that are most significant regarding the issue of headship are 1 Corinthians 11 and Ephesians 5. Both are permeated with ancient cultural traditions. Indeed, like so many other questions regarding women's roles, this one cannot be thoroughly answered without an understanding of Palestinian and Greco-Roman cultures of the New Testament era and without an understanding of Greek terms.

The answer to the basic question is simple enough—yes, the apostles affirmed male headship and wifely submission. But that answer alone sheds very little light on the issue until we have determined what headship means and until we have determined whether men (or husbands, in particular) are also expected to submit.

What is the meaning of *kephale,* the Greek term for "head"?

The little Greek word *kephale,* which is usually rendered "head" in English, has been the subject of countless studies and debates in recent years. Its significance was summed up a few years ago in a *Christianity Today* news article, "Battle of the Lexicons," about a meeting of the Evangelical Theological Society in Atlanta at which this word became the focus of debate. Speakers actually brought their lexicons to the podium as they sought to refute each other's research and conclusions on this one little Greek noun.

The battle continues today as scholars publish their latest findings. The stakes are high. If the Bible says the husband is the "head" ("ruler" or "authority over") of the wife, those who would advocate an egalitarian model for marriage and ministry are confronted with a serious obstacle.

Simply stated, the debate centers on whether *kephale* means "ruler" or whether it means "source"—though there are other shades of meaning that also come into the argument. Since *kephale* is usually rendered "head," the meaning is settled in the minds of most people. There is no debate that a prevalent contemporary usage of "head" in the English language designates one who has authority over a corporation, a country or any other entity that is being governed. But the question is whether our contemporary usage of "head" correlates with the usage in ancient times.

Alvera Mickelsen has done extensive research on the word *kephale*—all of which indicates that the most accurate rendering of the term is not "ruler" or "authority over." Some of her evidence is summed up as follows:

> The most comprehensive lexicon of the Greek language of that period [first century A.D.] now available in English is one compiled by Liddell, Scott, Jones and McKenzie that covers classical and Koine Greek from 1000 B.C. to about A.D. 600—a period of nearly 1600 years, including the Septuagint (Greek translation of the Old Testament) and the Greek of New Testament times. The lexicon lists nearly twenty-five possible figurative meanings of *kephale* ("head") that were used in ancient Greek literature. Among them are "top," "brim," "apex," "origin," "source," "mouth," "starting point," "crown," "completion,"

"consummation," "sum," "total." The list does *not* include our common English usage of "authority over," "leader," "director," "superior rank" or anything similar as meanings. There is an older Greek-Latin thesaurus published in 1851, but written primarily in the sixteenth century. It also gives no meanings such as "authority over," or "supreme over."

Philip Barton Payne has also done extensive study of this issue. As part of his research, he consulted three secular specialists in ancient Greek literature. They all verified that the idea of "authority" was not a recognized meaning of *kephale* in classical Greek. Nor does *kephale* appear as a synonym for leader, chief or authority. S. C. Woodhouse lists many Greek equivalents for "chief" and for "authority" and for "leader," but *kephale* is not listed as an equivalent for any of them. Apparently *kephale* is considered to mean "authority over" primarily by those who are trying to find God-ordained male dominance in the Bible.[1]

Mickelsen's research has not settled the issue on *kephale*. Bible scholars have quickly scrambled to find instances where *kephale* actually did mean "ruler," and their claims are countered by scholars who argue that their evidence is not substantiated.

It should be pointed out that most of the church fathers presumed that *kephale,* as it is used in 1 Corinthians 11 and Ephesians 5, meant "ruler" or "authority," but they, like interpreters throughout history, may have simply assumed that meaning because it fit well with their concept of what a woman's place is in relation to her husband.

The debate is certainly not over, and it probably never will be. The precise meaning of *kephale* in the "headship" passages of the New Testament is simply not known, and unfortunately we have no inspired or inerrant lexicons that can definitely settle the matter.

How is man the head of women as the Father is the head of Christ?

Now I want you to realize that the head of every man is Christ, and the head of the woman is man, and the head of Christ is God. (1 Cor 11:3 NIV).

"How can a woman be equal to a man when the Bible says the head of the woman is man?" This is the exact wording of a spirited question an African student fired at me in a class I was teaching at Moffat College of the Bible in Kijabe, Kenya, a few years ago. I was used to questions like his, so I simply responded with another question: "Is the Son of God equal to the Father?" There is only one answer to that question—at least at Moffat—and the student knew immediately that he was trapped.

But that issue was not so easily settled in the early church when the Arian controversy was raging. Arians taught that Christ was a lesser being than God the Father, and their argument was based in part on this portion of Scripture—that "the head of Christ is God." In response, orthodox churchmen insisted that headship in no way implied that the Son was less than the Father.

Today among orthodox Christians the doctrine of the Trinity and the deity of Christ is a settled matter, but we still must be careful in how we define "head" when we teach that God is the *head* of Christ.

When we look closely at the context in 1 Corinthians 11, the "source" definition seems in many ways most appropriate, though the "rule" meaning also holds true. As trinitarians we believe that God the Father and God the Son are equal—that one is not greater than the other. Yet it is true that God the Father was *over* God the Son during his earthly ministry, so it would not be heretical to infer authority or rulership from the statement, "The head of Christ is God." But a straightforward reading of the whole passage seems to indicate the connotation of origin. We know that God is not literally and physically the father of Jesus (as the Mormons claim), but the Bible repeatedly offers us this model of their relationship to each other. Thus it is entirely appropriate to think of the Father as the "father" or source or origin of the Son. Elsewhere Scripture supports this concept: "For God so loved the world that he *gave* his only Son" (Jn 3:16); "but when the fullness of time had come, God *sent* his Son" (Gal 4:4).

By the same token, we all in a sense have our origin in Christ. We learn from 1 Corinthians 8:6 that there is "one Lord, Jesus Christ, through whom are all things and through whom we exist." So the concept of "source" or "origin" is consistent with the teaching of Scripture.

But the best indication for the meaning of *kephale* in this particular passage comes from the context itself, where the issue of origin, not rulership, is predominant, particularly in verses 8 and 12: "Indeed, man was not *made from* woman, but woman *from* man. . . . For just as woman *came from* man, so man *comes through* woman; but all things *come from* God." Paul here interprets the word himself. He is talking about origins—creation and birth. Woman was taken from man in creation, man has his origin in woman through birth. We do not have to be scholarly textual critics to understand this; nor do we have to pit one lexicon against another. The plain meaning of the text is enough.

In the fifth century, Cyril of Alexandria came to the same conclusion regarding 1 Corinthians 11:3: "Thus we say that the head of every man is Christ, because he was excellently made through him. And the head of woman is man, because she was taken from his flesh. Likewise, the head of Christ is God, because he is from him according to nature."[2]

When the meaning of *kephale* is understood to be "source," it makes more sense in the context of 1 Corinthians 11. The only authority that is mentioned in this passage is the authority *(exousian)* a woman has on her head.

What did a head-covering signify to Paul?

A man ought not to cover his head, since he is the image and glory of God; but the woman is the glory of man. For man did not come from woman, but woman from man; neither was man created for woman, but woman for man. For this reason, and because of the angels, the woman ought to have a sign of authority on her head.

In the Lord, however, woman is not independent of man, nor is man independent of woman. For as woman came from man, so also man is born of women. But everything comes from God. (1 Cor 11:7-12 NIV)

Not long ago I heard a colleague refer to the above verses as a "desperately difficult" passage. Surely that was no exaggeration; he is not alone in his bewilderment. According to C. F. D. Moule, "St Paul's strictures . . . still await a really convincing explanation." G. B. Caird reflects similar sentiments: "It can hardly be said that the passage has yet surrendered its secret."[3]

One thing of which we can be sure is that Paul had no editor with a blue pencil in hand, demanding that he clarify his statements. The meaning has been left for Bible students through the ages to decipher, and no two of them, it seems, agree.

Indeed, there are several statements in this short passage that are very confusing and difficult to understand. Why, for example, ought a man not "cover his head, *since* he is the image and glory of God"? Has it not been a Jewish tradition through the centuries for men to cover their heads in worship with a skullcap, or *yarmulke*? Did a man's head-covering now mean something different in Corinth? Surely Paul was not suggesting that Jewish men who covered their heads did not recognize that they were in the image of God. So what did Paul mean? After a lengthy discussion on veils and head-coverings, long and short hair, and shaved heads, Evans concludes: "The difficulty in coming to a definite conclusion about the exact nature of the custom described here is perhaps an indication that we should be very wary about claiming biblical support for any instance of a particular form of headgear in the church today." What is clear in these verses is that Paul is giving strong support to the difference in custom between men and women.[4]

Paul's next statement about woman coming from man is based on the Genesis 2 creation account and in itself is not difficult to understand. But the next sentence, which he ties to the creation of woman from man, is bewildering: "For this reason, and because of the angels, the woman ought to have a sign of authority on her head." Why "because of the angels"? This is another desperately difficult phrase to understand, and scholars can only speculate.

What follows that phrase is more controversial. Paul does *not* say that a woman ought to have a "sign of" or "symbol of" authority over her head, as most translations have rendered the Greek here. Those words are left out, but based on that rendering, Bible commentators have taken the meaning a step further to argue that the woman has the sign or symbol of her *husband's* authority on her head—that her authority is a passive authority through her husband. W. M. Ramsay, an authority on the Greek world of the apostle Paul, wrote in 1907 that this passive meaning of the term was "a preposterous idea which a Greek scholar would laugh at anywhere except in the New Testament, where (as they seem to think) Greek words may mean anything that commentators choose."[5]

According to Walter Liefeld,

The most straightforward meaning of the expression taken alone would probably be that the woman ought to have authority over her own head. Therefore, it is more in accord with the context to propose that the authority possessed by the woman is the right to pray publicly. . . . Why does Paul say "authority over her *head*"? Is it that he is affirming both that she *has* authority to speak and that she ought to have a symbol that would give her that right? This would be a modest hair style or covering that would deflect accusations of shameful behavior in public.[6]

Whatever he has meant in the foregoing verses, in verses 11-12 of this passage Paul balances the scales, saying that neither the woman nor the man is independent of the other, and even as the woman was created from the man, so the man comes from woman in childbirth. Giving birth, in Paul's mind, may have included giving a man his very identity. "According to Jewish law, anyone who is born to a Jewish mother and has not abandoned Judaism, the religion of the Jews, is a Jew."[7] In the end, what it all boils down to is that "everything comes from God"—a fitting finale to these "desperately difficult" verses.

Does the Bible teach mutual submission of husband and wife?

The answer to this question was summed up in the title of an article in *Moody Monthly* in 1987: "Submission Is for Husbands, Too." Here Mark Littleton writes that "one of the most overlooked, misunderstood, yet fundamental aspects of marriage" is "the *mutual* submission of each mate to the other." How does the husband submit? "The way a husband is to be submissive is by loving his wife and sacrificing himself for her as Christ did for the church."[8]

Littleton's biblical basis for mutual submission is the well-known passage in Ephesians 5. The apostle Paul opens the chapter by admonishing the Ephesians to "be imitators of God, as beloved children, and live in love, as Christ loved us and gave himself up for us." Then in verses 21-33, Paul offers guidelines for families—a household code, as such a set of injunctions was known in ancient times. The passage opens with a summary statement, "Be subject to one another out of reverence for Christ."

Paul moves on to those familiar verses we have so often heard preached from the pulpit: "Wives, be subject to your husbands as you are to the Lord. . . . Husbands, love your wives, just as Christ loved the church and gave himself up for her." Actually there is no verb in the first sentence admonishing wives to "be subject." It is assumed by Bible translators as a follow-up from the previous verse, which admonishes mutual submission and introduces the entire passage.

What is most striking about this passage is that only three verses are focused on the wife, while seven verses are devoted to the husband. Why the extra attention to the men?

It is safe to say that in the ancient world Paul's admonitions to women did not amount to shocking news. That a wife should submit to a husband was obvious. That was part of the very fabric of society and culture. But that husband and wife were to "be subject to one another" had to be rather startling. And that a husband was to love his wife "as Christ loved the church" was certainly a standard far beyond what was expected of husbands in the ancient world.

If anyone squirmed in the pew of the first-century church, it surely must have been the husband, not the wife. Indeed, his standard must have seemed utterly impossible to meet. The wife's submission is equated with the church's submission to Christ—which is in reality not a very high standard—but the husband's love is to be comparable to the utterly incomparable love of Christ for the church, as it is described in Philippians 2:8: "He humbled himself and became obedient to the point of death—even death on a cross."

Does Paul speak to the issue of domineering wives?

While most women would not have been shocked by Paul's admonition for them to submit to their husbands, that is not to assume that all first-century women were automatically submissive. The words were not superfluous. They were given for a reason.

Marriage is a difficult relationship to maintain, and it needs all the selflessness it can get—from both partners. The husband ought not seek to dominate—nor ought the wife. Indeed, a little-talked-about condition that often cripples marriages is the domineering of a wife, who may give lip service to submission but does not practice it. A story that illustrates this in a lighthearted style is Mark Twain's "The McWilliamses and the Burglar Alarm." We pick up the story with Mr. McWilliams speaking:

> When we were finishing our house, we found we had a little cash left over, on account of the plumber not knowing it. I was for enlightening the heathen with it, for I was always unaccountably down on the heathen somehow; but Mrs. McWilliams said no, let's have a burglar alarm. I agreed to this compromise. I will explain that whenever I want a thing, and Mrs. McWilliams wants another thing, and we decide upon the thing that Mrs. McWilliams wants—as we always do—she calls that a compromise.[9]

There is no doubt more truth in these lines than many women would want to admit, and in Ephesians 5:21-24 Paul has a message for them.

The most constructive way to build a successful marriage is for each partner to strive to surpass the other in love and submission. That is a high ideal, but the rewards are priceless. Some, however, will argue that there must be a "head" or a chain of command. If not, who will be the tie-breaker when differences of opinion arise? I have a hunch that it is this "tie-breaker" mentality that leads to a lot of marital breakdowns. Good relationships do not require tie-breakers. Business partnerships work without a "head"—as do other partnerships. I have co-authored two books, and in both instances there were many tough decisions that had to be made—ones that my co-authors and I had to struggle through and hammer out. It was not always easy, but we were forced to consider each other and to make compromises, and in the end our partnership was stronger for it. So, too, can it be in a marriage.

Who is the "head of the home"?

The phrase "head of the home" is common in contemporary vocabulary, though it is not one that is common to the Bible—except in the sense of the owner who is in charge of the home. Today, the man is usually considered the "head of the home"—though not necessarily sole owner, because most wives have joint ownership with their husbands. Nevertheless, he is "head of the home." But is he really?

In 1 Timothy 5:14, Paul admonishes younger widows to "marry, bear children, and manage their households, so as to give the adversary no occasion to revile us." A man is also admonished "to manage his own household" (1 Tim 3:5, 12), but different Greek words are both rendered "manage" in the English. The one associated with men, *prostenai,* means "to be up front" or "to exercise leadership." The Greek word used in regard to young widows, however, has much greater force. It is *oikodespotein,* from where we get the word "despot." In the noun form, this word is commonly used in the Gospels to mean the owner or ruler of the household.[10] So Paul is instructing young widows to remarry, to bear children and to *rule* their households, thus implying that they are the "head" of the home.

Some might argue that the woman's ruling of the home simply defines her role—that a woman's proper place is in the home. Even the strongest defenders of male headship will not object if the wife makes decisions regarding what to have for dinner or what color of drapes to buy. But this is not the message of the New Testament. Yes, of course it was natural for women to have domestic responsibilities, but that should not necessarily be seen as the only or the ideal role for a woman. Jesus clarified this issue when dealing with Mary and Martha. Martha was rightly rankled when Mary sat as a disciple at Jesus' feet instead of helping her. After all, meal preparation and domestic duties were the responsibility of women, and Mary was shirking her rightful function as a woman. Jesus could have kindly reminded Mary of her rightful role—if, indeed, he believed that women had such roles—but he did not. Instead he said: "Mary has chosen the better part, which will not be taken away from her" (Lk 10:42).

Does the Bible command a wife to "obey" her husband?

This is a touchy issue for many evangelical Christians—especially as it relates to the wedding ceremony. After a wedding I attended recently, a number of people at the reception remarked upon the fact that the bride did *not* pledge to obey. Most of the comments were negative.

In the passage relating to husbands and wives in Ephesians 5, it is important to note that "the word *obey,* which occurs with regard to children and to slaves, is conspicuously absent in the section about wives. In addition, not one of the instructions to the husband pertains to ruling. All have to do with caring for and enhancing one's wife."[11] The same pattern is seen in Colossians 3:18-22, where wives are not commanded to obey, but children and slaves are.

In 1 Peter 2:18—3:7, the pattern is different. Here slaves are listed first, and children are not mentioned at all. "Slaves, accept the authority of your masters with all deference" (2:18). That is followed by, "Wives, *in the same way,* accept the authority of your husbands" (3:1). In both cases the Greek term rendered "accept the authority" is the same word used in Ephesians 5:21 for mutual submission *(submit yourselves* to one another). Paul's admonition to women is followed by one to men: "Husbands, *in the same way,* show consideration for your wives" (3:7). In this passage, Peter does give the illustration of Sarah's obeying Abraham and calling him lord, but he does not specifically say that all wives must obey and call their husbands lord; and as our earlier discussion noted, Abraham also obeyed Sarah.

While Peter does not call children to submit to parents in his first epistle, he does admonish Christians "to accept the authority of every human institution, whether of the emperor as supreme, or of governors, as sent by him" (2:13-14). It is interesting how often these verses are passed over by those who apply very literally the following section on wives' submitting to their husbands. Indeed, some of the most conservative ministers who sermonize on wifely submission are the most enthusiastic supporters of antigovernment uprisings—as occurred in China in 1989 and later in Eastern Europe. While it is true that these regimes were and are very repressive, Peter does not seem to be making exceptions in this passage. A literal application, then, would exclude supporting any such antigovernment action. And it would also tend to dampen spirits on the Fourth of July, a holiday commemorating American independence—won through a revolution—which has almost become a sacred celebration to some evangelicals.

What does the term "weaker vessel" mean in reference to women?
The phrase "weaker vessel" is found in 1 Peter 3:7 in the King James Version. That is the literal rendering of the Greek, but in the New RSV, the passage reads: "Husbands, in the same way, show consideration for your wives in your life together, paying honor to the woman as the weaker sex, since they too are also heirs of the gracious gift of life—so that nothing may hinder your prayers."

To refer to the woman as the "weaker vessel" has become common usage. In fact, a recent best-selling book on women in seventeenth-century England by Antonia Fraser is entitled *The Weaker Vessel*.

But what does the phrase mean? Most Bible scholars who emphasize male headship argue that the weakness has to do with position or authority. "A reference to authority fits context more naturally and makes more sense," writes Hurley. "It would seem unlikely that Peter would be saying, 'Remember that she is physically weaker and cannot lift as much as you,' or 'Remember that she cannot take as much beating as you.' It is quite likely that he would say, 'Remember that hers is the subordinate position and don't abuse your stronger position of authority.'"[12]

Bilezikian does not deny the association of authority with the expression, but he does not regard it as the standard: "Women may be considered the 'weaker sex,' especially since their subjection to male rulership at the fall, but now, in the new creation, they become 'joint heirs' with their husbands."[13]

Most modern Bible commentators, however, have concluded that the expression refers to physical weakness—in contrast to earlier commentators, who often used the phrase to support their belief in a woman's weaker intellectual or reasoning capacity. But to view the expression as primarily physical frailty is not necessarily indicated in the context. Faith Martin suggests simply that "a wife was the weaker partner, legally as well as physically, and a husband must not take advantage of her."[14] This explanation would fit the context, in that the next phrase refers to the husband and wife as "joint heirs," a phrase that seems to allude to the legal standing of husband and wife.

In what ways are wives "joint heirs" with their husbands?

Here again, the expression comes from 1 Peter 3:7 in the King James Version. It is a less repeated expression than "weaker vessel"—perhaps because it reflects very positively on women, and some preachers and Bible teachers are less likely to repeat the positive than they are the negative.

That women are "joint heirs" is no less than remarkable in the context of first-century Jewish culture. Peter is recognizing the woman's "full religious equality with man—a thought impossible for Judaism." He "is simply pointing out," writes Evans, "that before God, man and wife stand in exactly the same position and that this common inheritance will affect the way in which they relate to each other on all levels."[15]

Has the institution of marriage changed since Paul's day?

Ephesians 5 is the single most important passage on the husband-wife relationship in the New Testament. It, like Colossians 3 and 1 Peter 2—3, is a household code, or *Haustafeln,* a form that was common in the ancient world. In this code, Paul speaks not only of the husband-wife relationship but also of the parent-child relationship and the master-slave relationship. The sections are parallel and should be read in the same light. But as contemporary Christians, we obviously do not seek to apply the section on slavery as Paul meant it in his day. Some theologians in the nineteenth century, however, did just that, as they gave biblical support to Southern slaveholders.

Many contemporary biblical scholars seek to substitute the employer-employee relationship for the master-slave relationship, but in doing so they are forced to admit that this portion of the household code—the institution of slavery—has changed significantly since ancient times. Today an employee can join a union or quit a job and find another employer, or even become an employer and, as sometimes happens, hire the former employer as an employee. So the employer-employee relationship is a very fluid one. The same cannot be said for the marriage relationship, but it is unrealistic to suggest that the institution of marriage—unlike the institution of slavery—has not changed in two thousand years. Today in Western society wives have equal rights with their husbands before the law. They have opportunities for education and careers as never before in history. The institution of marriage has changed, but the principles of mutual love and submission remain.

What are some very practical concerns regarding male headship?
A topic of serious concern in recent years is the widespread abuse of male "headship"—particularly in Christian homes. Family violence surely is not a problem that has emerged in modern times, but the grim statistics pointing to its epidemic proportions have only surfaced in recent years, and Christian families are certainly not immune to these problems.

It is a concern for many Christians that the concept of male headship is being used, not to give sanction to a husband's abuse, but to keep a woman in an abusive situation by "beating her over the head with a Bible," as one friend of mine phrased it.

This issue of wife abuse was addressed by Elisabeth Elliot a few years ago when she was speaking before a large gathering of seminary wives at a well-known evangelical seminary. It would have been naive to assume that there were no battered wives in that audience. Yet in response to the question "Should a wife remain in a home where she is being physically abused by her husband?" Elliot pointed the women to 1 Peter 2, which speaks of slaves who were "beaten" and "endured" even when they had done no wrong. Elliot then quoted 1 Peter 3: "*In the same way, you women must accept the authority of your husbands.*" In her spontaneous commentary on these verses, she said, "I don't think that requires

PART 5

The Role
of Women in
Church History

17

Did the Influence of Women Decline after the New Testament Era?

The New Testament is unusual in presenting many named women who were active in ministry. Women were not among the twelve disciples, but they are featured prominently in the biblical text. Mary the mother of Jesus, Elizabeth and Anna are significant at the time of Jesus' birth. Mary and Martha of Bethany, Mary Magdalene and many other women were involved in Jesus' ministry, and Dorcas, Lydia, Phoebe and Priscilla were all active in the early church. But following the New Testament period, women's names do not appear so prominently on the pages of recorded history.

When women do appear in the historical narratives, they almost seem to jump out at the reader as an aberration. It was a man's world, and normally there was no reason to record the activities of women. But in some cases, the story simply cannot be told without their participation being noted. This is true of a letter that was sent from Pliny the Younger, governor of Bithynia to Emperor Trajan around A.D. 112. The letter is very interesting in that it offers many details and insights from a pagan perspective on the persecution of early Christians.

Pliny wrote to the emperor to request directions on punishing Christians—whether, for example, the age of the person and renunciation of faith made any difference. While asking for advice, however, he made it dreadfully clear that he was not passively waiting for a response. "So far this has been my procedure when people were charged before me with being Christians," he explained. "I have asked the accused themselves if they were Christians; if they said 'Yes,' I asked them a second and third time, warning them of the penalty; if they persisted I ordered them to be led off to execution." Pliny emphasized to Trajan that this procedure was working and that Christianity was decreasing in strength. But to obtain more information, he found it "necessary to inquire into the real truth of the matter by subjecting to torture two female slaves who were called 'deacons'; but I found nothing more than a perverse superstition which went beyond all bounds."[1]

This brief reference is a fascinating glimpse of women in ministry in the early second century. We do not know why Pliny chose two female slaves to torture, but they may have been the only leaders left in the church—the others having either renounced their faith or been executed. That they were deacons indicates that slaves and women apparently did hold office in the postapostolic church. And their "perverse superstition" was most likely their belief in such doctrines as the virgin birth, the bodily resurrection and the deity of Christ—evidence that they may have been fully capable at articulating their beliefs.

What was the role of women martyrs in the early church?
The most frequent references to women in the early church are to female martyrs. From Eusebius, the early church historian, we hear the painful stories of some of these women. Two particular women are mentioned in connection with the persecution in Alexandria around the mid-third century. "They led a woman called Quinta, who was a believer, to the temple of an idol, and attempted to force her to worship," he writes; "but

when she turned away in disgust, they tied her by the feet, and dragged her through the whole city, over the rough stones of the paved streets, dashing her against the millstones, and scourging her at the same time, until they brought her to the same place, where they stoned her." Later, "they also seized that admirable virgin, Apollonia, then in advanced age, and beating her jaws, they broke out all her teeth, and kindling a fire before the city, threatened to burn her alive, unless she would repeat their impious expressions." At first she hesitated, "but when suffered to go, she suddenly sprang into the fire and was consumed."[2]

One of the best known of the early women martyrs is Vibia Perpetua, a young mother living in North Africa who died for her faith after Emperor Septimus Severus issued an edict in A.D. 202 forbidding conversion to Christianity. Her husband, apparently an unbeliever, is not mentioned; he may have been dead or separated from her. She and her personal slave Felicitas were among a group of new converts participating in catechism classes. It would have been an easy matter for this young woman of high standing to simply say to the leader of the group that she and Felicitas had changed their minds—that with the publication of the edict it would make sense for them to forgo joining the church. But she did not.

Perpetua and Felicitas were imprisoned, as were the other catechists. Perpetua's father pleaded with her to renounce her beliefs and was beaten for trying to rescue her from prison. But in the end, both women stood firm in the face of martyrdom. They were first put in the arena with wild heifers, but when this torture became too bloody and the crowd shouted "Enough!" they were brought before the gladiator, whose job it was to behead them. As the story is told, he did not carry out the execution of Perpetua on the first attempt; with a cry of pain, she clutched his trembling hand and brought the sword down on her neck, and it was quickly over.[3]

Perpetua and Felicitas, like so many other women in the early church, passed the ultimate test of faith, and by doing so added to the cumulative testimony of martyrs—a testimony that powerfully served the cause of Christ.

Did women hold office in the postapostolic church?

Did Phoebe hold office? Was she a deacon? She is described with the Greek word *diakonos* in Romans 16:1. Whether women held office as deacons or deaconesses in the New Testament era is uncertain. Paul, however, seemed to open the door for such appointments in 1 Timothy 3:8-13. Here he is speaking of qualifications for deacons, and in verse 11, he turns his attention specifically to women, believed to be either wives of deacons or women deacons: "Women likewise must be serious, not slanderers, but temperate, faithful in all things."

It does appear from Scripture that women had churches in their homes—women such as Lydia and the "elect lady" and her sister in 2 John. But whether these women actually held office is unknown.

Some of these larger house churches became the sites of cathedrals and bishops' palaces. With women continuing to take leading parts in worship services, the idea of an order for those who thus served slowly evolved. These women were first called deaconesses and later canonesses. As they were ordained to assist in the services of the cathedrals, they began to live together nearby. According to Joan Morris, an Oxford University lecturer, women were the first to live in community. Also according to Morris canonesses were considered to be of apostolic origin. Augustine wrote their rules and later adapted them for men.[4]

Did these women perform the functions of ordained church officeholders? Again, so little has been handed down to us on the role of women in the early church that it is difficult to know. There are hints, however, especially in the Roman catacombs, that women may have functioned as clergy. "In the 'Cappella Greca' of the Catacomb of Priscilla, a second-century fresco has been found with seven women celebrating Holy Communion. On the table there are the chalice, the bread and the fish, symbolizing Jesus Christ. On either side are the baskets of bread." This, of course, does not prove that women administered Communion, but in a document written by Athanasius in the fourth century, he gave the following instructions: "If there are two or three Virgins with you, let them 'Give Thanks' over the bread together with you." His rationale for allowing these women to administer the Lord's Supper was that as an order of virgins, they were living lives devoted to God as though they were in heaven, and "in the kingdom of heaven there is neither male nor female, so that women pleasing to the Lord may receive the Order of men."[5]

The primary role of the women officeholders—or deaconesses—in the early church had nothing to do with administering the sacraments. "It should not be forgotten," writes Philip Schaff, "that many virgins of the early church devoted their whole energies as deaconesses to the care of the sick and the poor, or exhibited as martyrs a degree of passive virtue and moral heroism altogether unknown before." It was these women whom the early churchman Cyprian referred to as "the flowers of the church, the masterpieces of grace, the ornament of nature, the image of God reflecting the holiness of our Saviour, the most illustrious of the flock of Jesus Christ, who commenced on earth that life which we shall lead once in heaven."[6]

What was the role of widows and virgins in the early church?

Devoting themselves entirely to God's service, widows played an important role in the charitable ministry of the early church. This organized involvement can be seen in its initial stages in Acts 9:36-43, where we read that Dorcas, who "was devoted to good works," died. Peter was called; when he went to her room, "all the widows stood beside him, weeping and showing tunics and other clothing that Dorcas had made while she was with them." From this account it appears as though there may have been an "order" of widows who were devoted to good works.

It is entirely possible that it is for this "order" of widows that Paul is requesting support in 1 Timothy 5:3-16. Here he tells the believers at Ephesus to "honor widows who are really widows." Who is the "real" widow? "The real widow, left alone, has set her hope on God and continues in supplications and prayers night and day." He goes on to speak of a "list" for widows. This would imply that here was the beginning of an "order," whereby widows were supported in exchange for their devotion and ministry to God.

Another "order" of women that developed in the early church was simply known as "virgins." Paul's admonitions in 1 Corinthians 7 may have been a motivating factor. He writes: "To the unmarried and the widows I say that it is well for them to remain unmarried as I am" (7:8).

In the centuries immediately following the close of the New Testament it appears as though these "orders" became more organized as "ministries of commitment." The church fathers often spoke approvingly of these women, though in many instances more for their commitment to celibacy than for their actual ministry.[7]

By the fourth century, these orders of widows and virgins were becoming solidified into monastic communities. One of the earliest female monastic leaders was Macrina of Cappadocia, who vowed as a teenager to devote her life wholly to God. So powerful was her commitment that she influenced other family members to join her, including her widowed mother and her brother, Basil, who became a monastic leader in his own right. "In her community for women, Macrina taught the Scriptures to anyone who would come and listen. She also established a hospital where divine healing was practiced."[8]

How did the church fathers influence church tradition regarding women?
While the church fathers often praised the "widows" and "virgins," they had little positive to say regarding womanhood in general. Tertullian's views are well known, especially his denigrating depiction of women: "You are the devil's gateway." What is most astonishing about this phrase is that it is found in a manuscript Tertullian wrote for women to read, entitled *On the Apparel of Women*. It is hard to imagine that women would read such insults, but Tertullian apparently sought to win them over by addressing them as "best beloved sisters." He wasted no time in getting to the heart of the issue. Because of Eve's sin, the Christian woman should dress and behave appropriately "in order that by every garb of penitence she might the more fully expiate that which she derives from Eve. . . . Do you not know that you are [each] an Eve? The sentence of God on this sex of yours lives in this age; the guilt must of necessity live, too."[9]

How did the women recipients of this treatise—many of them devoted to a life of ministry—react? Did they roll their eyes and sigh? Did they clench their fists in rage? Or did they accept his judgment as their lot in life?

Clement of Alexandria was equally negative in his reflections on women—though at least he did not address his remarks to them personally. "Nothing disgraceful is proper for man," he wrote, "who is endowed with reason; much less for women, to whom it brings shame even to reflect of what nature she is. . . . by no manner of means are women to be allowed to uncover and exhibit any part of their person, lest both fall—the men by being excited to look, they by drawing on themselves the eyes of men."[10]

John Chrysostom is known for pronouncing judgment on women in one short sentence: "Among all savage beasts, none is found so harmful as woman." And John of Damascus, according to Schaff, collected "in his Parallels such patristic expressions as these: 'A woman is an evil.' 'A rich woman is a double evil.' 'A beautiful woman is a whited sepulchre.' 'Better is a man's wickedness than a woman's goodness.' "[11]

It is impossible to imagine that these opinions offered so freely on women did not have an impact on the church. The church fathers were revered not only in their day but also through the centuries that followed. Indeed, it was common practice for theologians down through the ages to quote the fathers as authorities to establish a basis of orthodoxy before giving their own opinions.

18

Did Women Find Meaningful Ministry in Medieval Catholicism?

W hat difference does it make whether or not women had meaningful ministry in the medieval period? Many Protestants would suppose that this is not part of their tradition anyway. But the medieval Roman Catholic church is very much part of our heritage as Protestants. Church history did not somehow take a mysterious leap forward in the fifth century and find itself suddenly nailing ninety-five theses to a church door in Wittenberg. The only way to find our way back to the postapostolic church from the vantage point of the sixteenth century is to cull through all that was good and bad in medieval Roman Catholicism. It is our church, and we cannot simply ignore that fact. And it is a particularly important era in regard to women's ministries.

The medieval period is known as a great era for monasticism. As new religious orders were founded, the numbers of men and women who joined monasteries and convents greatly increased. For many women in the Middle Ages, the convent was an appealing alternative to the rigors of married life. It offered opportunity for education that was otherwise not available, and it allowed women to savor the satisfaction of serving God.

In most instances these women resided in cloistered settings entirely apart from the general population and were bound by vows to remain in their convent as long as they lived. It was this isolation that most profoundly characterized female monasticism. Indeed, in my mind, one of the saddest aspects of women's ministry during the medieval period is that it was so inwardly and vertically focussed that it offered little benefit to those who were most needy.

Spirituality was a high priority for the medieval monastic woman, but there was far less concern to share that deep faith in God with their sisters who lived in the world and had few opportunities to delve into spiritual matters with a student of the Scriptures. Women in the villages were certainly not devoid of religion, but often their religious beliefs were filled with superstitions. These women surely could have benefited greatly from the ministry of women like Dorcas and Priscilla in the book of Acts, who offered humanitarian ministry and taught the Word of God.

The Poor Clares were typical of medieval female monasticism. That religious order began in 1212, when the twelve-year-old Clara of Sciffi escaped her home and convinced Francis of Assisi to establish the order of Clarisses, or Poor Clares.[1] Clara may have thought that this would be an opportunity to devote her life to serving the poor, but she was wrong. The pope imposed a strict rule: "No sister is to go out of the convent for any purpose whatsoever except to found a new community. . . . Perpetual silence is imposed on all the members of the community, and continuous fasting, often on bread and water."[2]

Men lived secluded in monasteries as well, but they generally had more opportunities to become involved in the lives of others, especially after 1200, when preaching friars spread out across Europe. The Franciscans were among them, but their female counterparts, the Poor Clares, remained cloistered. Clare described herself more than once as "the useless servant of the monastery of Saint Damian's." Though she spoke those words in a spirit of humility, the underlying message is of a deep sense of failure—feelings that may have been pervasive among these silenced and secluded women.

How did the issue of celibacy influence attitudes toward women?

Because it was widely held that woman was the cause of man's fall into sin, it was believed by many that a truly spiritual life of devotion to God must be free of sexual contact. Even social interaction with the opposite sex was viewed as harmful. We have all read about the hermit monks of the early centuries who went out in the desert to avoid temptation—especially sexual temptation. Often the devil would come to them in the form of a sensuous woman, and they would fight battles with these hallucinations.

But celibacy was not an ideal upheld primarily by men—especially in the earliest centuries of the church. "Celibacy was most common with pious virgins, who married themselves only to God or to Christ, and in the spiritual delights of this heavenly union found abundant compensation for the pleasures of matrimony." Thus, among many churchmen the idea of celibate nuns enhanced their view of women—though in some cases the nuns brought shame on their profession and only added to the scorn that was associated with their sex. "Many of these heavenly brides lived with male ascetics," writes Schaff, "under the pretext of a purely spiritual fellowship, in so intimate intercourse as to put their continence to the most perilous test."[3] Worse yet, according to an eleventh-century French bishop, there were many convents in which nuns were involved in prostitution.[4]

The practice of celibacy sometimes led to scandals involving some of the most celebrated churchmen of this era. While Jerome wrote lengthy letters to women praising the merits of virginity, he himself was rumored to have a questionable relationship with a close female friend and associate, Paula. To a friend he wrote, "The only fault found in me is my sex, and that only when Paula comes to Jerusalem." And again he wrote: "Before I knew the house of saintly Paula, my praises were sung through the city, and nearly everyone judged me worthy of the highest office of the Church. But I know well that it is through good and evil report that we make our way to the kingdom of heaven." Peter Abelard, a twelfth-century philosopher and monastic leader, created a scandal when he seduced his young student, Heloise, and was castrated as the penalty.[5]

It is interesting that both women whose names were associated with these scandals were influential leaders in their own right. Paula was one of the most respected Bible scholars of Jerome's day, and Heloise went on to become one of the great abbesses of the medieval period.

The ideal of celibacy, which these and so many other women upheld, gave them the opportunity to devote their lives to God. But it also had negative connotations—especially when it was viewed as the only way men could avoid the enticing evils of women, and when women were associated with the scandals that naturally too often shook the celibate communities.

Did medieval Catholicism foster a feminine Christianity?

Because of the large numbers of women in monasticism in the medieval period, and because of the heavy focus on the Virgin Mary, some historians have argued that the end result was a feminization of the church. They contrast medieval Roman Catholicism with Reformation Protestantism, which they argue was a very masculine form of religion. Such generalizations and stereotypes of masculine and feminine are not always useful. But in this instance it is interesting that medieval religion did place greater focus on the experiential side of the faith, emphasizing visions, miracles and inner spirituality, while Reformation faith placed an emphasis on biblical study and doctrinal issues.

In her analysis of medieval spirituality, Eleanor McLaughlin writes that both men and women of this era exemplified that which might be regarded as "feminine":

Dangerous though this suggestion be in its implication of stereotypes, I want to explore the notion that these holy women exemplified a human nature and a vision of divine nature that gave more weight to affectivity, love and the integration of love and intellect, than has been the usual, acceptable or mainstream idea of "human nature," as we perceive it, since the seventeenth century. This more "feminized" human nature was *not* seen as "feminine" by men and women of the pre-Reformation Church but rather as Christian, typical and in the image of God, who was Mother as well as Father, Love more than Intellect. Holiness called forth a Christian theology and an anthropology radically *less* androcentric than that which dominates Christian piety today.[6]

The issue of a feminine form of Christianity concerns some people today. If women were permitted to hold office and serve equally alongside men in ministry, would the church become feminized? We must be careful about stereotyping masculine and feminine spirituality, but at the same time we might do well to seek a balance between those aspects of our faith that would typically be viewed as feminine and those that are masculine. Reflecting on medieval spirituality can be beneficial in this respect.

How was Mary viewed in the church of the Middle Ages?

How are we as Christians to regard the Virgin Mary? Do we give her special honor as the mother of Jesus? Certainly that is appropriate, especially in light of Elizabeth's response when she heard that Mary had conceived: "Blessed are you among women" (Lk 1:42). Mary herself recognized this special honor when she said, "Surely, from now on all generations will call me blessed" (Lk 1:48). "The Blessed Virgin Mary" is an appropriate title for Jesus' mother, but only if it is balanced by Jesus' own description of her as a mere woman. "Who is my mother, and who are my brothers?" he asked, and answered his question by pointing to his disciples: "Whoever does the will of my Father in heaven is my brother and sister and mother" (Mt 12:48-50).

In the medieval Roman Catholic church, Mary became a virtual god in her own right. "Devotion to Mary reached a peak in the Middle Ages," writes Don Sharkey, himself a devotee of Mary. "The palaces of earthly queens were hovels compared with the palaces—churches and cathedrals—of the heavenly Queen. . . . Nearly every great church of the Middle Ages belonged to Mary. If it was not dedicated to her outright, it contained a Lady Chapel." But this veneration of Mary did not last, according to Sharkey. "It was in the sixteenth century, at the time of the Protestant Revolt, that millions of people turned away from their heavenly Mother. That revolt was one of the most tragic events of history. . . . Our Lady was neglected even by large numbers of Catholics. . . . Catholics continued to pray to her, but she did not play the prominent part in their lives that she should have. The world had truly turned from its Mother."[7]

Despite Sharkey's pessimistic analysis, the veneration of Mary has abated very little since medieval times—especially in areas of Europe and Latin America. Indeed, according to my friend Lori, who is a missionary in Spain, images of Mary are paraded through the streets on festival days, with people cheering and exalting their favorite virgin.

Today we often view this veneration as a phenomenon that occurs among the theologically illiterate, but Catholic theologians down through the centuries have defended Mary's perpetual virginity. In the medieval period they differed on the detail—some arguing that she was conceived sinless, others that she became sinless while in the womb—but there was no strong opposition, and over time the position of Thomas Aquinas came to dominate: "As a virgin she conceived, as a virgin gave birth, and she remains a virgin forever." It was not until 1854, however, that Mary's sinlessness became part of church dogma.[8]

What influence did medieval theologians have on the women's issue?

A mile from my home in Grand Rapids, Michigan, is Aquinas College, a small liberal arts school on a beautifully wooded campus. The school is named for the most highly acclaimed theologian and philosopher of the medieval Roman Catholic church, Thomas Aquinas (1224-1274). He was a Dominican monk who wrote massive theological works and Bible commentaries. So important is he that more space is devoted to him in my 1978 edition of *The New International Dictionary of the Christian Church* than to John Wesley—and for good reason. He had a powerful influence on the Christian church that is still widely felt today, and not just among Roman Catholics. According to Paul Helm, "The influence of Aquinas on Protestantism must not be minimized."[9]

Aquinas wrote on a broad range of topics, including issues relating to women and gender differences. In his view, women are controlled by their sexual appetites while men are governed by reason. Women's lives and concerns are trivial and are wholly dependent on men, while men need women only for procreation. Because of their inferiority as a sex, women are utterly incapable of filling important roles either in society or in the church. Consider these words from Aquinas's pen: "The woman is subject to the man, on account of the weakness of her nature, both of mind and of body. . . . Man is the beginning of woman and her end, just as God is the beginning and end of every creature. . . . Woman is in subjection according to the law of nature, but a slave is not. . . . Children ought to love their father more than their mother."[10]

Other medieval theologians and philosophers shared the sentiments of Aquinas. One was Bonaventura, a leading thirteenth-century schoolman. Aristotle, according to Bonaventura, spoke well when he said, "Woman is an embarrassment to man, a beast in his quarters, a continual worry, a never-ending trouble, a daily annoyance, the destruction of the household, a hindrance to solitude, the undoing of a virtuous man, an oppressive burden, an insatiable bee, a man's property and possession."[11]

It would be foolish to suggest that these attitudes, as they have been passed down from generation to generation, have no influence in the Roman Catholic (and Protestant) church today.

How did medieval "heretics" view women?

There are two categories of medieval "heretics": true heretics and true believers rejected by the official church. As "sectarian" movements with no official standing in a society permeated by *the* church, these groups flourished only through the active participation of the laity. Women and men worked side by side with few distinctions, and women even served in clerical positions during the foundational stages of these movements.

Two "heretical" movements that are now viewed by many church historians as forerunners of the Protestants were the Waldensians and the Taborites. The Waldensians were followers of Peter Waldo, who denied the authority of the Catholic church and insisted that the Bible was the only true rule of faith. In the early thirteenth century, eighty "heretics" believed to be Waldensians were burned at the stake in Strassburg; twenty-three of them were women. Among the Waldensians, women as well as men preached, and according to their enemies, women even officiated Communion and baptisms. The Taborites were radical followers of John Huss, who, like the Waldensians, believed that the Bible was the sole source of doctrine. Among them, women also served as preachers.[12]

It would serve as powerful historical support to an egalitarian position if only the biblically orthodox medieval sects had offered women active ministry and leadership. But some of the truly heretical religious groups, such as the Cathers of southern France, also permitted women prominent roles in ministry. The explanation for this phenomenon is not so much that these sects were following biblical precedent as that they were rebel movements that needed to marshal all the forces they had into active service.

What effect did visionary experiences have on women's ministry?

Visionary and miraculous experiences of all sorts have been important throughout the history of Christianity. According to Peter, on the Day of Pentecost, "Jesus of Nazareth was a man accredited by God to you by miracles, wonders and signs" (Acts 2:22 NIV), and the message of the new faith was "confirmed" by Paul, Barnabas and others through "miraculous signs and wonders" (Acts 14:3 NIV). In the centuries that followed the apostolic period, signs and wonders continued, and they were seen as evidence to "confirm" the message or to give an individual credibility.

This was particularly true with women. Unlike men, whose ministry was authenticated by rites and certificates of ordination and by the authority conferred on them through gradations of officeholding, women were generally on their own. Some wielded power as abbesses within their own religious orders, but recognition from the world outside was gained primarily through alleged miracles and visionary revelations.

It is important to emphasize that men, too, testified of miracles and visionary experiences. But women's monasteries were more often centers of charismatic activity than were men's. Did this have something to do with women's nature? Are women inherently more prone to be emotional and mystical? Caroline Bynum, a historian who has studied women's spirituality in the Middle Ages, argues against any such generalization, but she does offer interesting insights on why women may have developed this form of spirituality. She suggests that these visionary charismatic experiences authenticated women's roles in the church—particularly priestly roles that were officially denied them. Thus from God—if not man—they acquired "direct authorization to act as mediators to others."[13]

So did these visions emerge out of impure motives—a lust for power? To make that argument is to go beyond what I personally am willing to do. However, I do have a healthy skepticism for any visions or revelations that are claimed to be directly from God—*especially* if these messages do not correspond with Scripture. Such false messages were common during the medieval period. For example, the visions and revelations of Brigitta of Sweden and Catherine of Siena, affirming the sinlessness of Mary the mother of Jesus, contradict the teaching of Scripture.

It is important to point out that many of these medieval mystics were reformers in the church, and their visions and revelations were often aimed at church leaders and laity who were involved in corruption and other sins. Hildegard of Bingen pleaded for sinners to repent, vividly depicting—through her visions—the consequences if they did not. The "souls of the disobedient" would suffer in "a well deep and broad, full of boiling pitch and sulphur," filled with "fiery vipers" and blanketed with "a thickest darkness."[14] But even these visions were typically depictions not of hell but of purgatory—a notion that has little biblical grounding.

19

Did the Reformation Open or Close Doors for Women in Ministry?

D id the Protestant Reformation that swept though Europe in the sixteenth century deal a massive blow to medieval monasticism, only to deny women opportunity for ministry? This question has been much debated.

Many nuns who had been faithfully carrying out their vows in cloistered convents suddenly found angry Protestant mobs clamoring at their windows, demanding that they renounce their Roman Catholic faith and their vows of celibacy. But even if the nuns had been so inclined, the Protestants had very little to offer them in exchange. All they could tell these devoted women was to return to their families, and if they had no families, to find lodging elsewhere. Elderly nuns were often forced to leave the only home and family they had ever known.

Some of the Reformers recognized these crimes for what they were. Wrote Philip Melanchthon, "The preachers scream, swear, and storm, and do everything in their power to rouse the hatred of the masses against the poor nuns; they openly say that as the words were of no avail, recourse should be had to force."[1]

Should we conclude that the Reformation had a very negative effect on women's ministries? Arthur Glasser of Fuller Seminary argues that it did: "One of the tragedies of Protestantism is that it drove women from the cloistered life. . . . With the dissolution of the nunneries women lost their last chance of churchly service outside the narrow circle of husband, home and children."[2] But the picture is not quite that dismal. Women have always circumvented restrictions on ministry, and that was certainly true during the Reformation period.

Katherine von Bora is a prime example. Her feisty personality and dogged determination landed her the most eligible bachelor of the sixteenth century, Martin Luther. As his wife, she had opportunity for ministry, as did other women who married Protestant preachers. Their ministries were not confined exclusively to the home. Many of them reached out in very effective evangelistic and humanitarian ministries. This was also true of women who were not married to ministers—women such as Argula von Stauffer, whose husband fiercely opposed her ministry.

How did the three hallmarks of the Reformation affect women?
The three great hallmarks of the Protestant Reformation were salvation by faith alone, *sola Scriptura* and the priesthood of all believers. These affirmations profoundly affected men and women—though in some instances women to a lesser extent than men. The Pauline proclamation of salvation by faith alone transforms lives with no gender differentiation. It reaches to the very core of our faith and offers hope that is not found in a works-oriented religion. But the other two hallmarks failed to provide what they had promised. If Scripture alone is the authority, why were women denied equal opportunity to study it and then share its good news with others? And was the priesthood really for all believers, or was it primarily for male believers?

The Protestant Reformation was truly a reformation, but not to the extent that it might have been. The Catholics had adapted many facets of the Old Testament priesthood to suit their purposes, including the concept of an all-male clergy. But in doing so they ran roughshod over the New Testament concept of priesthood, especially as it is presented by the apostle Peter. To all believers—not just men—Peter wrote:

> Come to him, a living stone, rejected by mortals yet chosen and precious in God's sight, and like living stones, let yourselves be built into a spiritual house, to be a holy priesthood, to offer spiritual sacrifices acceptable to God through Jesus Christ. . . . But you are a chosen race, a royal priesthood, a holy nation, God's own people, in order that you may proclaim the mighty acts of him who called you out of darkness into his marvelous light. (1 Pet 2:4-5, 9)

It is quite clear that Peter is making references here to the Old Testament priesthood, which, in very different packaging, is now offered to all Christians. And not merely to affirm their standing as believers, but to compel those who are "called" to "proclaim" the message of Christ.

The hallmarks of the Reformation had great potential for eradicating gender distinctions in ministry, but somehow their full meaning was lost in a male-dominated world.

What was Martin Luther's view of women?

Luther's view of women was a mixed bag. He was a man of his time, and he often made crude comments about the opposite sex. "Take women away from their housewifery," he scoffed, "and they are good for nothing." But he knew better. When he received word that one of his courageous supporters was suffering persecution, his response reflected only deep admiration: "The Duke of Bavaria rages above measure, killing, crushing and persecuting the gospel with all his might. That most noble woman, Argula von Stauffer, is there making a valiant fight with great spirit, boldness of speech and knowledge of Christ. . . . She alone, among these monsters, carries on with the faith. . . . She is a singular instrument of Christ."[3]

Luther's view of women might be best summed up as ambivalent. He waffled on the issue—indeed, so much so that his effort to balance the scales at times became an amusing effort of gender tightrope-walking. Men are, of course, superior. He was a man who still had one foot in the Middle Ages, and he had to affirm that assumption. But women are also very exquisite creatures—though to a lesser degree than men, as he tries to convince us in his reflections on the creation account in his commentary on Genesis:

> Moses here places the man and the woman together in order that no one might think that the woman was to be excluded from the glory of the future life. The woman certainly differs from the man, for she is weaker in body and intellect. Nevertheless, Eve was an excellent creature and equal to Adam so far as the divine image, that is, righteousness, wisdom and eternal salvation, is concerned. Still, she was only a woman. As the sun is much more glorious than the moon (though also the moon is glorious), so the woman was inferior to the man both in honor and dignity, though she, too, was a very excellent work of God. So also today the woman is the partaker of eternal life, as the apostle writes (1 Pet. 3:7) that she is a coheir of grace. Therefore the woman should not be excluded from any honor which human beings enjoy, even though she is the weaker vessel.[4]

We see Luther qualifying his statements rather comically, almost as if his wife, Katie, were sitting next to him and giving him the elbow every time he wrote something negative about women. Nevertheless, he got the last word—"she is the weaker vessel."

Why did John Calvin restrict women in ministry?

Calvin's views concerning women in ministry have been a matter of debate in recent years. In the past it was simply assumed that he was a strong opponent of women in office, but challenges to that position have been supported with quotes from his writings. Regarding Paul's admonition in 1 Corinthians 14:34, that women be silent and not speak in church, Calvin wrote: "The discerning reader should come to the decision that the things which Paul is dealing with here are indifferent, i.e., neither good nor bad; and that none of them is forbidden unless it works against decorum and edification."[5]

Calvin valued his close associations with women—especially women who wielded political power. He spoke highly of Marguerite of Navarre and her daughter Jeanne d'Albret, and went so far as to send one of his most trusted ministers to serve as the private pastor to Renée of Ferrara. For Calvin, women were vital to the Protestant cause, but that did not mean they were fitted for leadership in the church. Renée wrote to Calvin complaining that she was not permitted to attend synod meetings. Her preacher-in-residence made that decision based on Paul's admonition that women should be silent in the churches and his fears that he would be ridiculed for having a church run by women—a common concern then and now.[6]

Calvin had other priorities, and he was not about to risk his reputation fighting for women's rights.

What contributions did women make as Reformers?
While the Protestant Reformation did not offer women full-time career ministries like those offered through the monastic system of the Catholic church, women did find their way into ministry—as ministers' wives and as Reformers in their own right. Indeed, their prominence in the Reform movement demonstrates that no official prohibition can keep women out of ministry. They did not need or desire the cloistered convents of monasticism. They were women of the world who could not be restrained by four walls and a vow of silence. Visionary experiences and miracles were not their specialty. They prayed and they worshiped, but theirs was primarily a ministry of action. This is seen in the life of Argula von Stauffer, who boldly defended Luther's writing before an assembly of German princes in Nuremberg in 1523. As we have seen, Luther praised her valor.

Katherine Zell is another example. She married Matthew Zell, a priest-turned-Protestant-Reformer, and became very active in the parish ministry—so active that at her husband's funeral she felt compelled to stand up and assure the people that she was not striving to become "Dr. Katrina," as rumor had it. "I am not usurping the office of preacher or apostle," she insisted. "I am like the dear Mary Magdalene, who with no thought of being an apostle, came to tell the disciples that she had encountered the risen Lord." But her assurances were not enough to stop the criticism. Her involvement in ministry expanded after her husband's death, and she felt obliged to defend herself: "A disturber of the peace am I? Yes indeed, of my own peace. Do you call this disturbing the peace that instead of spending my time in frivolous amusements I have visited the plague infested, carried out the dead? I have visited those in prison and under sentence of death. . . . Is this disturbing the peace of the church?"[7]

Besides heading a massive refugee program in Strassburg, for homeless victims of the Peasants' War, Zell ministered as an evangelist, wrote tracts, edited a hymnbook and served as a hostess to traveling ministers (including Ulrich Zwingli and John Calvin). She was a Reformer in her own right and should be remembered as such. Indeed, the answer to the Church History 101 test question "Name three great Reformers" should not necessarily be "Luther, Calvin and Zwingli," or "Luther, Calvin and Melanchton," or "Luther, Calvin and Knox"; it could just as correctly be answered, "Luther, Calvin and Zell."

What was the female role in advocating religious toleration?
Some time ago, as I walked through the library lounge at Calvin College, where I teach as an adjunct professor, I picked up a copy of *Cheers,* a parody edition of the student newspaper *Chimes.* As I paged through it, an editorial column titled "Integrating Faith and Partying" caught my attention. The new game on campus, so the parody went, was called "Servetus"—named for "the heretic who was burned at the stake in John Calvin's Geneva." The idea of the game is "to think of a new excuse why JC was justified in giving Servetus the torch. . . . If you give a reason that is ethically equivalent to saying 'everyone in the 16th century was doing it' then the whole table has to drink a shot of tequila. . . . That's the party equivalent of a home run."[8]

The not-so-subtle sarcasm was aimed at our double standards—excusing Calvin's intolerance because "everyone was doing it" while rejecting that same excuse for behavior that is unacceptable today.

While I found this little piece amusing—especially since my own church tradition harks back to Calvin's Geneva—I also found it a bit unsettling. This student satirist knew well that the fact that "everybody was doing it" is too often our only justification for the terrible religious intolerance that was prevalent in the sixteenth century. What a shame it is that Reformed people were the perpetrators of what is sometimes referred to as the cruelest joke of the Reformation—drowning Anabaptists, whose only crime was their practice of believers' baptism by immersion. "If that's how they want to be baptized, we'll baptize them," said the religious oppressors—those ancestors of mine.

Actually, everybody *wasn't* doing it. Our church history books have not given the whole story—and some of those who were most vehemently opposed to religious intolerance were women.

Katherine Zell rose above her male counterparts in this respect. "Why do you rail at Schwenckfeld?" she demanded of a Lutheran Reformer. "You talk as if you would have him burned like the poor Servetus at Geneva. . . . You behave as if you had been brought up by savages in a jungle. The Anabaptists are pursued as by a hunter with dogs chasing wild boars. Yet the Anabaptists accept Christ in all the essentials as we do."[9]

This same spirit of religious toleration is reflected in the writings of other women Reformers, in some instances in defense of Catholics who were under heavy persecution. Concern for them prompted a plea for help from Renée of Ferrara to Calvin. "Monsieur Calvin, I am distressed that you do not know how the half in this realm behave," she wrote. "They even exhort the simple to kill and strangle. This is not the rule of Christ. I say this out of the great affection which I hold for the Reformed religion."[10]

We simply cannot excuse Calvin and other Reformers for not taking a strong stand against religious intolerance. No, everybody wasn't doing it.

20

Why Have Women Historically Found Ministry in Sectarian Movements?

At the time of the Protestant Reformation and in the centuries following, sectarian movements arose—many of which developed into today's respected religious bodies. In the early years, however, they were viewed with suspicion and outright hostility by the "respectable" denominations. Like the "heretics" of the medieval period, these groups severed their ties from the institutionalized churches, and in doing so they opened doors of ministry to laity, both men and women. Often in sectarian movements—at least in the early stages of development—visions and direct revelations are claimed as proof of God's endorsement. Such a religious mentality by its very nature does not discriminate between male and female. Women were as inclined—or more so—to claim special spiritual illumination as were men. So while men may not have overtly encouraged women preachers and prophets, this "theological loophole"—the sanctioning of visions and revelations—"left the door ajar" for women to enter.[1]

Why were the early Quakers rumored to be a women's cult?

The door was left ajar for women in almost every sectarian movement in the post-Reformation era, but in none more than the Quakers. Indeed, there were so many women actively involved in the initial stages of that movement that it was rumored to be a "women's cult." The Quakers—officially the Society of Friends—were founded by George Fox, but equally important in those formative years was Margaret Fell, who later became his wife. One of my former colleagues—a church history professor—commented to his class, in reference to her, that one way to become famous in a religious movement is to marry the founder. That may be true in some cases, but my colleague was slighting Margaret Fell when he put her in this category. She was a prominent leader in the movement long before she married Fox, and during the marriage the two were often separated, going their separate ways preaching, or imprisoned in different jails.

Although Margaret was ten years older than George, she outlived him by more than a decade, and during that time she was able to hold the movement together amid dissension. Her booklet *Womens Speaking Justified* was a well-reasoned defense of women's ministries based on biblical texts.

Other Quaker women served with equal distinction. In fact, many of the most noted Quakers were women. Elizabeth Hooton, Mary Fisher and Mary Dyer all sailed to the American colonies as missionaries only to be imprisoned or exiled or worse. Dyer was hanged in Boston for her refusal to discontinue her preaching. The most celebrated of all the Quaker women, however, was Elizabeth Fry. She was an English prison reformer who single-handedly transformed Newgate Prison and influenced similar reform at home and abroad. Indeed, her work was so remarkable that it caught the attention of foreign dignitaries. When Frederick William IV, King of Prussia, visited England, he asked to have a meeting with her. John Randolph, a Virginia legislator, contrasted his visit with her to his experiences at the British Museum, Parliament and the Tower of London, commenting that they "sink into utter insignificance in comparison to Elizabeth Fry."[2]

What role did women play in early Methodism?

The most fascinating woman in early Methodism was not actually a Methodist. She was Susanna Wesley, an avowed Anglican, who as a teenager turned away from her father's Nonconformist beliefs. She married Samuel Wesley, an Anglican priest, and in the years that followed gave birth to nineteen children, among them John and Charles Wesley. Her marital problems are well known, especially the incident that prompted her husband to abandon her and the children. When she refused to say "amen" to his prayer for King William—she being a supporter only of the Stuart line of royalty—he retaliated by leaving home, insisting, "if we have two kings, we must have two beds." This was not his only absence. His term in debtors' prison, brought about by charges from his own parishioners, also left Susanna alone—but certainly not without resources of her own. Indeed, the Sunday church services she began for her own children soon attracted the whole community—so many that some had to be turned away. When Samuel complained, she wrote back: "I cannot conceive, why any should reflect upon you, because your wife endeavors to draw people to church. . . . As to its looking peculiar, I grant it does. And so does almost anything that is serious, or that may in any way advance the glory of God, or the salvation of souls." Years later John referred to his mother as a "preacher of righteousness"—a fitting description.[3]

Among the followers of John Wesley were many women who carried on the tradition of preachers of righteousness. Wesley himself was initially less than enthusiastic about women preachers, but he soon realized that they were the backbone of his movement. One such woman was Mary Fletcher, who was married to one of the movement's prominent leaders. After his death, she continued in the ministry, preaching at times to crowds numbering more than three thousand. Her greatest legacy, however, was her success in building harmony between the Methodists and Anglicans—an accomplishment that very few men were able to equal.[4]

Another woman who played a crucial role in early Methodism was Lady Selina, Countess of Huntingdon. Her wealth made her an important figure in the movement, but she was far more than a financial benefactor. Her various estates were turned into chapels, and she opened a school to train preachers—a band of itinerants that became known as the "Huntingdon Connection." She was deeply involved in doctrinal issues, strongly supporting the Calvinist position held by George White-field. At one point she dismissed the Arminian followers of John Wesley from her training school, but her dominant inclination was to bring about reconciliation in a movement that was torn by doctrinal contro-versies.[5]

There is another woman in Methodism whose story deserves mention. She was my grandmother, Ida Carlton. I will never forget one Sunday many years ago when we arrived for dinner just as she was coming home from church. She was noticeably upset. Though she was nearly eighty, she had faithfully walked more than a mile to and from church every Sunday. On this day, however, she was determined not to go back again. The minister had admitted in his sermon that he did not believe that Jesus was God. She was too old to find a new church, and she died not long afterward. Her funeral was conducted by the man who did not believe that Jesus is God.

Most of the women in Methodism have not been great leaders. They have been ordinary women like my grandmother who simply believed the message that Wesley preached. Today the Methodist church is turning away from that biblical foundation. It may be left to the women—leaders and laity—to bring the church back to its heritage.

How did the Salvation Army view women?
It is sad when church history texts name William Booth as the founder of the Salvation Army and go on to describe that organization with no mention of the cofounder, Catherine Booth, William's wife. But that is often the case. "As so frequently happens in the writing of history," laments Patricia Hill, "the women have simply disappeared."[6]

Catherine Booth was a preacher's wife and the mother of eight chil-dren, but that did not prevent her from becoming a humanitarian leader in her own right as well as a preacher to audiences ranging from slum missions to affluent congregations. She was a forthright feminist whose views powerfully influenced the development of the Salvation Army. Indeed, there were no gender barriers in that organization—at least in the early years. The Booth daughters all became regional leaders—most notably Evangeline, who served as commander in the United States and was eventually promoted to general.

Women served as evangelists, many beginning as teenagers. Eliza Shirley was sixteen when she became an Army lieutenant, and soon after that she was preaching to large crowds of people who filled a Philadelphia warehouse. She was only one of an enthusiastic band of "Hallelujah lassies" who spread out over the globe to serve the needy and save souls.[7]

The tradition of strong women in the Salvation Army continues today. In 1986, Eva Burrows, an Australian, became the general in charge of the worldwide, one-and-a-half-million-member movement.

What role did women play in nineteenth-century American revivalism?
Since colonial times, revivalism has been a prominent feature of American religion. The names of the great revivalists are very familiar: Whitefield, Edwards, Finney, Moody, Sunday, Graham. But women also were known on the evangelistic circuit and often provided an added flavor to what was sometimes perceived as an all-male profession.

In the early years of the nineteenth century, Clarissa Danforth captivated crowds in New England. People who were attracted by the sensation of a woman preacher often came away converted. Though she was a Freewill Baptist, in Rhode Island "almost all houses of worship . . . were opened for her, and ministers and people in multitudes flocked to hear." One revival lasted out for nearly a year and a half.[8]

It was among the Methodists that women found the greatest opportunities for revival ministries. Jerena Lee, a Black woman and a member of the African Episcopal Church, traveled widely during the early decades of the nineteenth century. She faced considerable opposition from ministers in her own denomination, but clung to her powerful and personal sense of calling.[9]

Another Methodist woman known for her evangelistic preaching was

Maggie Van Cott, who was on the "sawdust trail" for thirty years during the last half of the nineteenth century. At the height of her career, she preached some four hundred sermons and made more than seventeen hundred converts in a single year. Her ministry was so influential that she was sometimes compared to evangelist Dwight L. Moody. The most widely acclaimed woman evangelist of the nineteenth century—another Methodist—was Phoebe Palmer, often referred to as the "Mother of the Holiness Movement." As a social activist, she was the founder of the Five Points Mission and other benevolent works, but it was her revival ministry that brought her recognition from the masses. She traveled with her husband in the United States, Canada and England, where hundreds were converted in single meetings. It is estimated that some twenty-five thousand people were converted as a result of her evangelistic ministry.[10]

21

What Can We Learn from the Role of Women in the Non-Western Church?

T oo often when we discuss women's issues—whether in the church, the home or society at large—we think only in terms of our own culture. And when we devise solutions to problems, our approach reflects solely a modern Western perspective. I have to catch myself short in this regard all the time—especially as international students challenge my perspective on a particular issue. But this is not a problem peculiar to me. Western feminists have been guilty of making generalizations and offering solutions that are presumed to suit women in all cultures, and they are discovering that non-Western women will not simply fall in line.

Women in many respects have been the backbone of the non-Western Christian church, and as such they have much to say to Western Christians. Although they have often found themselves in very subservient roles in society and in the home, their Christian faith has liberated them for pivotal roles in ministry.

How has Christianity influenced the role of women in other cultures?
Christianity has had a powerful impact as it has confronted other cultures—and this impact has been felt by women in a particularly remarkable way. In modern oppressive societies women are often treated much as they were in the early nineteenth century when Ann Judson wrote of their plight in Burma, telling of child marriages, female infanticide, and women who were held down by the "tyrannic rod" of their husbands. "The wife receives the appellation of *my servant,* or *my dog,* and is allowed to partake of what her lordly husband is pleased to give her at the *conclusion* of his repast."[1]

One of my favorite stories of how Christianity has powerfully influenced women in other cultures is that of Kana, a woman from Irian Jaya. In the midst of a repressive culture, the gospel had set her free, and she reached out with this freedom to minister to other women, on one occasion speaking before a vast audience at a women's retreat:

"When the gospel came to us Dani people, we were told that the gospel was for the men," she reminded them. "The men said we women did not have souls, so we did not need the gospel message. The men crowded around the speakers of the good news. We women were told to sit out on the edges of the crowd and to keep the children quiet so the men could get all of the profit from the message."

So convinced was she that she wasn't a full human and did not have a soul that she questioned her own reality. "Once I was in a group when a photo was taken by the missionary," she related. "I was so excited I would not wait until the picture had been developed and came back. When word came that the picture had arrived, I elbowed my way through the crowd to see if my face would show up or if, as the men insisted, I would not appear because I was only a spirit." She was ecstatic. "There I was! . . . I had shown up the same as the men had! I, too, was a real person."[2]

Kana's story does not end there. The gospel had made her free, and she realized that this freedom meant responsibility. There were others who had not heard this glorious message, and now she had an obligation to God and to them to share her newfound faith.

What role have Bible women played in world evangelism?

The term "Bible woman" is unfamiliar to most Christians today. Yet Bible women were the backbone of the church in many areas of the world in the late nineteenth and early twentieth centuries, and in some areas they continue to play an important role today. Like the indigenous male evangelists, they reached out to their own people, often working closely with missionary women. They were generally more effective in ministry than the missionary, because they knew the language and the culture and were able to go where the missionary was unwelcome. This was true in China, where Rosalind Goforth, a Presbyterian missionary from Canada, relied heavily on Mrs. Wang, a dedicated Bible woman, to break down barriers that Goforth herself could not have penetrated. In one instance, Mrs. Wang pursued a hostile woman—known as "the Old Autocrat"—who controlled her village's clan, and was able to persuade her to permit the gospel to be preached in her village.

Some Bible women were barely literate and had to rely on memorized passages of Scripture as they preached in the villages. Others, however, were quite well trained. By 1900, there were forty female training schools in China alone, and in India there were more than thirty such schools.

Bible women served in a variety of ministries, including evangelism, medical work, teaching, music and foreign missions. They worked long hours and were often away from home for days and weeks at a time. Yet their pay was barely enough to sustain them. They depended on the hospitality of strangers as they moved from town to town, always facing the threat or the reality of persecution.[3]

The ministry of Bible women is foreign to us—truly foreign. Today this ministry continues in many parts of the world, though on a diminishing scale. It is a pattern of ministry that more closely reflects that of the New Testament era than does the type of ministry we are familiar with in the modern Western world. The Bible women's humble, informal style that is characterized more by house churches than multimillion-dollar ministry complexes, and by Bible studies more than thirty-minute, three-point sermons. It is a style that is far more compatible with unpretentious servanthood than with ordained clerics in robes or pin-striped suits.

What can different cultures say to us about women in ministry?
I have often found that missionaries and non-Western Christians have unusually profound insights on Scripture. Because of their experiences in other cultures and their own struggles in cross-cultural communication, they are able to grasp subtle meanings in language or recognize cultural peculiarities more quickly. They are not quite so handicapped by parochialism as most Americans are.

Olive Rogers' insights are an example. Paul's admonitions in 1 Corinthians 14:34-35, for women to be silent and to ask their husbands for clarification at home, make much more sense in light of her insights:

When in Old Delhi once, I visited the golden domed temple of the Sikhs. Being a woman, I was taken round to a back entrance and then through several rooms, till I reached the upper gallery where the ladies gathered. I sat on the richly carpeted floor and surveyed the scene. Suddenly, as so often in the East, the Scriptures became alive! We were high above the main body of the temple. The worship—intoning of the Sacred Book, and instructions for salvation—being carried on down below was pertinent only to the men, for they alone have souls to save. I tried in vain to hear what was going on, but the women were sitting around in groups gossiping, amused at the play of their children, careless of the fact that they were in a place of worship. For them a visit to the temple was merely an opportunity to escape from the monotony of an existence behind the four walls of their homes, where they reign supreme in their own quarters, but where their lives seldom encroach upon those of their men-folk, who do all the work involving contact with the outside world.

Not many months later I attended one of the Christian conventions held annually in S. India. Day after day thousands of men and women sat under the large leaf shelter. The men's section of the "pandal" was quiet and orderly as they listened to the Word, taking notes with assiduous care. The women's half was another matter. All the children were there, restless, demanding and noisy, and many of the women were sitting in groups chattering.[4]

This picture of worship may be very similar to what Paul confronted

22

How Have World Missions Affected Women's Ministries?

T he title to this chapter might more appropriately be, "How Have Women's Ministries Affected World Missions?" Each has had a profound effect on the other. Women have made monumental contributions to the efforts of world evangelism. Even those who most strongly defend male headship generally agree with that analysis—with some rare exceptions. John R. Rice, for example, who was in other respects a missions enthusiast, spoke in negative terms of women's involvement—especially when it entailed speaking in churches in the homeland:

> The deputation work of great missionary societies has suffered greatly at the hands of women missionaries. If godly, Spirit-filled men, manly men, should go to the churches with the appeal that those whom God has called for his work should come prepared for toil and sweat and blood and tears, it would do infinitely more for the mission cause than the prattle about dress and customs and food, with . . . slide pictures of quaint heathen groups presented so often by women missionaries,

largely to groups of women and children. We have debased the cause
of foreign missions by not keeping it on the high vigorous plane which
the New Testament gives mission work. . . . It violates the command
of God for women to speak before mixed audiences of men and wom-
en, and to take the pulpit in the churches. And we may be sure that
the work of the gospel of Christ among the heathen is not prospered
by this sin.[1]

Rice's sentiments have clearly not prevailed. Women have had more
opportunities for ministry within the mission context than in any other
setting. Indeed, it has been under the cover of "mission" that women have
been allowed to preach and teach and plant churches all over the world—
including North America—and to speak from the pulpit in established
churches in their homeland. As far as women have been concerned,
mission has been to the modern world what monasticism was to the
medieval world—except that mission has provided far more opportunities for proclaiming the gospel to a lost world. Here, outside the official
hierarchy of the church, women's ministries have flourished. Women
have worked shoulder to shoulder with men in the most difficult and
challenging situations, grateful simply for the opportunity to serve.

Why were women initially barred from missionary work?

The answer to that question is simple and straightforward. Women were
initially barred from missionary work primarily because of two passages
of Scripture: 1 Timothy 2:11-12, which enjoins women not to teach and
usurp authority, and 1 Corinthians 14:34, which asks women to be silent.
If women could not preach and teach and have authority, so the denominational leaders reasoned, how could they be missionaries? So for the
first several decades of the modern missionary movement, women were
barred from serving as missionaries. They could be missionary wives or
they could function in support capacities on the home front, but they
could not actually be missionaries themselves. Married women served
alongside their husbands, but single women were forced to marry or to
stay home.

The "call" of God, however, was stronger than the opposition from men, and during the last four decades of the nineteenth century, single women began going abroad as missionaries without the blessing of the church. Yet they were not without strong male supporters. Men such as J. Hudson Taylor, founder of the China Inland Mission, and Fredrik Franson, founder of TEAM (The Evangelical Alliance Mission), recognized that the unfinished task of world evangelization was far too enormous for men alone to accomplish. "We face the circumstance," wrote Franson in 1897, "that the devil, fortunately for him, has been able to exclude nearly two-thirds of the number of Christians from participation in the Lord's service through evangelization. The loss for God's cause is so great that it can hardly be described." Franson's logic was powerful and helped turn the tide in favor of women in mission:

It is amazing how one can get such a false idea that not all God's children should use all their powers in all ways to save the lost world. There are, so to speak, many people in the water about to drown. A few men are trying to save them, and that is considered well and good. But look, over there a few women have untied a boat also to be of help in the rescue, and immediately a few men cry out; standing there idly looking on and therefore having plenty of time to cry out: 'No, no, women must not help, rather let the people drown.' What stupidity.[2]

What is the significance of the women's missionary movement?
The women's missionary movement began around 1860, when women began establishing societies to sponsor and support single women as missionaries. Married women had served faithfully as missionary wives, and in many instances their accomplishments had been remarkable. Ann Judson, for example, conducted evangelistic work among the Burmese people while translating portions of Scripture into Thai. But, like that of other missionary wives, her ministry was limited in its duration. Most married women were so involved with domestic cares and having babies that their mission work was severely restricted. If they survived a dozen years they were fortunate. After Ann Judson died, her husband married twice more. One missionary to China buried seven wives there.

The urgent needs in world mission, then, more than any other factor, thrust single women into the forefront of the missionary enterprise. The impetus actually came from a man, David Abeel, an ordained minister from the Reformed Church in America who was serving as a missionary in China. He recognized the need for women missionaries who could devote their entire lives to ministry, and he challenged women in his denomination to respond.

The response, however, did not come until more than two decades later, in 1861, when Sarah Doremus, who had been deeply involved in urban ministries, organized the Woman's Union Missionary Society. The word *union* was very significant. She herself was Reformed, but the founding committee was made of women from other denominations, and the first woman commissioned for service was a Baptist. In the years that followed more "female agencies" were founded; by the turn of the century the number had reached forty, and the women's missionary movement was on its way to becoming the largest organized women's movement ever.[3] The women's missionary movement was unique in that for the first time in history women could take up leadership positions in evangelistic outreach on a large scale. Women in monasticism did not have any such autonomy; they were strictly limited by the Roman Catholic church. In most instances the women's mission organizations were independent of outside control, and their united efforts gave them remarkable strength in numbers. The Central Committee for the United Study of Foreign Missions published millions of textbooks and sponsored summer schools for missions studies that attracted thousands of women.

In assessing the whole movement in 1910, Helen Barrett Montgomery wrote: "It is indeed a wonderful story. . . . We began in weakness, we stand in power. In 1861 there was a single missionary in the field, Miss Marston, in Burma; in 1909, there were 4710 unmarried women in the field. . . . Then the supporters numbered a few hundreds; today there are at least two millions."[4]

By the early decades of the twentieth century, the heyday of the women's missionary movement had passed. Denominational boards were now accepting single women as missionaries, and the women's societies began merging with the denominational boards. The result was a major loss of power and influence once wielded by women.

Mission textbooks have by and large failed to recognize this powerful arm of the modern missionary movement. Indeed, some books fail to mention it at all, while emphasizing other movements of far less consequence. The women's missionary movement is part of our religious heritage—one that offers many challenges for both women and men today.

Was the women's missionary movement a feminist movement?

This question would not even be posed had not a major book on the subject by R. Pierce Beaver been published under the title *American Protestant Women in World Mission: A History of the First Feminist Movement in North America*. Most people would not associate feminism with missions, but the term *feminist* is used in different ways by different people. If, in using the term, Beaver meant that women took charge of their destinies and vowed to enter the missionary enterprise despite gender barriers, his case is well founded. But if the term is used in a broader and more general sense to describe a women's "rights" effort, the women's missionary movement could hardly be described as feminist.

Beaver says that in response to the intransigence of male mission leaders, "the women revolted and formed the first women's board."[5] His own evidence, however, offers very little indication of a revolt. Time and again women deferred plans to organize mission agencies or to expand their outreach because of male opposition. Had their spirit been one of revolution, they would have been less sensitive to the fact that their mission work was perceived as a threat to the male establishment.

Jane Hunter, author of an important study on women missionaries published by Yale University Press, takes issue with those who would argue that these women had feminist inclinations: "For feminism to have gained a foothold among the women's missionary community would have entailed the replacement of the underlying premise of women's mission work, self-denial, with its opposite, self-advocacy."[6]

Elisabeth Elliot has taken the argument a step further, suggesting that missionary women did not need to demand equal rights because of the opportunities they already had in mission work: "Today strident female voices are raised, shrilly and ad nauseam, to remind us that women are equal with men. But such a question has never even arisen in connection with the history of Christian missions. In fact, for many years, far from being excluded, women constituted the majority of foreign missionaries."[7]

Elliot is wrong both in her logic and her facts. That women were in the majority does not mean they enjoyed equality. Moreover, women missionaries did raise the question of equality. Lottie Moon, the most celebrated Southern Baptist missionary, is a prime example. "What women want who come to China is free opportunity to do the largest possible work," she wrote. "What women have a right to demand is perfect equality."[8]

Despite her rhetoric, however, Moon was not incited by feminism. Motivation is a key issue here. She and women missionaries generally were motivated by the needs of others rather than their own. They may have looked and acted very much like feminists when they launched the women's missionary movement in 1861, and when they individually fought for ministry opportunities equal to men's, but beneath the surface the issues were very different.

Why are women permitted more latitude overseas than at home?
The initial opposition to women's serving alongside men in mission faded by the early twentieth century. Indeed, virtually all mission boards were accepting single women as candidates. This was not because church leaders had re-examined Scripture and determined that women could rightly preach and teach; it was more a matter of pragmatism. Women had determined that they would serve in mission, and there was very little that denominational board leaders could do but accept that fact.

Leaders of independent faith-mission boards had long since accepted women. The situation was similar to the one that has prevailed in sectarian movements: evangelism was first and foremost in their minds. Few of these mission leaders even contemplated the inconsistency of denying women ministry in their homeland while encouraging such ministry abroad.

This inconsistency was easily tolerated, because at a distance of thousands of miles women were out of sight and out of mind, and thus could be dismissed by church leaders. Besides, they were teaching and preaching to "natives," not real men—so went the understood rationale. This division between preaching in the homeland and preaching on the mission field has been largely taken for granted and continues today—though in some instances evangelical mission boards have curtailed women's missionary activities in recent years as a result of the backlash against feminism. In most cases, however, women still have far more freedom in foreign settings, with little opposition from those who perceive themselves as traditionalists.

In fact, traditionalists often encourage women to pursue roles overseas that they are denied at home. A student of mine not long ago told me that she had talked with another seminary professor about a ministry of teaching theology on the Bible-college level. He told her that such a role was not proper for a woman, but then went on to encourage her to continue her studies and pursue the same ministry in missions—where presumably she would be teaching "natives."

The distinction between "natives" and "men" was brought home to me some years ago. I was talking to a man who was associated with the Plymouth Brethren—a religious movement that has been known for severely restricting women's roles. I commented to him that in the past Plymouth Brethren women had had ministries teaching men, and I mentioned Florence Young, who had taught thousands of men in her Bible studies. He was certain that I was mistaking the Plymouth Brethren for some other group of Brethren. I insisted otherwise, giving him further details of her ministry in the Solomon Islands. With that geographical revelation, he reacted with sudden comprehension—"Oh, you mean she taught natives?"

That explained it. She was not teaching "men" after all.

23

Have Women Made Gains in the Church in the Twentieth Century?

The role of women in the church in the twentieth century will perplex future historians. On the surface it will appear as though women made great gains—as though the closed doors of the early decades had been opened wide by the final decades of the century. Where once women could not even cast a vote in a church meeting, they had come to the point of leading the meetings, and no office or position was denied them. But those historians who dig deeper will discover that the mainline churches that were offering women the greatest opportunities were simultaneously declining in membership and influence. Some of these churches, which once had stood firm on the historic orthodox faith, were becoming too sophisticated to take the Bible at face value. The gains that have been made, then, are mixed at best.

And historians will find that the story has been entirely different among the more conservative churches. At the turn of the century, these denominations had little influence and were generally scorned by outsiders. In these circles, however, women had much greater opportunity for ministry. This was the era of the internationally acclaimed Evangeline Booth of the Salvation Army, and of the well-known Pentecostal leaders, including the celebrated Aimee Semple McPherson. And even in tiny fundamentalist and holiness denominations, women were ordained as evangelists and preachers.

But as the decades marched on, the opportunities for women declined—at the very time that these denominations were gaining respectability and influence. Indeed, by the end of the century, as evangelicals of all stripes were dominating the religious scene, a conservative reaction had set in, denying women the ministries they had once so freely enjoyed.

How did leaders of the Social Gospel view women's issues?

One of the most prominent religious developments of the early twentieth century was the Social Gospel movement—a movement that is typically associated with mainline denominations. Among the best-known leaders were Walter Rauschenbusch, Washington Gladden and Lyman Abbot. True to their more liberal mainline denominational associations, these men were not supporters of women in ministry. Rauschenbusch, who is frequently referred to as the "father of the Social Gospel in America," praised women for their emotional sensitivity but also insisted that it was a liability in that it could "warp her judgment and make her less safe for teaching and administration."[1] Women served at the grass-roots level of the Social Gospel movement—but not in leadership roles, except where more conservative evangelicals were prominent.

The Social Gospel in its broadest sense was a diverse movement that spanned the entire religious spectrum. Most historical analysis has been applied to the more liberal elements, but that is changing since the publication of *Salvation in the Slums: Evangelical Social Work, 1865-1920* by Norris Magnuson. Magnuson points out that some of the most effective social work among prisoners and the unemployed and homeless was conducted by deeply committed evangelicals, working with such organizations as the Salvation Army, the Christian and Missionary Alliance, the Volunteers of America and inner-city missions. And true to the evangelical heritage, women were prominent not only at the grass-roots level but also in leadership positions.

Among the women wielding powerful influence among the evangelicals were Catherine Booth, Phoebe Palmer and Frances Willard, as well as many lesser-known women who directed the work in rescue missions. These women, according to Magnuson, were "liberated" women of their day, and they and their male co-workers generally supported suffrage, the "feminist" issue of the day.[2]

What was the women's role in the rise of the Pentecostal movement?
Like many other so-called sectarian movements in past history, the Pentecostal movement seemed to be custom-made for women with a call to ministry. The emphasis on spontaneous charismatic experiences did not easily allow for gender distinctions. Women could hear the voice of God with just as much certainty as could men. And with the conviction that they were propelled by the power of the Holy Ghost, they preached with as much might as did the Spirit-filled brethren. In that sense, Pentecostalism was an equal opportunity employer.

Indeed, it was the testimony of a woman that launched the Pentecostal movement into the twentieth century. The setting was the Bethel Bible School, near Topeka, Kansas. "It was after midnight and the first day of the twentieth century when Miss [Agnes] Ozman began 'speaking in the Chinese language' while a 'halo seemed to surround her head and face.' "[3] This midnight prayer meeting was the precursor to the Azusa Street Revival that began in 1906.

Most Pentecostals today would concede that there were many excesses in the early years, and it is not my purpose here to evaluate the movement. But it should be noted that women were in the forefront of this movement, which has since spread worldwide in an amazing demonstration of the power of the Holy Spirit. They served as denominational leaders, preachers, evangelists, Bible-school teachers and missionaries with freedom not previously experienced, except in smaller movements such as the Quakers. Few would argue that in some instances women

Pentecostal leaders became consumed with their own grandeur. Aimee Semple McPherson, one of the most celebrated evangelists in the early decades of the twentieth century, is an easy target in this regard. She was a crowd-pleaser who played up to her audiences with a dramatic flair, never seeming too concerned that her eccentricities might demean the cause of Christ. Nor was she particularly careful about her personal life: she left her first husband to go on the road as an itinerant evangelist, later remarried, and finally claimed to have been kidnapped—a story challenged by reporters, who insisted that she was hiding out with another man.

Yet, when she died, McPherson left behind the Foursquare Gospel church—a denomination that has been very active in mission at home and abroad—and she also left behind many converts who had found Christ through her ministry. She cannot be excused for apparent moral lapses or for the flamboyance that may have discredited the gospel, but her ministry does demonstrate the power of God that often prevails despite sin and failure.

How has the women's movement affected Catholic women in recent decades?

Despite the Roman Catholic church's official teaching that women may not be priests or carry out the functions of priests, the actual practice of the church is not so cut and dried. Women have circumvented such obstacles since medieval times, and they continue to do so today. Due to a shortage of priests in recent decades, nuns have often been the only resident spiritual leaders available to the laity. This is particularly true in Latin America and other areas of the Third World, but it is also true in North America, as Tony Campolo relates:

> Recently I spent some time with a Roman Catholic bishop who explained to me how women had been a godsend to many of the churches in his diocese which lacked priestly leadership. He explained that nuns were serving as the pastors for many of his rural congregations, although the people did not actually call them pastors. These nuns visited the sick, taught the catechism, preached the homilies, and

even served Holy Communion. He explained that once a month, he or one of his auxiliary bishops would visit each of these female-led parishes, perform the mass, and sanctify the bread and wine. These "sanctified elements" would then be stored until worship time, when they would be given to communicants by the nuns. When I pointed out that these nuns did everything that priests do and therefore should be ordained, he agreed. Then he added, "Most people in these parishes would also agree, but you know how the church is." Indeed I do.[4]

The Roman Catholic church, more than any other religious body, contains a wide diversity of opinion on the issue of women's roles. Because of splintering, individual Protestant denominations are far less diverse. If a particular Presbyterian body's stance on women's issues, for example, does not suit someone's tastes, there are many others from which to choose. Not so for Catholics. Within this one church we find extreme traditionalism and extreme feminism.

William Marra, a Catholic theologian and philosopher who teaches at Fordham University, argues that a woman's place is in the home and that any woman who wants a career should remain "celibate." He represents a wing of the church—which includes the pope and other high officials—that strongly opposes women in office, while most of the laity would be more moderate or feminist in their orientation.

At the other extreme of Catholic belief are feminist theologians who regard the Bible as a book that is tainted with sexism. The most widely recognized Catholic feminist is Elisabeth Schüssler Fiorenza, the author of *In Memory of Her: A Feminist Theological Reconstruction of Christian Origins*. While she continues to view the Bible as Christian revelation, she qualifies its validity: "Biblical revelation and truth are given only in those texts and interpretive modes that transcend critically their patriarchal frameworks and allow for a vision of Christian women as historical and theological subjects and actors."[5]

What is the status of women in mainline churches?

The situation today in most mainline denominations is significantly different for women from what it is within Roman Catholicism—although the changes did not come without bitter conflict. The Anglican church and its American counterpart, the Episcopal church, are striking examples. In less than two decades Episcopal women have gone from being barred from the priesthood to being consecrated bishop, as Barbara Harris has been. And today, for the first time in history, the head of the Anglican church, Archbishop of Canterbury George Carey, affirms women in the priesthood.

Interestingly, the events of recent years have erupted in stark contrast to the prevailing conditions in mainline denominations in past generations, when restrictions on women's ministry were more severe than they were in evangelical circles. Indeed, during a time when many mainline churches were drifting into liberalism and modernism, women continued to be shut out of ordained ministry. Biblical and historical arguments were marshaled in support of male supremacy, while many cynically suggested that the opposition was more a matter of power than a matter of orthodoxy.

By the 1960s and 1970s, however, most mainline bodies, including the Methodist, Episcopal, Presbyterian, Lutheran, United Church of Christ, and Disciples of Christ parent denominations, had renounced gender barriers affecting women, and women were finding their way into the highest levels of church leadership. The rationale was fairness and feminism—very often with little emphasis on scriptural support. The effects of higher criticism had shaken the belief in an authoritative Bible, and in the minds of many a biblical basis for ministry was not essential.

Many feminists in mainline liberal churches argue that the Bible—and particularly the writing of Paul—has been the source of the problem for women. They insist that both Old and New Testaments must be stripped of patriarchy before their teachings can be applied to the contemporary church. In that sense they differ from evangelical feminists, who argue that through Christ women are beyond the curse and that the teachings on women in the Gospels and the Epistles have been misinterpreted to wrongfully restrict women.

It is important to point out, however, that there are many evangelical women involved in ministry in mainline churches—women who have been nurtured in an evangelical faith or who have rediscovered their evangelical roots. Other women have sought out mainline denominations because they have been denied ordination by their own denominations. In many cases these women are having a very positive impact on their churches. I know of one woman who was called to be the senior pastor of a liberal church partly on the basis of her gender. Not only was she deemed an excellent preacher, but she offered the church an opportunity to atone for its sex bias of the past. But as soon as her ministry began, the church realized that it had gotten more than just a woman preacher. She was thoroughly evangelical, and during her tenure she led the church back to its evangelical roots. Her story is one that can be repeated again and again as women reaffirm their Christian heritage and accept the challenges that await them in mainline denominations.

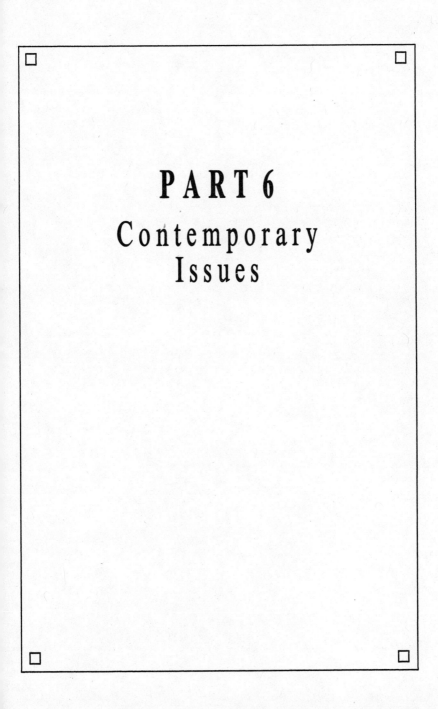

PART 6

Contemporary Issues

24

Is the Bible
a Sexist Volume?

I s the Bible—the inspired Word of God—sexist? Many people today, among them Episcopal Bishop John S. Spong, would argue that it is. Spong has written a book entitled *Rescuing the Bible from Fundamentalism*. The Bible is sexist, he argues, because its authors were sexist. A prime example is the apostle Paul, whom Spong describes as a "self-loathing repressed homosexual."[1]

At first glance, Bishop Spong's claims are too ridiculous to consider. But we cannot dismiss the fact that he is a man of influence whose apparent contempt for Scripture is filtering down to ordinary people in the pews.

So how do we respond? Is it possible that the very Word of God is sexist? We must always remember that the books of the Bible, while inspired by God, were written in a linguistic style consistent with the cultural mores and the authors' personal idiosyncrasies. Language is not static, and we cannot expect that what was written hundreds or thousands of years ago will necessarily sound good to our ears today. From a modern perspective portions of the Bible could be deemed sexist, but that does not mean that they were written with a spirit of sexism. The truth of this hit home to me a few years ago when I read a review of my book *Guardians of the Great Commission: The Story of Women in Modern Missions*. In this case the issue was not sexism, but rather racism and ethnocentrism. The reviewer wrote:

> The book might be seen in places to be condescending toward indigenous races and cultures. For example, in the introduction, Tucker selects a quotation to exemplify a woman as "guardian of the Great Commission." The quotation, without disclaimer or comment speaks of Africans as "poor but affectionate and well-meaning people, who though black enough their skins may be, have never-dying souls."[2]

It had never occurred to me that anyone would be offended by that opening quotation from Ann Martin Hinderer. What the reviewer failed to mention was that the line preceding the words she quoted read: "When I see what is needed, I feel that if I had twenty lives I would gladly give them to be the means of a little good to these poor but affectionate and well-meaning people. . . ." But, even more important, the reviewer failed to mention that these words were written in the 1850s. Hinderer was not exhibiting racism or ethnocentrism. She was a woman of her time, who was willing to give her very life for the African people. Yes, I could have made a disclaimer, as the reviewer suggested, but I would have been disclaiming my way all through the book, and I was confident that my readers were sophisticated enough to sort out the linguistic anachronisms.

So it is with Scripture. There are many linguistic anachronisms. Language and culture have changed since the first century. The Bible is a timeless volune, but it was written in the context of the times.

Have biblical texts been changed in order to diminish women's roles?

This is a touchy issue—so touchy that one is almost labeled a heretic for even broaching the subject. If we cannot trust the biblical text, then we might as well throw our whole faith overboard. We can, however, trust the biblical text as a whole—and in particulars—and I have never heard anyone within orthodox Christianity suggest that because of some variances, any doctrine or particular message of Scripture is questionable. But there are minor instances of what appear to be textual changes, and in some cases they tend to diminish the role of women.

Often we hear a minister who is waxing eloquent on a passage of Scripture introduce a nuance not apparent in English by saying, "In the original Greek . . ." or "In the original text. . . ." The fact is that there are no *original* Bibles or portions of the original Bible available. The only manuscripts we have are copies, dating from the second century and later. These copies have minor differences as a result of errors or changes made by the copyists, and it is up to professionals known as textual critics to determine which of the texts are closest to the originals.

That there are some variations does not mean that the Bible should be regarded as unreliable. The late F. F. Bruce, a renowned textual critic, has compared the biblical text with other ancient texts (Caesar's *Gallic War,* Thucydides' *History,* and the like) and found it to be far superior. There are many more ancient copies of the Bible or portions of the Bible, and they are much older than manuscripts for other writings. He further emphasizes that "the variant readings about which any doubt remains among textual critics of the New Testament affect no material question of historic fact or of Christian faith and practice.[3]

Regarding the issue of women and distortions in the text, it is very important to emphasize at the outset that nothing of *major* significance has been changed. The case for or against male headship or women's involvement in ministry, for example, does not hinge on any of the passages where there are variants. Acts 17 is an example. Here the Western text, which is more recent and considered less reliable by textual critics, inverts the women and men in verse 12, where Luke relates that many in Thessalonica believed, "including not a few Greek women and men of high standing." The Western text changes the order, mentioning the men first. The same is true in Acts 18:26, where Aquila's name is listed before Priscilla's; the most reliable texts show Priscilla's name first.

And Luke's mention in Acts 17:34 that Damaris, a woman from Athens, joined Paul and believed is omitted entirely from the Western text. According to Bruce, "the Western text consistently plays down any prominence given to women."[4]

While nothing of major significance has been found to have been changed by early copyists, there is evidence that 1 Corinthians 14:34-35 has at least been tampered with—evidence that has prompted Gordon Fee, a highly respected (and evangelical) textual critic, to argue that those two verses admonishing women to be silent and not to speak in church were added by a copyist. The tampering involves the placement of the verses. In the Western text, the verses do not appear after verse 33 but after verse 40. Fee points out that "displacements of this kind do not occur elsewhere in the New Testament," and thus he believes it likely that a copyist simply added the verses. He also points out that the passage reads smoothly—indeed, perhaps more smoothly—without these verses, and that certain terms contained in the two verses are "not typically Pauline." Further support for his argument is that these verses seem to contradict Paul's discussion three chapters earlier of women praying and prophesying.[5]

Fee's position is certainly interesting in light of the known discrepancies in the Western text in Acts 17—18, but until early manuscripts are found that actually show the omission of these two verses in 1 Corinthians, his arguments must be viewed as well-reasoned speculation, and only that.

Have Bible translations or paraphrases distorted women's roles?

Assuming the texts are reliable concerning women—as I do—have Bible translators distorted women's roles? Bible translators have the difficult task of making the Hebrew and Greek language of some two thousand and more years ago meaningful to modern Christians. Many terms and concepts are difficult to render with precise accuracy in English, and it is more difficult yet to do so in languages to which biblical concepts are entirely foreign. Bible translation is most certainly not an exact science; thus it does allow for the bias of the translator to arise. Most translations, however, have been done by teams of translators, so it is less likely that individual bias comes through. Still, we cannot entirely dismiss the fact that translation teams have been almost exclusively male.

In most cases any male bias that has entered the text is subtle—perhaps unconsciously rendered—and does not significantly alter key texts. But even subtle distortions can have negative effects on our understanding of women's roles in the church. Why, for example, did the King James translators render the Greek word *diakonos* as "servant" when it refers to Phoebe (Rom 16:1) but as "minister" when it refers to Tychicus (Eph 6:21)?

The Living Bible, which is a paraphrase, renders *diakonos,* as it relates to Phoebe, as "dear Christian woman," while Tychicus is designated "faithful helper."

The King James Version and the Living Bible are not the only versions that have subtle translation flaws diminishing women's roles. Even the Revised Standard Version was not beyond such defect. In 1 Corinthians 11:10, for example, the Greek word *exousian,* elsewhere rendered "authority" or "power," is here rendered "veil," presumably because the translators thought it more proper that a woman have a veil rather than authority over her head. The simple truth is that is not what the Bible says.

Faith Martin points out other problems with the RSV. The Hebrew word *chayil* is rendered "brave" when referring to men and "good" or "virtuous" when referring to women. The same is true with words in the New Testament:

> The Greek word *sophrosune* means "sane" or "self-controlled." The Revised Standard Version translates it "modest" when women are discussed (1 Tim. 2:15) and "sensible" when men are the subject 1 Tim. 3:2). If Paul used the same word for men and women, why didn't the translators do the same? Translators have given us brave and sensible men but kept the women virtuous and modest. The translators have made subtle decisions with enormous implications at a level where the ordinary reader is helpless to discern their prejudice.[6]

Less serious problems in translations occur when Greek terms such as *anthropos,* meaning "human being" or "person," is rendered "man." This occurs frequently in the New International Version and in the King James. As a child, I memorized 2 Corinthians 5:17: "If any man be in Christ, he is a new creature . . ." from the King James. In fact, that verse is both underlined and highlighted in my old, worn, "loose-leaf" King James Bible. But how much better it sounds to me now in the New RSV: "So, if anyone is in Christ, there is a new creation. . . ."

Is it important to have a gender-sensitive Bible translation?

For me the choice of a Bible translation is a rather personal matter. In recent years I have primarily used the NIV for my study and devotional reading. But transferring my loyalties to the NIV from the King James did not come easily for me. I had a vested interest in the King James Version. Indeed, as a member of BMA (Bible Memory Association) for many years, I had memorized hundreds of verses from that translation, and it was disconcerting to realize that my pastor and most of the people in the pews were using another version. My somewhat reluctant decision to switch from the King James to the NIV was prompted in part by the readability of the newer version. It simply made sense to me to use a Bible that was written in a more contemporary style.

Now I am faced with the decision again. Having realized that the NIV is dated in some respects, ought I consider another translation that is even more contemporary in style? The question is very important to me as a writer and speaker who often uses biblical quotations. In my writing and speaking, I have become very aware of gender inclusivity. For example, I seek to avoid the third-person singular pronoun "he" as a generic term, and I no longer use "man" to refer to human beings. And if I did, my editors would surely delete them from my writing before publication. So should I continue to use a Bible such as the NIV, which is not consistent with my own style and that of the vast majority of writers today? For me the answer is no—not if there is a translation that is both accurate and gender-inclusive.

What Bible translation embodies both accuracy and gender inclusivity?

As much talk as there has been in recent years regarding inclusive language, there has been no major version of the Bible that is gender-inclusive until 1990, with the publication of the New Revised Standard Version. The edition was not without controversy. Heading the revision team was Bruce Metzger, a New Testament professor from Princeton Theological Seminary. "While Metzger is conservative on matters of doctrine," writes Richard Ostling of *Time* magazine, "he is willing to avoid male nouns and pronouns—where the original Hebrew and Greek texts allow it."[7] For example, the NRSV translates Matthew 4:4 "One does not live by bread alone," instead of "Man does not live by bread alone."

Not surprisingly, the revision has been controversial. Feminists have charged that the revision team was not going far enough to eradicate sexist language, while traditionalists have insisted that the team sacrificed meaning for inclusivity. Since the new version appeared in 1990, however, reviews have been mostly favorable and sales have been higher than expected. "Destined to become the new standard in mainline Protestant churches—including the Methodist, Presbyterian, Episcopalian, Evangelical Lutheran, Reformed Church in America and Disciples of Christ," the NRSV had already sold nearly two million copies in the first several months following publication.[8]

The NRSV, however, ought not to be seen merely as a Bible for feminists and mainline denominations. Reviews from evangelical scholars have also been favorable. My colleague Donald A. Carson, for example, is widely recognized for his brilliant scholarship but would never be mistaken for a feminist. In light of that, his assessment, presented at the Annual Meeting for the Society of Biblical Literature, is worth noting:

> The NRSV translators have taken great pains to eliminate the sexual bias inherent in the English language, whenever the reference is to people generically, to people who are not gender-specified. On the whole, their efforts are judicious, thorough and effective, as perhaps one should expect from a Committee chaired by Prof. Metzger, among whose many gifts is that most uncommon one, common sense. A generic "man" often becomes a plural ["those"] (as we saw in Ps. 1); "fathers" often becomes "ancestors," "brothers" often becomes

"brothers and sisters." By my less than exhaustive count, "one" is used sparingly, "someone" a little more frequently, and "anyone" rather too much. . . . Masculine pronouns for Deity are thinned out, but not neutered, and not feminized. . . .

But what is clear is that for use in any context where virtually all the people are sensitized to inclusivist language (not the least the university environment), the NRSV sounds incomparably more modern than its closest rivals.

Carson goes on to give an overall assessment of this version:

If I were offering a rather personal evaluation of the NRSV on a scale of one to ten, with ten signalling perfection, I would, in a US school, assign about 9.0; or, in the British and Canadian tradition from which I spring, where, on a scale of ten, perfection is attained about 8.5 or 9.0 (leaving the rest of the scale unused), I would assign 7.5 or 8.0— B+ or A-. Since my students will testify how stingy a marker I am, that means the NRSV is a jolly good piece of work.[9]

How have commentators distorted the meanings of words and passages?

One of the first rules of Bible study that I learned in my hermeneutics course in college was to be aware of the personal biases that would naturally surface as I sought to interpret a text—and to be aware also of the biases of Bible commentators whose work I might refer to. Liberation theologians have challenged us in this area as well. We too often approach the Bible from our Western, middle-class perspective and fail to recognize that our interpretations might be entirely different from those of a theologian from, say, Uganda.

It is no secret that most Bible commentaries have been written by men. Is it possible, then, that there is a male bias—not necessarily an overt and oppressive male bias, but perhaps a subconscious bias of which the commentator is utterly unaware? And if that is possible, is it unreasonable to imagine that such bias might subtly emerge when the commentator is dealing with passages that reflect on women's roles or offer models of biblical women?

Take Mary the mother of Jesus. Charles Ryrie emphasizes that she is a model of womanhood who offers lessons "mostly related to the home." For support, he cites James Hastings, who offers another male perspective: "Mary was of a retiring nature, unobtrusive, reticent, perhaps even shrinking from observation, so that the impress of her personality was confined to the sweet sanctities of the home circle. . . . We see in the little that is told of her what a true woman ought to be."[10]

Responding to these male appraisals, Dorothy Pape writes:

Mary may well have been retiring and home-loving, but with the possible exception of the angel's announcement of the coming conception, the scriptural record never shows us Mary at home. She is hurrying off to Elizabeth, then going to Bethlehem for the census, then to Jerusalem for purification rites, down to Egypt, back to Nazareth, then to Jerusalem again for the Passover, to Cana for the wedding, to Capernaum, to a city near the Sea of Galilee with her other sons to persuade Jesus to come home, and finally to Jerusalem again. It therefore requires an exercise of imagination to learn from her lessons "mostly related to the home."[11]

How does the issue of biblical authority bear on the women's issue?
A key biblical doctrine of Protestantism is that the Bible alone is our rule of faith. *Sola Scriptura*—Scripture alone—was Martin Luther's challenge to Roman Catholicism, which then and now places church dogma alongside the Bible as authority. The doctrine of *sola Scriptura* has been tested through the centuries by various elements in the church, from cultic movements claiming to have new written revelations to charismatics claiming to receive direct messages from God. Now the doctrine is being tested again in a very subtle way.

Yes, Scripture is our only authority, the argument goes, but there is a pastoral authority that operates alongside biblical authority, so that the one standing in the pulpit has authority in his own right. Thus a woman, who is not permitted to have authority, cannot be a pastor or preach from the pulpit.

The argument falls apart very quickly in real life, as we see authority being abused on the one hand and utterly ignored on the other. In some instances pastors take on authority to the point of being "cult" leaders. Their followers are under their strict control. But in most instances pastors have no real authority at all. If members disagree with the content of the preaching or disapprove of the conduct of the preacher's wife, they simply leave the church—and in my mind the game of "musical churches" is played all too often today.

But the church with no real pastoral authority, despite the negative side effects, certainly transcends the cultic effects of *real* pastoral authority, because Scripture is our *only* authority. Even when the authoritarian pastor is claiming to align himself fully with Scripture, there is a danger when the people look at him as their authority rather than the Bible. The typical pastor who has no real authority may have a semblance of authority, but it is based entirely on Scripture; thus if that pastor preaches something that is contrary to Scripture, discipline should be meted out.

So whether the individual in the pulpit is a man or a woman, the real authority lies in Scripture, and the preacher has authority only insofar as the preaching reflects the truth of Scripture. And the precise truth of Scripture (as interpreted by the preacher) has nothing to do with gender.

The claim of pastoral authority can lead to various levels of inconsistency. For example, a man in a church that I know well removed his family's membership because the senior pastor held that women could be pastors and exercise the authority that position entails. The man was convinced that the pastor's position was not biblical, but in taking the action he did, he was disregarding the very pastoral authority that he was claiming to be defending.

Those who would argue for pastoral authority claim that Paul recognized such authority. That may be true, but times are very different today. In Paul's day, the New Testament had not even been formulated, and those who taught had real authority. But since the completion of the biblical canon, Scripture *alone* is our authority.

Does the doctrine of inerrancy affect the women's issue?

Inerrancy, much debated in recent years, has been strongly defended by conservative evangelicals and fundamentalists. Simply stated, those who hold to inerrancy believe that the Word of God is inspired and without error in the original writings. The belief has nothing whatever to do with the women's issue per se, but in an effort to discredit biblical feminists, some traditionalists have exploited this doctrine. "Biblical feminists do not believe that God has given us his word true and trustworthy," writes Susan Foh. "The biblical feminists have abandoned the biblical and historic position of the God-breathed, inerrant Scriptures."[12]

Foh's charges are simply untrue. I do not know of anyone identified as a "biblical" or "evangelical" feminist who would claim that Paul's admonitions regarding women are in actuality errors in the Bible. Biblical feminists deal with these passages straightforwardly, exegeting the Greek language with as much respect for the text as traditionalists do.

But if inerrancy is not the issue, hermeneutics, the science of biblical interpretation, is. Biblical feminists do interpret texts differently from traditionalists, but not as differently as is sometimes supposed. Very often biblical feminists are accused of diminishing Paul's admonitions to women by making them culturally conditioned. But traditionalists do the very same thing. While they take Paul's statements regarding teaching and having authority literally for all times, they do not regard his teaching on fashion in the same way. So they, too, see the Bible as being culturally conditioned.

Biblical inerrancy and hermeneutics are vitally important issues, but they should not be exploited for the purpose of discrediting a differing position.

25

On What Basis
Do Churches Today
Deny Women
Ordination?

Ordination confers authority on an individual, and if Paul does not permit a woman to have authority, she cannot be ordained—so the reasoning goes. The meaning of "authority" *(authentein* in the Greek) in 1 Timothy 2:12 has already been dealt with; suffice it to say that this little verse has granted men far more—and women far less—authority than Paul ever intended. But for many traditionalists, this verse is only a supporting clause to the real thrust of the argument. Headship is the core of the matter.

Foh makes this case, and in some respects her defense is similar to that of Roman Catholics who insist that the priest is the vicar of Christ and thus must be male. According to Foh,

God has forbidden the teaching and ruling offices in the church to women, and he has appointed the husband the head of his wife. . . . By creating the man first, God established him as the head of the human race. There is a sense in which the woman is included in the man, is represented by him, but the reverse is not true. (And so in the one-flesh union, the husband is the head; the male elders in the church can represent the whole congregation—men and women.) The male is representative by God's appointment or decision, not because men are valued more or are superior in being. Since God has given this representative ability to the male, Christ, as the head, source, and representative of the church, had to become incarnate as a man.[1]

As a Protestant whose heritage goes back to the Reformation, I bristle when I hear that only a man can represent me before God. The Reformation proclaimed, among other things, the priesthood of all believers. Foh further supports her argument with the fact that "only men could be priests and elders in the Old Testament."[2] The New Testament, however, shows us that Jesus is our High Priest. We do not need an earthly priest to intercede for us. The Holy Spirit is the one who "intercedes, with sighs too deep for words" (Rom 8:26).

Some would suggest that denying women ordination has to do with much more than a select few Scriptures where ordination is not even mentioned. Mary Stewart Van Leeuwen tells of a six-year-old boy who had a ready answer for his Sunday-school teacher's question, "What is a church council?" With no hint of humor, the little boy responded that it is "a bunch of guys who get together once or twice a month to try and figure out ways to keep girls out of their club."[3] It is a bit cynical to equate church officeholding with an all-male club, but sometimes even extreme analogies are worth pondering.

What is the biblical basis for ordination?

"There has never been, and never will be, a scriptural basis for ordination of women"—so declared Jay Van Sweden in a letter to the editor of a church magazine. To that letter Carma Van Liere responded: "In the sense that Mr. Van Sweden and the Reformed Church in America and I use the term 'ordination,' there has never been and never will be any scriptural basis for it at all."[4]

Is she right? Is there no scriptural basis for ordination as it is understood today? It may surprise many people that ordination—the issue that has caused more controversy regarding women than any other in the church today—is more a product of church tradition than of biblical precedent.

Precisely for that reason, a number of sectarian religious movements have refused to practice ordination. Among those groups are the Quakers, founded by George Fox (who disdained the "priestly" class, be it Catholic or Protestant), and the Plymouth Brethren, founded by John Nelson Darby. Darby was dogmatically opposed to ordination and anything else that set clergy apart from laity; his view is forcefully expressed in the title of his booklet "The Notion of a Clergyman: The Sin against the Holy Ghost in This Generation."

Ordination serves a purpose in our churches, but we ought to be very careful not to give the custom more status than it deserves.

How did ordination become a part of church tradition?

As the Christian church became institutionalized in the centuries following the close of the New Testament, formal ordination rites became a part of initiation into ministry. "The earliest record of an ordination rite is found in the *Apostolic Tradition of Hippolytus* (A.D. 200-220)," according to Marjorie Warkentin, in her book *Ordination: A Biblical-Historical View.* "By the fourth century there are many references to such a ceremony, particularly in the *Apostolic Constitutions.*"[5]

By the time of the Reformation, the rite of ordination had become one of the most hallowed ceremonies in the Roman Catholic Church. It was one of the "Seven Sacraments" and as such was believed "to imprint an indelible character on the soul." But among Protestants, ordination had a much lesser status. Indeed, John Wesley, an ordained Anglican, was able to say: "Give me one hundred preachers who fear nothing but sin, and desire nothing but God, and I care not a straw whether they are clergymen or laymen; such alone will shake the gates of Hell, and set up the kingdom of heaven upon earth."[6] In any discussion of ordination from a historical perspective, it is worth noting that some of the greatest preachers of all times, including Charles H. Spurgeon and Dwight L.

Moody, were not ordained. Others were ordained who probably should not have been. Billy Sunday is an example. When he applied for ordination to the Presbyterian denomination in 1903, he was unable to answer many of the theological questions asked him. He made no apologies except to say they are "too deep for me." Finally the examining board agreed to ordain him on the grounds that "God has used him to win more souls to Christ than all of us combined." Sunday apparently did not view theological knowledge as a requisite to ordination: "I don't care if you're ten miles off in theology if you're right in your heart. Nobody was ever kept out of heaven because he didn't know theology. . . . I don't know any more about theology than a jack-rabbit knows about ping-pong, but I'm on my way to glory."[7]

How does ecclesiology affect ordination?

Even if it could be established with certainty that clerical ordination was instituted in the New Testament, there would still not be agreement among the various denominations as to what ordination entails. Indeed, it is not enough to ask whether there are biblical grounds for the ordination of women. One must first determine the ecclesiastical framework out of which the question arises. What requirements does the particular church body demand for ordination? And what are the functions of the ordained individual? Only then can one seriously consider the issue of ordination—a practice that has developed through the centuries and that varies significantly from one church tradition to another.

Ordination is often associated with the biblical "laying on of hands," as in Acts 13:3, when the church leaders in Antioch "laid their hands on [Paul and Barnabas] and sent them off." This was not a formal ecclesiastical ceremony, and it is as appropriate today as it was then. I am reminded of a church service some years ago when my good friends Joan and Bud Berends were invited to come forward to have the elders lay hands on them. They had taken early retirement from their jobs in order to serve as missionaries in Kenya. How appropriate that they, like Paul and Barnabas, should have hands laid on them before leaving on their missionary journey. It was a simple act of commissioning in which ecclesiastical or gender considerations would have been utterly inappropriate.

How has women's ordination been defended historically?

The ordination of women is often perceived to be a recent phenomenon, but history records that women have been ordained since the early centuries. Women were formally ordained, generally as deaconess, though not without resistance from male clergy and laity. Indeed, a standardized prayer used during the fifth and sixth centuries defended women's ministries in an effort to silence the opposition.

> Eternal God, Father of our Lord Jesus Christ, Creator of man and woman, who didst fill Miriam and Deborah and Hannah and Huldah with the Spirit, and didst not disdain to suffer thine only-begotten Son to be born of a woman; who also in the tabernacle and the temple didst appoint women keepers of thine holy gates; look down now upon this thine handmaid who is designated to the office of deacon, and grant her the Holy Ghost, and cleanse her from all filthiness of the flesh and of the spirit, that she may worthily execute the work instructed to her, to thine honor and to the praise of thine Anointed; to whom with thee and the Holy Ghost be honor and adoration forever. Amen.[8]

A more contemporary defense of women's ordination was given by Luther Lee, a Wesleyan Methodist minister, on the occasion of Antoinette Brown's ordination in 1853. Lee emphasized that ordination does not "make a minister" or give a person the "right to preach the gospel." No ceremony could accomplish these things for Brown. "If she has not that right already, we have no power to communicate it to her." Neither does ordination qualify one for ministry, he went on to say, and it could not "confer on her any special grace for the work of the ministry." What then was the purpose of ordination? "To subscribe our testimony to the fact, that in our belief, our sister in Christ, Antoinette L. Brown, is one of the ministers of the New Covenant, authorized, qualified, and called of God to preach the gospel of his Son Jesus Christ.[9]

For most women in ministry throughout Christian history, clerical ordination conferred by a church body has not been the central issue. The opportunity simply to preach the gospel was paramount, and that is why tens of thousands of women have gone abroad or served in their homelands as "missionaries," even without official ordination. In the minds of most of them, they are "ordained" by God—if not by man.

How does the "call" of God affect ordination?

The "call" to ministry is a difficult issue to deal with; it is a subject for a book in itself. The term is not generally used in Scripture in reference to a lifetime career ministry. Rather, it is typically used in the sense of God calling someone to salvation or for a very specific duty, such as Paul's much heralded Macedonian call. However, it is important to point out that Paul was also "called to be an apostle" (1 Cor 1:2)—to serve on the front lines for Jesus Christ—and in that sense men and women, through the centuries, have identified their call to career ministries.

It is interesting that throughout church history the emphasis on the call has gone through successive phases. During the foundational stages of religious movements, the call to ministry was generally viewed as an essential component to authenticate one's ministry—especially where lay ministry was the norm and training institutions were not available. But as these movements developed and became institutionalized and clerical offices were formalized, the "call" was de-emphasized. It is not surprising, then, that women have found greater opportunities for ministry in developing religious movements than in established ones, and that they have held onto the concept of the call to authenticate their ministries.

That mentality among Christian women continues today, as is illustrated by a letter to the editor of the *Church Herald,* published by the Reformed Church in America:

> Men and women in the New Testament church who were called to preach did not go to college or seminary. They were not examined by the classis or called by the local congregation. Some of them, like Peter and the woman at the well in Samaria, were called by Jesus himself. Others were called by the Holy Spirit, like Paul, Timothy, Priscilla and Aquila, and the four daughters of Philip.
> The calling of the Holy Spirit is still necessary. I like the idea of

training people who have been called so that they will be able to address the needs of the institutional church, but there is nothing in Scripture that says the candidates for ministry must pass a course in church history since the Reformation. . . . The only thing that is required by Scripture, or ever will be, is the call of God.[10]

It is difficult to argue against this line of reasoning in light of Scripture and in light of an individual's very personal sense of call. And while it is true that ideally the "call" will be validated by a body of believers, such ought not to be seen as an absolute necessity. Many individuals who have demonstrated a powerful call to ministry have been opposed by their very own people and churches. Included among them are women whose sense of calling was so certain that nothing could deter them. Others, however, stumbled under the strain of opposition and turned away from the gospel ministry. Florence Nightingale is an example. As a young woman she sensed a call to serve God in the church, but that call was never fulfilled. Speaking of the church, she wrote, "I would have given her my head, my hand, my heart. She would not have them. She did not know what to do with them. She told me to go back and do my crochet in my mother's drawing room. 'You may go to Sunday school if you like,' she said, but she gave me no training even for that. She gave me neither work to do for her, nor education for it."[11]

Why is ordination so important to many women today?

If Spurgeon, Moody and a host of women missionaries through the generations could have extraordinary ministries without ordination, why are many women demanding that privilege today? Are they not able to have effective ministry without a certificate of ordination?

The issue is not primarily effective ministry. It is recognition—recognition by either an ecclesiastical body or a regulatory agency that they are qualified to perform certain functions of ministry.

As a Baptist, and as the senior pastor duly called by a congregation, Spurgeon did not need the rite of ordination to perform the duties normally carried out by a senior pastor. He would have gained nothing through ordination.

But today, especially in denominations that are more structured than Baptist groups, and in a society that is regulated at every turn, ordination is not only desirable but often a necessity. Unless they are ordained, women are generally ineligible for certain positions and benefits such as military chaplaincy and tax credits. Indeed, when ecclesiastical bodies refuse to ordain women, it often means that a female doing the same work as her male counterpart receives less actual remuneration, because she is not eligible for a housing allowance and other tax breaks. She may be a director of Christian education or seminary professor—professions her denomination does not regard as off-limits to women—but because she is not ordained her compensation is less than her colleagues'.

26
Has Modern Feminism Influenced the Church?

Of course modern feminism has influenced the church. It has influenced every aspect of society. The real issue is how far that influence has extended. Some people suggest that it has been momentous and charge that the church has accommodated itself to the spirit of the age. They attribute women's involvement in ministry and women's ordination to feminism.

It is true that in recent years mainline churches have opened their doors wide to women, largely as a result of feminist protest. But long before this time women were filling important leadership roles in the church. This was particularly true in evangelical and Pentecostal churches, where women had little concern about equal rights per se but felt constrained to preach the gospel by what they perceived to be a powerful "call" from God Almighty. Thus, in the past, it has been a sense of call and commitment—rather than feminist instincts—that has most influenced women to seek ministry.

What is the definition of feminism?
The term *feminism* is difficult to define, partly because there are many degrees and varieties of feminists. "The only definition of feminists that fits them all," writes Patricia Gundry, "is probably that of Alan Alda: 'A feminist is someone who believes women are people.' "[1]

Such a "definition" is thought-provoking, but it does little to clarify the meaning of the term. The obvious inference is that anyone who is not a feminist does not believe women are people. Such an insinuation is as untrue as it is unfair. There may be "nonfeminists"—or traditionalists— who do not believe women are people, but I have never encountered one. Dare I say that some of my best friends are traditionalists, and they all affirm my full humanity.

Obviously Alda and Gundry are suggesting that not all people who say they believe in the full humanity of women act as if they do, and if they acted that way they would be feminists. Gundry goes on to qualify the meaning further: "The vast majority of feminists are moderates, people who want to change laws and practices to grant full personhood to women, nothing more and nothing less. And rather than disrupt the family, most feminists want to upgrade it and make family life more satisfying for women and men. There is even a national feminist organization composed entirely of homemakers (HERA, Homemakers Equal Rights Association)."[2]

It is significant that Gundry refers to an equal rights association, because for many American feminists equal rights has been the heart of the issue. A feminist is someone who believes women ought to have equal rights with men. Give women equal rights, and the sex discrimination problem will be solved. But not all women who claim to be feminists would agree. Some argue that women are equal but *different,* and that treating them the same as men unfairly discriminates against them.

Sylvia Hewlett, an economics professor at Barnard College, found this to be true in her own personal experience and in her study of working women. In *The Lesser Life,* a book with the telling subtitle *The Myth of Women's Liberation in America,* she writes: "To ignore biological difference, as many American feminists choose to do, is to commit a double folly. In the first place, it ensures that most women will become second class citizens in the work place. For *without public support policies few women can cope with motherhood without hopelessly compromising their career goals.*"[3]

A footnote to the equal-but-different debate pertains to the issue of women's restrooms in public buildings—particularly theaters, concert halls and sports arenas. Because women are different, the argument goes, they need special privilege—more facilities—not simple equality with men. This issue came before the Pennsylvania legislature in 1990, and in December of that year, Governor Robert P. Casey signed into law the "potty parity" bill—a law that promises to shorten the lines for women in many of the state's public facilities.

So what is the definition of feminism? That depends on whose book you read, and to some extent, what year it was published. Feminists today, much more than their sisters a decade or two ago, are concerned with the differences between men and women, and they quickly recognize that simply giving women equal rights will not necessarily offer women equal opportunity in the workplace or in society at large.

How many "feminisms" are there?

One of the major difficulties in defining feminism is that it is not a monolithic outlook on life. Feminists come in many different stripes, and their agendas can often be quite different. The National Organization for Women (NOW) is representative of liberal feminism—the feminism most dominant in America, which places political equality above all other objectives. Hewlett, on the other hand, is more representative of social feminism—a European style of feminism, which emphasizes a woman's unique role in society and sees a need for special privilege for women in certain circumstances.

Marxist feminism, now on the wane, is a philosophy that views women's fight for equality as merely one aspect of a much larger battle—that age-old conflict of class struggle. Radical feminism is the brand of feminism that most frightens people. Radical feminists, according to Rosemarie Tong, "believe that neither their liberal nor their Marxist sisters have gone far enough. They argue that it is the patriarchal system that oppresses women, a system characterized by power, dominance, hierarchy, and competition, a system that cannot be reformed but only ripped out root and branch. It is not just patriarchy's legal and political structures that must be overturned; its social and cultural institutions (especially the family, the church, and the academy) must also go."[4]

A more recent development in feminism is known as postmodern feminism. "More than any other type of feminist thought," according to Tong, it "has an uneasy relationship to feminism." It has a much more positive view of women's roles in society. It recognizes that women are the "second sex"—that they are the "Other" outside of the acknowledged power-base in society. But postmodern feminists do not regard that a disadvantage. "Otherness, for all of its associations with oppression and inferiority, is much more than an oppressed, inferior condition. Rather, it is a way of being, thinking, and speaking that allows for openness, plurality, diversity, and difference."[5]

The variety of beliefs under the label of feminism ought to caution us to avoid using the term too loosely. To call someone a "feminist" is to apply a very imprecise label.

What is "Christian" or "biblical" feminism?

Christian or biblical feminism is not typically viewed as a separate category of feminism as is liberal feminism or social feminism. It is rather a philosophy of feminism that has grown out of a Christian world view or has been significantly influenced by it, and as such it would not contradict biblical truth. Some people scorn the idea of a biblical feminism, insisting that women who espouse it have accommodated themselves to the spirit of the age and in doing so have twisted biblical truth. Beverly LaHaye writes, "Within the church are 'Christian' feminists who believe that much of what is taught about women in both the Old and New Testaments is simply a result of 'cultural conditioning'—not God's specific instructions to His people."[6]

Such appraisals utterly fail to shed light on the issue. To understand biblical feminism, we must first of all recognize that it is not a position that has suddenly arisen with the advent of the modern feminist movement. From the time of Jesus and the apostle Paul the Christian faith has been a liberating force for women, and women have found this to be a great consolation. Well-reasoned books articulating Christian feminism have appeared since the Reformation. Most notable are Margaret Fell Fox's *Womens Speaking Justified,* in the seventeenth century, Catherine Booth's *Female Ministry; Or, Woman's Right to Preach the Gospel* in the late nineteenth century, and Catherine Bushnell's *God's Word for Women* and Jessie Penn-Lewis's *The Magna Charta of Woman* in the early twentieth century.

Christianity has also been found to be a liberating force in overseas mission, as the gospel confronted other religions and cultures. Christianity offered women the glorious promise that in Christ there is no longer Jew or Greek, slave or free, male or female, for all are one. This message has had a revolutionary effect on families once bound by religious systems that keep the wife a virtual slave to her domineering husband.

Biblical feminism is not simply a by-product of secular feminism. It is deeply rooted in Scripture and has been publicly articulated for centuries. In my own Christian pilgrimage, secular feminism had very little influence on my thinking. I completed my doctoral studies at a secular university during the 1970s, but somehow the feminist movement passed me by. I knew of Germaine Greer, Gloria Steinem and Betty Friedan, but I ignored them. It was not until the early 1980s, when I was teaching at Grand Rapids School of the Bible and Music, a conservative fundamentalist school, that my views began to change. I was assigned to teach a course in women's ministries, and as I began to delve into the biblical basis for women in ministry, I began to see inconsistencies and inaccuracies in what I had always been taught. This led me to a reappraisal of the whole issue and has brought me to my present understanding.

What is the definition of "traditionalism"?
The term *traditionalism* or *traditionalist* is a misnomer in that it suggests

the position comes from a belief that has been long-held and widely taught. Such is the case regarding many aspects of "traditionalism," which would place the woman in a subordinate position to the man in the home, the church and society at large. But what is often spoken of as "traditional" is not that at all. The "traditional" family, for example, is not the "nuclear four"—a mother, a father and two kids in the suburbs, with the father spending long hours away from home and the mother busying herself with school and community functions. This is a recent innovation which bears little resemblance to the family of generations and centuries ago.

The "traditional" position on women in ministry, which would deny them access to leadership, is also misleading, considering the fact that women in past generations have often had greater opportunities for ministry than they do today.

Nevertheless, "traditionalist" is the most common term used to denote someone who believes that in the home, church and society, women ought to be cast in supporting rather than lead roles. This position is bolstered by the belief that male headship was instituted at creation and extends to the end of time. The claims of traditionalism are perhaps best spelled out in a 1991 collection of essays entitled *Recovering Biblical Manhood and Womanhood.* In one of the articles, Raymond Ortlund makes a terse statement that sums up the ideology: "The woman was made *from* the man (her equality) and *for* the man (her inequality)."[7]

Traditionalists are found in every religious group, from fundamentalist Baptists and Roman Catholics to Mormons and Jehovah's Witnesses. In every instance, Scripture is deemed the basis for women's secondary status.

How does the history of feminism speak to contemporary issues?

It is interesting that churchmen in every age have perceived feminism as a threat to society in general and family life in particular. In the 1830s and 1840s, "the woman question," widely debated in England, focused on the education of women. Some "feminists" of the day were involved in founding women's colleges, and the "traditionalists" were despairing over what that would do to marriage, the home and the female sex in general. They argued that education "would encourage rivalry between the sexes, make women dissatisfied with their divinely-appointed roles in society, and disrupt the complementarity that is at the heart of the marriage relationship."[8]

A similar reaction was voiced when women began entering careers that had traditionally been limited to men. John James, a well-known nineteenth-century Congregational minister in Birmingham, England, wrote a book on female piety. He argued that women should be denied employment outside the home: "Neither reason nor Christianity invites woman to the professor's chair, or conducts her to the bar, or makes her welcome to the pulpit, or admits her to the place of ordinary magistry. . . . The Bible gives her a place of majesty and dignity in the domestic circle: That is the heart of her husband and the heart of her family. It is the female supremacy of that domain, where love, tenderness, refinement, thought and feeling preside."[9]

The debate on women took another turn in the early twentieth century, when women's suffrage and birth control became hot issues. In 1920, the editor of the Missouri Synod *Witness* warned of the ominous effects of women's suffrage: "Many women will be so busy about voting and political office that the home and children will have no attraction for them, and American mothers and children, like Christian charity, will be a rarity." Birth control was also associated with feminism: "The new woman hates children, and is madly exerting her ingenuity in frustrating the ends of matrimony."[10]

Church history is a great teacher—particularly in revealing how the do's and don'ts of one generation are sometimes reversed in the next. Today, Beverly LaHaye, who decries contemporary feminism, enthusiastically embraces the feminism of an earlier generation. A political activist herself, she fervently pleads with her followers to get involved in the political process—not only in voting but in campaigning for particular causes. In her book *The Act of Marriage,* co-authored with her husband, she devotes an entire chapter to birth control, with no admonitions against it.

27

Does Women's Equality in the Church Negatively Affect Men?

T his is a fundamental question. When women make gains, do men suffer losses? It is a legitimate fear. In our competitive capitalistic society, we naturally assume that no one can "win" unless others lose. If a woman is added to a church staff or a woman is elected to the church board, then there is one less position available for a man.

But true ministry should not be viewed in a spirit of competition. We need *more* people reaching out with the gospel, not fewer, and if there are not enough prestigious senior pastor positions to go around, something is wrong with our ministry outlook overall. The New Testament pattern of ministry did not have all the best-qualified leaders bunching up in one place, but spreading out where the gospel had not yet been preached. We need to resurrect that pattern once again.

Does opening church offices to women "feminize" the church?

"Feminism in the church is a blight that has grieved God," wrote the late John R. Rice, who went on to say, "I have no doubt that millions will go to Hell because of the unscriptural practice of women preachers." These are strong words, but Rice was convinced that women in leadership would feminize the church: "The truth is that men know that which is so plain in all nature, that God did not intend a woman to be in authority over men. It is unnatural and inefficient. Then do you wonder that in the modern sissyfied churches the average he-man will have no part?"[1]

Aside from the sexist rhetoric, did Rice have a legitimate concern about men deserting female-led churches? He is certainly not the only Christian leader to be troubled by the prospect of feminized churches. The fears, however, are not substantiated by the facts. Studies have shown that women in leadership do not scare off men. One study that surveyed Pentecostal denominations in 1936 found that Aimee Semple McPherson's Foursquare Gospel had the highest ratio of men to women (65:100), while the male-dominated Assemblies of God had a male-female ratio of only 59:100.[2]

Nor are there feminized churches on the mission field. Here is where the signs should be most obvious, since a majority of missionaries in the twentieth century have been women, and many of them have been church planters. "A woman-dominated church has not been created," writes Tim Stafford in an article entitled "Single Women: Doing the Job in Missions." He continues, "I defy anyone surveying the church in Kenya to tell me which part was planted and nurtured by women and which by men. There is no difference. You will not hear stories about women missionaries out of control, dominating men or falling into cultic or heretical teaching because of the authority they have been given. These male nightmares have proven groundless."[3]

How do women and men complement each other in ministry?

How men and women complement each other intellectually or emotionally is often a contentious issue, because almost anything that is said can be shredded to bits as some sort of sexist stereotype. Yet it is difficult to argue that there are no differences between men and women—be it innate or socially acquired. The very fact that women are usually the primary caregivers in the home and in the extended family gives them a different perspective on life from the one men would normally have—regardless of whether that makes them more "nurturing," as many social scientists would suggest. Women are typically more outwardly emotional than are men, and they often have a perceptiveness akin to a sixth sense—call it women's intuition, if you will. All this adds up to a potential difference in how a woman would handle decision making and problem solving.

For these and other reasons, there are distinct advantages in having both women and men in leadership roles in the church and in Christian organizations. When my own church—on the year of its one-hundredth anniversary—ordained its first two women elders, the flavor of the consistory meetings began to change. The women did not seek to dominate the discussions or introduce a feminist agenda, as doomsayers would have predicted. The change was more subtle. According to one of the male elders, who had previously served for two terms with men only, the women were often alert to needs and problems among families in the church of which the men were completely unaware. The two women were very actively involved in volunteer church ministry, while the majority of the male elders were too busy working at their sixty-hours-a-week jobs to take time to reach out to needy families in the congregation.

Women's voices are also essential in the professional ministries of the church and in overseas mission. The latter has been a particular concern of mine. For generations women have actively served in the front lines of mission outreach—in the trenches, so to speak—but they are rarely involved in mission strategizing and planning. The decision-makers are men. Most mission boards are headed by a male director and an all-male board. How unfortunate that they have been deprived of the female perspective, especially when dealing with religious pluralism, family matters, crosscultural communication and charting the course for partnership with nationals—issues that women have been grappling with for decades.

Has feminism caused females and males to lose their identity?

The fear that feminism will create a unisex society has been raised by traditionalists ever since the advent of the modern feminist movement. How can a woman be a woman and a man be a man, so the argument goes, if we have unisex hair salons, unisex clothing and, worst of all, unisex toilets? The consequences, they caution, may well be devastating.

The first time I used a bona fide "unisex" toilet was several years ago in the middle of the night somewhere along Interstate 75, on a trip from Michigan to Florida. Zombielike, I crawled out of the back seat of the car and asked the gas-station attendant where the restrooms were. "We've got a unisex one around the back," was his less than friendly response. That woke me up. It was during the era when Phyllis Schlafly was warning that such was the hidden agenda of feminists. I had not previously paid much attention to the debate, but suddenly the issue was one I could not ignore—or maybe I could. Minutes later, as I stumbled out of that little 4x4 space and back into the car—with my sexual identity fully intact—it occurred to me that unisex toilets were the only kind we had at home, and they served their purpose quite well.

In a more serious vein, there is genuine concern about the loss of sexual identity in this modern age. In the widely circulated "Danvers Statement," which outlines a strongly traditionalist position, the first in a list of rationales for the statement is "the widespread uncertainty and confusion in our culture regarding the complementary differences between masculinity and femininity."

How critical is this problem of gender identity? I have a feeling that it has been overdrawn. In my mind it would be a real tragedy if the line between masculinity and femininity became obliterated, but I think the anxieties of traditionalists are probably excessive. We must keep in mind that "appropriate" renditions of femininity and of masculinity are constantly changing. I was reminded of that by a 1990 *Time* article subtitled "Male Ponytails Hang in There as a Style for All Seasons." To many traditionalists, men's wearing ponytails is simply another example of loss of gender identity, but this style is not a product of a feminist unisex agenda. The ponytail was "the Founding Fathers' favorite hairstyle," as the article points out, and who could ever accuse the founding fathers of being effeminate?[4]

So before we make quick judgments about what is truly masculine and truly feminine, we must step back and look at the issue from a historical and cultural perspective. If men start wearing scarves on their heads, does it mean they have capitulated to a unisex style, or have they simply adapted a clothing style that has long been traditional for men in Arab cultures? Does increased female involvement in college athletics lead to gender "uncertainty and confusion"? I hope not. In my recent experience in teaching a high-school Sunday-school class, I found that girls are still very much girls and boys are boys. After three decades of feminism, very little seemed to have changed. The boys were more physically aggressive than the girls, and their interests focused more on professional sports than on fashion. The girls were more giggly and appeared to have closer relationships with each other than the boys did. For better or for worse, gender differences like these are still around and probably always will be.

28

How Do Women Fare in Today's Church?

There is a positive and a negative side to women's status in the church today. Many mainline denominations have dropped all gender barriers to ministry. If a woman feels called to pastoral ministry and desires to be ordained, that option is open to her. Still, in most instances she will find more difficulty obtaining a parish than her male counterpart. On the grassroots level, there is still an uneasiness in some sectors regarding a woman pastor.

In many conservative evangelical churches, on the other hand, gender barriers to ministry have increased in recent years. Some churches that once ordained women, such as the Evangelical Free Church in America, have discontinued the practice.

This is true in missions as well. Where once women had virtually unlimited opportunities to minister, they now face restrictions. "When I entered the Mission in 1954," writes one single woman missionary, "I had a great deal of freedom in giving out the Gospel. . . . As the years went by, particularly in the 1960s, I noticed that there was more hesitancy to let women lead in biblical teaching."[1]

In most instances the changes have been subtle, but some missions have actually made the new restrictions part of their policy. This has been true of the Rural Home Mission Association, which no longer permits women to serve as pastors, as once was the case—largely by default. In a policy statement, the mission conceded that women had served in these roles previously but, due in part to "clear scriptural injunctions on this matter," such ministry would not continue. "All this does not reflect in the least upon the past effectiveness of any lady workers. . . . Ladies now active need not fear hasty or ill-conceived actions."[2]

This trend is also evident in the Reformed Presbyterian Church of North America, as Faith Martin testifies: "My own denomination has not escaped this reactionary pressure. I can remember not so long ago when women took turns with men in leading the prayer meeting; that practice has been stopped in some congregations. I have observed the gradual removal of single women from our mission fields and women teachers from the Sunday school. Where will it end?" Martin answers her own question by saying, "It is too early to predict the outcome, but if the present trend continues, women will find their role even more restricted and more at odds with Scripture."[3]

Mission-board representatives will be quick to insist that, despite any such setbacks, opportunities still abound for women in evangelical ministries today, as they have in recent generations. But, as in the past, most of these opportunities involve positions that depend on deputation for financial support. Most mission or parachurch appointments require raising one's own support. There are many "blessings" involved in deputation, as administrators of these organizations quickly point out—but not so many as to prompt a voluntary switch from salary to deputation by pastors and church staff—positions generally filled by men.

How strong is the "traditionalist" movement in the church today?
Today the traditionalist movement is probably stronger in the church

than it has been at any other time in this century. There has been a backlash against the feminist movement, and traditionalists have begun to organize. It is an unfortunate circumstance, but the evangelical church is becoming more and more divided into two camps: those who oppose women in leadership positions and those who affirm them. It is difficult to escape the conflict. One of the first questions fired at candidates who are seeking pastorates is, "What is your position on women?" Even seminary professors and missionary recruits are required to take a stand.

This was not the case in years gone by. But today, with more and more women entering seminaries, the battle lines are being drawn. If we don't stop them now, so the reasoning goes, how will we ever stop them a few years down the road? In the minds of some it is almost comparable to a Gulf War rationale for stopping Saddam Hussein early.

The most conspicuous organized response to "evangelical feminism" has been what some have termed the "Danvers Movement"—a name based on the Danvers Statement, a document published several times in *Christianity Today* in 1989 by the Council on Biblical Manhood and Womanhood. The agenda for the movement is to "publish books, articles, pamphlets. Hold seminars for scholars as well as large conferences for laypersons. And pray that the Lord would bring evangelicals to consensus on these issues rather than allowing controversies and divisions."[4]

Even before the publication of the Danvers Statement, however, the traditionalist position was not without powerful influence and structure—most prominently represented by Concerned Women for America, headed by Beverly LaHaye. Membership in that organization has been estimated to number anywhere from 200,000 to 500,000 or more, but whether those statistics have any credibility is doubtful. Some years ago I wrote to the organization just to find out for myself what it stood for, and I received a membership card with my name already printed on it. In effect, that makes me a "card-carrying traditionalist."

What leading evangelical figures openly support women in ministry?
There are a number of Christian leaders who stand out for their strong support of women in the church today. Some do so at a risk, knowing

that their ministry might be in jeopardy because of their stand. Compelled by their conviction, they speak out despite the criticism.

Stuart Briscoe is one such individual. His Plymouth Brethren background and his associations with conservative Christian Bible conferences and institutions have not provided a natural platform for a "liberal" perspective toward women, but he has nevertheless taken a strong stand on the issue of women in ministry, as he himself testifies:

Frankly, as a pastor, a husband and a father, I have a dread of burying someone else's talents, particularly those bestowed on women.

Accordingly, I have tried to scrutinize my views, the place of tradition, the thrust of theology and the force of my prejudices. Repeatedly, I have come back to this fact: If the Lord has given gifts, I had better be careful about denying freedom for their exercise.

More than that, I need to ensure that the women in my life have every encouragement from me to be what He called and gifted them to be. A major part of my life must be spent . . . caring for, nurturing, encouraging and developing gifted women, because they aren't the only ones who will give account for their stewardship.

As a man in a male-oriented church, I may one day be asked about *their* gifts, too. I would like to be able to say I did considerably more than burying.

A talent is a terrible thing to waste.[5]

Another well-known evangelical leader who has given strong support to women in ministry is Tony Campolo. In his book *Twenty Hot Potatoes Christians Are Afraid to Touch,* he touches the hot potato of women preachers. He opens the chapter by telling a story of being billed as a conference speaker with a woman who was to share the ministry. He had known her previously and looked forward to the fellowship their families could have together, but the time together was filled with turmoil. "Neither of us was prepared for the barrage of criticism that came from Christian people who felt that having a woman as a preacher was unbiblical."[6]

Yes, indeed, the issue is a hot potato. But Campolo faces it head-on, willing to risk his good name among evangelicals by taking a strong stand in support of women in ministry—and women preachers in particular.

"I think that some of us are just catching on to the implications of the ways in which Christ changed the status of women," he writes. "Christendom is still keeping women from its most prestigious pulpits, but it won't be long before we will all be forced to grow up and grasp the message about women that God has been trying to declare to us for the last two thousand years."[7]

Other highly visible men who have taken a public stand in favor of biblical equality are Richard C. Halverson, longtime pastor of Fourth Presbyterian Church in Washington, D.C., and chaplain of the Senate; Stephen A. Hayner, president of InterVarsity Christian Fellowship; Bill Hybels, senior pastor of Willow Creek Community Church in Barrington, Illinois; and Arnold T. Olson, elder statesman of the Evangelical Free Church of America.

Are evangelical women effectively modeling leadership today?
The vast majority of evangelical leaders today are men. The leading ministers, evangelists, radio and television personalities, mission and parachurch executives, and seminary and Bible-college faculty members are male. The Christian world is far behind the secular world in this regard.

Yet there are women who are modeling effective leadership in evangelical circles today, and it is important for women and men to know about them and their work. Some are in pastoral positions, but very few of them have risen to positions of prominence in their denominations. Gone are the days—earlier in this century—when Aimee Semple McPherson, Mary Woodworth-Etter, Alma White and Kathryn Kuhlman were the best-known figures in their denominations. Today there are virtually no women preachers of note among evangelicals—at least in North America.

Naomi Dowdy is the senior pastor of a large church in Singapore. When she arrived in that country in 1975, it was not her intention to be a pastor. She was an evangelist, and she purposed to reach out from her headquarters there to other parts of Asia. But that was before she was invited to serve as the pastor of a tiny church of fewer than fifty that was torn by dissension. She agreed, and within four years the attendance had grown to nearly one thousand. Today the attendance at church services is over two thousand, and a theological center has been established with an enrollment of more than one hundred.[8]

Another woman who effectively serves in pastoral ministry is Luz M. Dones de Reyes, from Puerto Rico, who started with a tiny Baptist church of twelve in 1971. Within a decade it had grown to nine hundred—the largest church in the area.[9]

Apart from pastoral ministry there are women who have excelled in other types of leadership positions in a very male-dominated world. Roberta Hestenes is a prime example. Her picture was on the cover of the March 3, 1989, issue of *Christianity Today,* with the caption "Taking Charge: Once reluctant to lead, Eastern College president Roberta Hestenes blazes the trail." The article details her pilgrimage from an illegitimate child in a dysfunctional family to the president of a Christian liberal arts college and shows how her strength of character has been molded as she has successfully confronted one obstacle after another.

Although she is a committed feminist, Hestenes has resisted making demands: "I have not been an angry woman pushing on doors that people wouldn't let me go through. I've been a reluctant woman, and people have said, 'Come and help.' . . . My theme has to be gratitude. I love Christian work. The opportunity to teach the Bible, to lead people to Christ, to build a group program—I have always been very, very grateful for that."[10]

Other women who are role models in leadership positions include Rebecca Manley Pippert, an author, evangelist and Bible teacher; Marchiene Rienstra, an ordained minister, retreat speaker and author; Jill Briscoe, a pastor's wife, conference speaker, women's ministries consultant and author; and Mary Stewart Van Leeuwen, a college professor, lecturer, author and former senior editor of *Christianity Today.* They are but a few of the exemplary Christian women who have assumed important positions of leadership in contemporary evangelicalism.

Does ordination offer women equal opportunity in ministry?

Most of the mainline churches today ordain women for pastoral ministry. These churches would include some of the nation's largest denominations, such as the United Methodists, the Presbyterian Church USA, the Evangelical Lutheran Church and the United Church of Christ. But a church policy that permits women to be ordained does not ensure that women will have equal opportunity for ministry. This has been the case in the Reformed Church in America, which officially permitted women's ordination to the office of minister of the Word in 1979. Ten years later, Kristine Veldheer testified that, despite the official ruling, very little progress had been made:

> The greatest frustration for me is the benign neglect I experience within the church. There appears to be a discrepancy between the theology of the RCA and its practice. Despite the fact that women are allowed to attend the seminaries, getting that first call can be problematic. Finding places to complete supervised ministry during seminary was an experience in finding churches that would consider a woman for the task. I have not experienced any intentional negligence in seminary or in being ordained to the ministry. However, I felt strongly a lack of intentional support for women which manifests itself in selling the women short to keep peace in the ranks. . . .
>
> I see a future for women in the RCA that is cloudy at best. Although some of the pioneers are doing well within the RCA today, there appears to be a major storm brewing in the distance. This storm will either clear a path for women to enter the church as equal partners or will force a major change in which women will have to face the reality of looking elsewhere permanently to do ministry."[11]

How do parachurch organizations regard women in leadership?

It is not unusual for women to be given secondary roles in parachurch ministries, just as they are in the church. This is perplexing in many ways. Any restrictions Paul may have placed on women in Ephesus and Corinth related to the church, and even if these restrictions were still fully valid for today—as traditionalists argue they are—they would be relevant only to the church. What do Paul's restrictions have to do with someone who is working in a campus ministry that is separate from the church itself? This is one of the inconsistencies of the modern traditionalist approach. Some organizations, such as Campus Crusade for Christ, do not permit women to be campus directors. They may be associate directors, but they must always answer to a male leader. In other campus and specialized ministries where women have traditionally served on an equal basis with their male counterparts, the role of women is currently under review. Is it too cynical to suggest that in some instances this re-evaluation is prompted by "political" pressure, not by the outreach needs of these ministries?

How does Mother Teresa's ministry speak to women and men today?
Although Mother Teresa is a Roman Catholic and holds some beliefs I do not agree with, I have found her to be a tremendous inspiration in my own life, and I think she ought to challenge both women and men to reflect more seriously on the nature of ministry. Ministry is servanthood and as such ought to be performed with a profound sense of humility. I need to be reminded of that often, and one powerful reminder is the example of Mother Teresa, especially as it is related by Dee Jepson, the wife of a former U.S. senator.

On one occasion, Jepson attended a Capitol Hill luncheon in honor of the Albanian-born nun. "In came this tiny woman, even smaller than I had expected, wearing that familiar blue and white habit, over it a gray sweater that had seen many a better day. . . . As that little woman walked into the room, her bare feet in worn sandals, I saw some of the most powerful leaders in this country stand to their feet with tears in their eyes just to be in her presence."

Jepson later reflected on how Mother Teresa ought to serve as a model for true womanhood, but I think her observations are equally applicable to men:

As I listened that afternoon, I thought, "Don't forget this, Dee. Here in this little woman, who doesn't want a thing, never asked for anything for herself, never demanded anything, or shook her fist in anger, here's *real* power." It was a paradox. She has reached down into the gutter and loved and given. She has loved those the world sees as

29

How Does the Women's Issue Affect Contemporary Family Life?

S ince the time of creation, "family" has been a fluid concept. In some cultures, cousins and aunts and uncles are as much a part of the family as brothers and sisters. This is foreign to me. My father was one of eight children, and on his side of the family are cousins whom I have not seen in years and would not recognize if they were to appear at my door today. I take no pride in this, but it is a reminder that for better or worse, family life has changed from what it was only a generation or two ago, and is vastly different from most ancient or tribal cultures. My lack of extended family connections is largely a result of the migration from farms to cities in recent decades. My father had close contact with his brothers and cousins, who all lived in a farming community in northern Wisconsin, but the present generation has moved away. I have sisters in Rhode Island and Madison and brothers in Minneapolis and Columbus. None of us has made our home near Spooner, Wisconsin. I sometimes think that it would be nice if we all lived there close together. But it's only a sentimental fantasy. Times have changed, and we cannot return to a bygone era.

Today, we see another transition in family life—this one most directly involving the mother, but having significant consequences for the whole family. The loss of the "traditional" homemaking mother is painful to many. Of course there are many women today who are primarily home-makers, even as there are extended families living near each other in farming communities, but the era of the 1950s that glorified Mom in an apron has passed. The modern homemaker is more often wearing jeans and is more concerned about preparing quick, nutritious meals than baking bread and cupcakes. She is concerned about her own diet and exercise, and though she "stays at home," she is contemplating the day when she will join her sisters in the work force.

Is the "traditional" family biblical?

If a "traditional" family is a breadwinning father, a homemaking mother and two or three children—preferably living in the suburbs—it is a family that has no relevance in my own experience. But it is this "traditional" family that has been on the decline in recent years, and many Christians are deeply concerned. In light of these legitimate concerns, it is important to ask, "Is the 'traditional' family biblical?"—a question posed by Rodney Clapp in the title of an article in *Christianity Today:*

There is good reason to doubt the Gospels are as profamily as we often pretend they are. After all, in their accounts Jesus is unmarried, and his 12 disciples are either single or leave families as decisively as they drop their fishing nets. Even the boy Jesus exhibits a startling detachment from his biological family. . . . And in echoing his childhood words in the temple, he deems that his true mother, brothers, and sisters are not his biological kin, but those who do the will of God are (Mark 3:35).[1]

But if the "traditional" family is not biblical, then what is? Again, Clapp's insights are helpful. Based on his study of 1 Corinthians 7 and other passages in Paul's epistles, he concludes that our primary focus should not be the "traditional" family, but the "family of faith"—Paul's phrase in Galatians 6:10. "For the Christian, church is First Family," writes Clapp. "The biological family, though still valuable and esteemed, is Second Family. Husbands, wives, sons, and daughters are brothers and sisters in the church first and most importantly—secondly they are spouses, parents, or siblings to one another."[2]

Certainly the traditional family is to be cherished, but only in its proper place—a place that is secondary to the family of God. The words of Jesus are piercing: "Whoever loves father or mother more than me is not worthy of me; and whoever loves son or daughter more than me is not worthy of me; and whoever does not take up the cross and follow me is not worthy of me" (Mt 10:37-38).

Has feminism destroyed the family?

Feminism is often viewed with alarm in Christian circles, and the concerns are not altogether unfounded. Secular feminism (in all of its forms), like other worldly philosophies, is basically humanistic and thus does not automatically mesh with biblical teachings—especially on issues involving abortion and gay and lesbian lifestyles. But secular feminism is not as menacing as some traditionalists have insisted. Family breakdown is not simply a product of the feminist movement, as Beverly LaHaye has claimed. According to her, "The philosophy of rebellion and hatred underlying modern-day feminism has been largely responsible for the destruction of the American nuclear family."[3]

Studies now show that the so-called traditionalist lifestyle of modern America—with the breadwinning husband who is absent from the home ten to twelve hours a day—has been a significant contributor to family dysfunction. But even more surprising are the studies indicating that it is among churchgoing families that abuse is also prevalent. "I would like very much to be able to say that the statistics for wife abuse and father/daughter incest are dramatically lowered when church affiliation is taken into account—but the facts are otherwise," writes Mary Stewart Van Leeuwen. "In recent years we have discovered that although eighty per cent of sexual abuse and family violence occurs in alcoholic families, *the next highest incidence of both incest and physical abuse takes place in intact, highly religious homes."*[4]

So we must be very cautious not to blame feminism for family problems that may be more accurately ascribed to a patriarchal system. But beyond that, we ought to be willing to credit feminism for positive influences in society. Indeed, it has been feminism, more than any other influence, that has propelled fathers into a greater parenting role in recent years. Many of my friends who now have grown children regret that the age of meaningful fathering did not come earlier. One middle-aged father confessed to me that he envies his son, who has a very close and special relationship with his children—one that my friend had assumed to belong only to mothers.

Feminists have also been largely responsible for bringing long-overdue changes in the workplace—changes that we often take for granted. The concept of equal pay for equal work, for example, is now widely accepted on all levels of society. Few people would argue that we ought to go back to the time—only a decade ago—when the night cleaning woman was paid less than the third-shift male janitor for doing the same work. This, too, is a family issue. Without comparable pay, many single mothers would find it impossible to make ends meet. It is true that gross inequities between male and female still persist in the workplace, but what gains women have made in recent decades have come largely as a result of feminist protest.

What impact has "family theology" had on the church and home?
The term "family theology" has been used to describe the views of such individuals as Tim LaHaye and James Dobson, who in recent years have placed a greater emphasis on the nuclear family than was common in past generations. Dobson's radio program, "Focus on the Family," points to that emphasis by its very name. But has "family theology" gone too far?

Many mission leaders and others feel that it has. The family has become such a high priority that young couples are questioning their call to missions because of family considerations. "Family has become a god in many churches, thereby throttling many potential missionaries," writes

James Reapsome, editor of *Evangelical Missions Quarterly*. "Some churches are putting the married state, home comfort, and the education and happiness of children before world evangelization."[5]

It is difficult to argue against the married state and the happiness of children, but these were not the number-one priorities of Jesus. "Family theology" is not biblical theology.

Do mothers who work outside the home adversely affect family life?

If I had wanted to be a bit contentious in posing this question, I could have asked: "Do fathers who work outside the home adversely affect family life?" But the fact of the matter is that the question as it stands is far more applicable to family lifestyle. Historically mothers have been the "keepers of the home"—and especially among middle-class families in recent generations. The change we are seeing today, then, is one that involves a role change for women more than men.

This role change for women is positive in many respects. It often allows them a far greater sense of fulfillment than they are able to enjoy at home. This is due in part to the fact that the diverse activities of our homemaking mothers and grandmothers have been drastically reduced by modern technology. My mother's activities involved cooking meals from scratch for a husband and five kids, sewing, washing clothes with a wringer washer and hanging them out on the line, gardening, canning, and helping with the farm work when she finished all of that. In comparison, my homemaking activities are trivial. I have one child, a washer and dryer, a microwave oven, lots of prepared food and Velcro. If I did not work outside the home or write books, I might turn on the soap operas to occupy myself.

But the fact remains that the increase of mothers in the work force has resulted in a serious child-care problem, especially for preschoolers and latchkey kids. Children are our greatest assets, and we dare not neglect them. It has also meant that all too often the mother is working what has become known as the "second shift." After coming home exhausted from work, she does another eight hours of work to keep the family functioning. This is unfair not only to her but also to the family—and to the marriage relationship. How many women really desire sexual intimacies after working a second shift?

An obvious solution is greater involvement on the part of the husband. But that still does not solve the problem of child care. Parents must do much soul-searching and practical planning to work out a schedule that does not shortchange the family. If the motivation for earning two paychecks is to pay for a bigger house in the suburbs and a boat, there is a serious problem with priorities.

So if only one parent stays home or works only part-time, which one should it be? This is a question every couple must answer for themselves. I personally do not see anything wrong with what is sometimes referred to as role reversal—the husband staying home and the wife working. But for me working part-time has been ideal, and I would not trade it for anything. My home office is a perfect place to grind out books, and part-time teaching has allowed me the interaction I need with students and colleagues. I, for one, do not envy those who work away from home forty or sixty hours a week. But not all women have a choice in the matter.

A few years ago I wrote an article for *Christianity Today* on working mothers.[6] I thought it was a very balanced article that either would be ignored or would draw fire from both sides. As it turned out, however, the vast majority of negative letters came from those who strongly opposed women's working outside the home. None of these letters, however, even made an effort to address one of the central themes of my article—that many women have no choice but to work. They are single mothers or women whose husbands are unemployed or underemployed—women with no real alternative to working.

What place do singles have in a family-oriented society?

One of the most serious defects of a strong "family theology" or a "traditional family" position is that there is no valid slot for singles in the configuration. Families consist of mothers and fathers and children living together under one roof. But such does not reflect reality. Singles—including the never married, as well as the widowed, separated and divorced—make up a high percentage of our society. And even if the last two categories are deemed flawed, that still leaves a large number of singles who cannot identify with an emphasis on "family theology."

The apostle Paul, in 1 Corinthians 7, regards the single life as a high calling. This is a difficult passage for most Protestants. We view the emphasis on celibacy in the Roman Catholic church as misdirected, and we can see the problems that have resulted from it. But it is entirely possible that we have gone to the other extreme, so that subconsciously we view singles as somehow defective. Fortunately, that attitude has been changing in recent years in America, but singles in other cultures still face very negative attitudes. The only thing that will change that for Christians is a solid biblical theology on family issues.

Is it possible to be a "pro-life" feminist?

One of the most fiercely debated issues in our land today is abortion, and it is no secret that the vast majority of feminists argue for a "pro-choice" position. Some "right-to-life" proponents refer to that position as a "pro-abortion" stance, but in reality it is not. "Pro-choice" is just that—giving women the *choice* whether or not to have an abortion. For most Christians, such a choice is not an option, and the real issue has nothing to do with women's rights. The issue is the definition of life—whether a fetus is a human life. If abortion is comparable to taking another person's life, then feminism or traditionalism has nothing to do with the issue. Surely feminists do not argue that women ought to have greater license to murder than men do. The only defense of a "pro-choice" position is one that claims that abortion is more of a surgical procedure than a taking of life. With that premise, a pro-choice position is valid. But as Christians we stand on biblical principles and on a strong anti-abortion church tradition that goes back to the very first centuries of the Christian era.

To answer the question, then, there is no inconsistency in the term "pro-life feminist." But, as Ron Sider and others have pointed out, the "pro-*life*" person ought to be concerned with more than life before birth. Sometimes the "pro-life" lobbies are the most adamantly opposed to social programs that would help single mothers who have chosen to carry their babies to term rather than abort them. This is sad. As Christians we must strive to be consistent—to be "pro-life" on all levels.

Do evangelical feminists endorse homosexuality?

To suggest, as some traditionalists have, that evangelical feminists endorse homosexuality is comparable in my mind to suggesting that traditionalists are wife-beaters. Yes, there are traditionalists who are wife-beaters—some who would actually justify physical "discipline" of the wife as part of the husband's headship responsibility. I have heard more than one person make a case for that position. But I am certainly not going to suggest that traditionalists can be characterized as wife-beaters—though I may feel that their position more easily lends itself to that false interpretation than the feminist position does.

The same can be said regarding the issue of homosexuality. Except in a few isolated cases, evangelical feminists do not endorse homosexuality. From a secular sociological perspective, I can understand how an individual might be able to make the connection between homosexual rights and women's rights. But from a biblical perspective there is absolutely no connection—if indeed sex outside of marriage is sin. Arguing that because the Bible affirms women's equality with men and supports women's involvement in ministry it also affirms women in promiscuous sexual relationships would be utter nonsense.

Time and again the Bible affirms women in ministry. Nowhere—absolutely nowhere—does it affirm homosexuality. To bring the two issues together by suggesting that if we ordain women the next step will be to ordain homosexuals is utterly ridiculous. They are two separate issues, connected only by the fact that both groups of people are generally denied leadership roles in the church.

Evangelical feminists, above all others, ought to be concerned about recent efforts to reinterpret the Bible on the issue of homosexuality. Those who argue that certain passages that have traditionally been interpreted to condemn homosexuality are more properly interpreted to renounce homosexual prostitution gain little through such an argument, because they still have to deal with the many biblical texts that forbid sexual activity outside of marriage.

Having said that, however, I want to emphasize how important it is that Christians show loving concern for homosexuals and lesbians. Some years ago, while involved in a mission project, I became well acquainted with a young woman, a lesbian, who was struggling with this trial in her life. In fact, she had joined the mission project to escape her lesbian lover and to recommit herself to God. Sometimes I was put to shame by her love for God and her deep spirituality. We would pray together, and she would plead with God to take away this burden from her. Yet, in her own strength, she seemed so helpless. She would date young fellows and pretend to be interested in the opposite sex, but she confessed to me that it was all a put-on. Her only sexual feelings that were real were for other women. More than anything she wanted to be straight—to have a family and be accepted in the Christian community.

I say with great sadness that after I left the mission project, this young friend of mine found another lover—believe it or not, a married woman missionary. I feel sorry for her and thank God that I do not have sexual desires for other women. But we cannot excuse practicing homosexuals and lesbians. Celibacy is a time-honored lifestyle among Christians. Catholic priests and nuns, single missionaries and single Christians generally are expected to refrain from intimate sexual relationships. Homosexuals and lesbians can make the same commitment.

30

How Can Gender Reconciliation Best Be Attained?

I t is very unfortunate that the women's issue has created rancor and ill will among individual Christians and within denominations—so much so in some instances that the gospel of Christ has been shamed. A goal for all Christians—whether traditionalists or feminists or somewhere in between—ought to be gender reconciliation. We bring disgrace on the body of Christ when we cannot work together in love. If we win the argument or win the vote but fail to demonstrate love, we do not have the mind of Christ, as the apostle Paul reminds us: "Do nothing from selfish ambition or conceit, but in humility regard others as better than yourselves. Let each of you look not to your own interests, but to the interests of others. Let the same mind be in you that was in Christ Jesus" (Phil 2:3-4).

Paul was very straightforward when he admonished his followers to get along with each other, but he himself was well aware that certain conflicts were not easily resolved. When he and Barnabas locked horns over whether to take John Mark with them on a missionary journey, they parted ways. Barnabas took John Mark, and Paul went out with Silas, and in the end the ministry was expanded. In some instances, a parting of ways is the only viable resolution. If the members of a denomination cannot live in harmony on an issue of such magnitude as women in the church—one that affects more than half its members—it is often better to separate than to endure a prolonged period of animosity and bitterness that diminishes the testimony of the gospel.

But even in a parting of ways, love and harmony should be a primary concern—each group affirming the other in their desire to follow God's Word and in their desire to reach out with the gospel of Christ.

Why is the women's issue so difficult to deal with in the church?

Unlike "purely doctrinal" issues—if there really are such—the women's issue is one that affects Christians on a very practical level. For example, if a congregation is divided on eschatology—some holding to premillennialism and the others to amillennialism (as is the case in my own congregation)—the opposing views usually do not clash in a way that affects the week-to-week activities of the church. But the women's issue involves more than one individual's private conviction, and it cannot easily be swept under the rug. If those in the congregation who support women in church office elect women as elders, those who disagree must nevertheless live under the authority of those women in leadership. And the opposite is also true. If those who oppose women in office are in the majority, the women who wish to serve as elders may never have the opportunity to do so.

So the issue is not easily settled, unless those whose position is not in force can, with God's grace, peacefully abide by the prevailing practice. This willingness to acquiesce has in the past typically fallen to women who desire church office. In the future the burden of bowing to the will of the majority may well fall on those who oppose women in office.

Perhaps the best way for those on the two sides of the issue to make peace is to focus on issues that bring them together. I think of John Piper in this light. He is the pastor of Bethlehem Baptist Church in Minneapolis and is well known as an outspoken advocate of the traditionalist point of view. I have spoken at his church—not on women's issues, but on the subject of missions. John is an enthusiastic supporter of world missions, and his church is a powerful testimony to that commitment. It is this common concern that brings us together. Whatever our differences are on women's issues, we can come together in our common commitment to reach the world for Jesus Christ. John agrees: "Our passion is not to become the watchdogs of where women serve. Our passion is to join hands, with all God's people, *in God's way,* to 'declare his glory among the nations' (Psalm 96:3)."[1]

Is strife between the sexes inevitable?

Some people have suggested that the battle of the sexes is inevitable—that it became a fixed reality in the course of human history as a result of the "curse." Along this line Susan Foh writes,

The "curse" here [Genesis 3:16b] describes the beginning of the battle of the sexes. After the fall, the husband no longer rules easily; he must fight for his headship. The woman's desire is to control her husband (to usurp his divinely appointed headship), and he must master her, if he can. Sin has corrupted both the willing submission of the wife and the loving headship of the husband. And so, the rule of love founded in paradise is replaced by struggle, tyranny, domination, and manipulation.[2]

Apart from the fact that there was no "rule" exercised in paradise—except for the "dominion" Adam and Eve had over the animals—Foh's scenario is harsh and unduly pessimistic. History does confirm male domination, but does it as generally demonstrate that the wife's "desire" is to "control" her husband? I think not. Also, Foh does not here acknowledge history's culmination in *redemption.* The story of creation and the Fall is incomplete without the story of redemption—especially when one is speaking of the "inevitable" results of the Fall.

Through Christ's redemption, we have the power to overcome sin. This includes the sin of male domination—as well as female domination, where that applies. War between the sexes is not an inevitable. It is not a natural fallout of the debate over women's full equality in the church, the home and society at large. That has been demonstrated time and again as women and men have worked together in equal partnership in the home, the church and the secular world.

It may seem trite, but love—agape love—is the only way to overcome animosity between the sexes. The message of 1 John is powerful in this regard:

Beloved, let us love one another, because love is from God; everyone who loves is born of God and knows God. Whoever does not love does not know God, for God is love. God's love was revealed among us in this way: God sent his only Son into the world so that we might live through him. In this is love, not that we loved God but that he loved us and sent his Son to be the atoning sacrifice for our sins. Beloved, since God loved us so much, we also ought to love one another. (4:7-11)

Christianity leaves no room for the "battle of the sexes." It does not allow for the contempt for men that is often evidenced in radical feminism, nor does it allow for what seems to be an underlying hatred of women among some men—a perversion that is sometimes found inside the church. John makes his point very clear: "Those who say, 'I love God,' and hate their brothers or sisters, are liars; for those who do not love a brother or sister whom they have seen, cannot love God whom they have not seen. The commandment we have from him is this: those who love God must love their brothers and sisters also" (1 Jn 4:20-21).

Has radical feminism hindered gender reconciliation?

There is no doubt in my mind that radical feminism has had a negative effect on the debate over women's roles and has magnified the differences between men and women. As a historian, however, I am not surprised by that fact. Almost every revolutionary movement in modern times has generated radicals who carried the movement too far—often creating a backlash that ultimately erased many of the gains the initial revolutionaries had achieved.

As revolutions go, the women's movement has been mild. Perhaps because it is a *women's* movement, it has not been violent. But in its own way, it has progressed through the typical stages of a revolution. It is helpful to keep that in mind when the words of radicals are quoted as a warning against feminism. These voices are those of legitimate feminists, but they do not represent the majority.

Radical feminism, by its very nature, is anti-male. An underlying assumption of the philosophy is that "men are corrupt and women are innocent." Lesbianism, in the minds of many, is the most logical response to a degenerate patriarchal society. Indeed, some radical feminists refuse to consider heterosexuals as true feminists. In an article entitled "Lesbians in Revolt," Charlotte Bunch writes, "The very essence, definition, and nature of heterosexuality is men first."[3]

Before we totally dismiss radical feminists, however, we ought to attempt to understand their anger and to be challenged in some ways by it. Indeed, men could profit from simply listening to some of their rhetoric. Rosemarie Tong sums up one aspect of their grievances in a series of provocative questions that should cause all men to pause for reflection: " 'Look,' says the radical feminist, 'and see for yourself who has the upper hand in all heterosexual relationships—it is man.' 'For whom does prostitution exist?' 'For whom does pornography exist?' 'Who rapes whom?' 'Who harasses whom?' 'Who batters whom?' And so on."[4]

Perhaps we need to hear more male voices speaking out against the sins of their sex. Too often we hear only the sopranos and altos in the chorus of voices denouncing rape (and date rape), pornography, wife-beating and child sexual abuse. Yes, we need more male voices in the choir.

Why are women often their own worst enemies?

The feminist-traditionalist controversy is very often a conflict not between men and women but between women and women. Indeed, it is often suggested that the most vocal adversaries of feminism are women themselves. Women—believe it or not—were among the strongest opponents of women's suffrage. They truly believed that female involvement in a man's world of politics would damage the family.

Today, some of the strongest opponents of women's holding church office and women's rights in the workplace are women. There are a number of reasons for this, not the least of which is the rhetoric of radical feminists. Another contributing factor is a certain arrogance that some career women have—or have had in the past—in comparing themselves with full-time homemakers. And perhaps the opposite is sometimes true as well. Still another reason women oppose women is fear of the un-known—a sense of insecurity about the changing roles of women in society.

Suggesting that women are their own worst enemies, however, implies that women ought to be a monolithic voting bloc. Pollsters do identify trends in women's voting patterns, but these are not nearly as strongly predictable as trends reflecting racial solidarity or workers' solidarity. This lack of solidarity is the natural outcome, as some feminists have cynically pointed out, of women's "sleeping with the enemy." When labor "goes to bed with" management, there are cries of "foul," and the hard-liners demand that the marriage be severed. But the same is not expected of women, and rightly so. Women and men are brought together by common interests and intimacy that will always take precedence over gender differences.

This is how male-female relations ought to be. It is a healthy state of affairs, but there are some negative repercussions—especially for women. Until women have equality with men, their close and often dependent relationship with males contributes to their vulnerability. This vulnerability ought to draw them together in a sense of solidarity—a bond that they have with other women in an unequal society.

Is a woman's dependence on a man a sign of vulnerability?
No man—or woman—is an island. We all depend on others to help us through life. But to be too dependent is to be vulnerable, and women—married women particularly—often find themselves dangerously vulnerable in relation to the men in their lives. It is essential for women to be self-sufficient—as men generally are—or at least to have an insurance policy for self-sufficiency. Christian women are often less prepared for

independence than women in general. They very often cannot fathom the possibility that their marriage vows could be broken. They trust God and their husbands to keep their marriage intact. A good marriage certainly needs not only trust in God but also trust in one's spouse, but not the kind of blind trust that would leave the wife vulnerable.

The fact of the matter is that married Christian men do run off with other women. It happens. It may be true that the other woman is married and has left her husband high and dry, but he is almost certainly not as financially vulnerable as the abandoned wife, who may not be employed but will likely be granted custody of the children. Yes, it happens, and women ought to be prepared for the possibility—even more than they are prepared for the possibility of a husband's death. We all know more young divorcees than widows.

We have insurance for other potential catastrophes—for automobile accidents, for deaths, for fires: why not for abandonment by a husband? Glance across your congregation next Sunday. How many people do you see whose house has burned down? Yet they all have fire insurance. Glance again, and count the women whose marriages have failed. Did they have insurance—not a policy as such, but preparation for the unexpected?

No-fault divorce, once heralded by feminists, has turned out to be one of the great travesties of modern times. It often leaves women in a virtual state of poverty. Indeed, a study done in California in the 1980s indicated that after a divorce women suffer a 73 per cent decline in their living standard, while men enjoy a 42 per cent gain. How can a woman prepare herself for such a potential catastrophe? Having her own career or part-time career is certainly one option. Updating credentials and education is also crucial. Establishing a credit line and then staying out of debt (which are not mutually exclusive) also help. The bottom line is that women who depend solely on their husbands for support are most vulnerable.

Is a woman misled in thinking that her *role* affects her *worth*?
This, according to some traditionalists, is one of the most distorted mis-

conceptions of feminism. *"There is no necessary relation between personal role and personal worth,"* writes Raymond Ortlund (his italics). "Feminism denies this principle. Feminism insists that personal role and personal worth must go together, so that a limitation in role reduces or threatens personal worth. But why? What logic is there in such a claim? Why must my position dictate my significance? The world may reason that way. . . . But the world's reasoning is invalid."[5]

I do not know of anyone who would say there is a *necessary* relation between personal role and personal worth. A business executive, for example, has no greater worth than the night janitor who cleans the office. And, no one, I hope, would suggest that a *White* business executive is of greater worth than a *Black* janitor. But if someone were to suggest that "business executive" is a role limited to Caucasians, and that African-Americans cannot fill that role, then the issue of personal worth is very relevant. Why is the African-American denied a particular role solely on the basis of race? Is the African-American inferior or less worthy in some respect? Past generations have made this case, but that makes it no less abhorrent.

The case for women is no different. If *all* women are denied certain roles solely because of their gender, it does relate to their worth—to their lack of equality—just as it does for African-Americans. Ortlund may argue that the Bible upholds this lack of equality, or lack of equal worth, in regard to women, but he should not suggest that to women this should make no difference—that it should not make them feel inferior or unworthy. That reasoning has not worked with African-Americans, and it will not work with women either.

How should we respond to gender differences?
Gender difference is not simply a fact of life to be tolerated. It is the ultimate achievement of God's creative genius—a glorious reality that ought to be cause for celebration. I am absolutely convinced of that. My bias comes through not so subtly in a fictional story I wrote for another book. Here, I try to give just a glimpse of this gender difference from Eve's perspective.

Eve squinted as she opened her eyes. She felt a twinge of dizziness, but caught her balance. . . . She took a deep breath—the air pushing through her lungs for the first time. Where was she? *Who* was she? . . . Then in her momentary confusion, she was startled by a sound. . . . She turned and there he stood. His presence awesome. Everything else seemed insignificant. He was looking at her—his eyes delighting in what he saw. She suddenly became conscious of her beauty. She took her eyes off him and looked at herself. He was like her. They were the same. Yet, they were different. He was Adam. She was Eve. His taut muscular masculine body—her soft shapely feminine form complemented the other perfectly.

I know my feminist friends will criticize me for not giving Eve muscles, but face it, she was only moments old. Adam had been around for a while and had all the spare time he needed for body-building.

I treasure my femininity and am ever grateful that I differ from men in more than anatomy. I value my interaction with men, but with my women friends I experience a unique meeting of minds that is woven out of the very fabric of our femininity. "Women's ways of knowing" is an appropriate phrase that is often used by feminists, and along with that are cultural traditions that celebrate the gender differences. It is essential, in my mind, that we carry on these traditions and cultivate new ones. It is not all bad when a family upholds a tradition of three generations of women working together in the kitchen preparing Thanksgiving dinner. Nor is it a bad idea if *new* traditions are cultivated that offer the men and boys a similar intergenerational camaraderie as they carry out the clean-up afterward.

Conclusion

The women's issue is a very important one—not merely a peripheral concern that can be set aside while "essential" matters are dealt with, as it often seems to be treated. Individuals and congregations ought to be firmly convinced that they are "rightly dividing the word of truth."

This is a phrase from 2 Timothy 2:15 (King James)—a verse that I learned from childhood applies particularly to a dispensational view of Scripture. But I've since come to believe that the passage can be applied even more appropriately to the women's issue and to women in ministry. It is obvious that Paul is writing these words most specifically to Timothy, but like all Scripture it can and ought to be applied in a very personal way in our own lives. To women who are facing opposition on this matter, I can hear Paul gently instructing them how to respond to those who would deny them ministry: "Remind them of this, and warn them before God that they are to avoid wrangling over words, which does no good but only ruins those who are listening. Do your best to present yourself to God as one approved *by him,* a worker who has no need to be ashamed, rightly explaining the word of truth."

Women, as workers in the Lord's vineyard, have no need to be ashamed, but it helps if they can justify their presence by rightly explaining the word of truth. To do so they need to be able to go back to the beginning—in good dispensational style—and show how God has worked at different times and in different periods of history.

We cannot rightly explain women's roles without properly understanding how women were affected by the creation, the Fall and redemption. Beyond that, we need to understand the intertwining of the gospel and culture—and more specifically the apostle Paul's missionary principle—and how that relates to us today. Nor can we leave out the many centuries of church history and how God worked through women, despite the opposition they faced in the institutionalized church. And our understanding is not complete without a knowledge of contemporary issues relating to women.

Besides "rightly explaining the word of truth," a time-honored means of justifying one's position is to point out the fallacies of the opposing view. Here, those who would affirm women's equality and full opportunity for ministry have a considerable advantage. The traditionalist model is filled with inconsistencies—especially when an attempt is made to apply Scripture to the contemporary situation. Why, for example, is the passage on widows in 1 Timothy 5 virtually ignored, while the much shorter passage on women teaching and having authority in 1 Timothy 2 is held high as a standard? Why are women not permitted to speak or have authority, while New Testament admonitions requiring head-coverings and forbidding pearls, gold jewelry and braids are ignored? The list goes on and on.

An even more difficult problem for traditionalists is how to apply the prohibition on women's speaking and teaching in today's church. A "literal" reading of Scripture says they must be silent. But, of course, virtually no one is that literal today. Women can speak—if they just give testimonies, or sing, or ask questions in Sunday-school class (even though

Paul said they should ask their husbands at home). And they can teach, if it involves teaching children or other women—or in some cases teenagers, or a mixed class of adults (if there is at least one other adult class taught by a man, or in extreme cases if there is simply no other capable teacher). The exceptions are endless.

But the traditionalist will quickly remind us that these exceptions involve Sunday school. Paul was talking about *church*. Sunday school was not even invented until Robert Raikes came along in 1785. But again we find serious inconsistencies in the argument. What really was a New Testament *church*? Was it remotely like our formal Sunday-morning worship services? Or is it possible that it would be more analogous to a Sunday-school class or home Bible study—where women's involvement is typically not challenged by traditionalists? Some traditionalists would concede that a woman could even speak (or preach) in a Sunday-morning service, providing she is "under the authority" of the pastor or elders. So from a traditionalist perspective, there seems to be no limit on varieties of do's and don'ts for women in ministry.

The egalitarian position is not filled with these inconsistencies. It would simply say that whatever ministry is open to men is open to women. It would likewise show that Paul's apparent restrictions on women in ministry were not as stringent as they often seem to be, and that they were colored by culture—even as his restrictions on women's fashions were.

But if the egalitarian position is so consistent and biblically sound, why has it been rejected by the vast majority of Bible commentators and churchmen throughout history? That is a difficult question to answer. On other issues where there are at least two distinct positions that can be drawn from the Bible, church history is filled with debates. The debate over Calvinism and Arminianism, for example, developed centuries before Calvin and Arminius were on the scene, and it continues to this day. The Calvinists marshal all their prooftexts and logic against the Arminians, who are well prepared to take on the battle.

Why then has the women's issue been systematically ignored, despite the fact that all the logic and and the prooftexts are so readily available?

Is it possible that this simply was not a male issue, or that, worse yet, it was perceived as an anti-male issue? It is no secret that virtually all the commentators and church*men* have been *men*. Today men have taken on the issue and, along with women, have turned it into a real debate. But why, I ask myself time and time again, did it take until the 1970s before men in large numbers in all the relevant fields of study came forward to present a solid opposing case on this issue?

There were, of course, exceptions, but they were generally men who were concentrating so heavily on reaching out with the gospel that they did not take time to write commentaries or to function in high positions of church leadership.

And here is the heart of the issue. When the church is outwardly focused, energy is expended on mission and evangelism and there is little time to fight battles to keep women out of ministry. With the realization that there is far more work to be done than workers to do it, the issue of gender becomes inconsequential. The future of women in ministry, then, depends largely on the focus of the church. If our theologians and biblical scholars remain confined to their ivory towers, the future looks bleak, but if they come out and confront the needs of the world, they will quickly realize that men and women must work in true partnership to get the job done.

Notes

Introduction
[1] From Eric Marshall and Stuart Hample, eds., *Children's Letters to God* (New York: Pocket Books, 1966); quoted in *Reader's Digest,* March 1967, p. 97.

Chapter 1: Is God Masculine?
[1] Susan Foh, *Women and the Word of God: A Response to Biblical Feminism* (Grand Rapids, Mich.: Baker, 1979), p. 153.

[2] Letha Scanzoni and Nancy Hardesty, *All We're Meant to Be: A Biblical Approach to Women's Liberation* (Waco, Tex.: Word, 1974), p. 21.

[3] Paul K. Jewett, *Man As Male and Female* (Grand Rapids, Mich.: Eerdmans, 1975), p. 168.

[4] John R. Rice, *Bobbed Hair, Bossy Wives and Women Preachers* (Murfreesboro, Tenn.: Sword of the Lord, 1941), p. 68.

[5] Jay Adams, *Christian Living in the Home* (Phillipsburg, N.J.: Presbyterian & Reformed, 1972), p. 89.

Chapter 2: Is the Term *Father* for God Figurative or Literal?
[1] Jerald and Sandra Tanner, *The Changing World of Mormonism* (Chicago: Moody Press, 1980), pp. 174-80.

[2] Dorothy Clarke Wilson, *Climb Every Mountain: The Story of Granny Brand* (London: Hodder & Stoughton, 1976), p. 77.

[3] Herbert Lockyer, *All the Women of the Bible* (Grand Rapids, Mich.: Zondervan, 1985), p. 302.

[4] Quoted in James R. Edwards, "Does God Really Want to be Called 'Father'?" *Christianity Today,* 21 February 1986, p. 27.

[5] Miriam Starhawk, *Yoga Journal,* May-June 1986, p. 59.

[6]Jim Spencer, "Women Discover a Spirituality They Can Call Their Own," *Chicago Tribune,* 25 October 1987, sec. 6, pp. 1, 7.

[7]Ibid., p. 7.

Chapter 3: Do Jesus and the Holy Spirit Have Feminine Characteristics?

[1]Paul K. Jewett, *Man As Male and Female* (Grand Rapids, Mich.: Eerdmans, 1975), p. 168.

[2]Susan Foh, *Women and the Word of God: A Response to Biblical Feminism* (Grand Rapids, Mich.: Baker, 1979), p. 159.

[3]Aida Besançon Spencer, *Beyond the Curse: Women Called to Ministry* (Nashville: Thomas Nelson, 1985), p. 22.

[4]Quoted in Caroline W. Bynum, *Jesus As Mother: Studies in the Spirituality of the High Middle Ages* (Berkeley, Calif.: University of California Press, 1982), p. 114.

[5]Ibid., p. 117.

[6]Ibid., p. 131.

[7]A. B. Simpson, *When the Comforter Came* (New York: Christian Publications, 1911), pp. 11-12.

Chapter 4: Does the Creation Account Support Male Headship?

[1]James Hurley, *Man and Woman in Biblical Perspective* (Grand Rapids, Mich.: Zondervan, 1981), p. 216.

[2]Gilbert Bilezikian, *Beyond Sex Roles* (Grand Rapids, Mich.: Baker, 1985), p. 25.

[3]Evelyn Stagg and Frank Stagg, *Woman in the World of Jesus* (Philadelphia: Westminster, 1978), p. 16.

[4]Quoted in Mary Hayter, *The New Eve in Christ: The Use and Abuse of the Bible in the Debate about Women in Christ* (Grand Rapids, Mich.: Eerdmans, 1987), p. 101.

[5]John R. Rice, *Bobbed Hair, Bossy Wives and Women Preachers* (Murfreesboro, Tenn.: Sword of the Lord, 1941), p. 68.

[6]Rousas J. Rushdoony, "The Doctrine of Marriage," in *Toward Christian Marriage: A Chalcedon Study,* ed. Elizabeth Fellersen (Nutley, N.J.: Presbyterian & Reformed, 1972), p. 14.

[7]John Calvin, *Genesis* (Grand Rapids, Mich.: Eerdmans, 1948), p. 129.

[8]Raymond C. Ortlund, Jr., "Male-Female Equality and Male Headship," in *Recovering Biblical Manhood and Womanhood,* eds. John Piper and Wayne Grudem (Wheaton, Ill.: Crossway, 1991), p. 98.

[9]Hurley, *Man and Woman,* p. 173.

[10]Jane D. Douglass, "Christian Freedom: What Calvin Learned at the School of Women," *Church History* 53 (June 1984): p. 167.

[11]Ortlund, "Male-Female Equality," pp. 102, 104.

[12]Ibid., p. 102.

Chapter 5: What Was the Relationship between Adam and Eve before the Fall?
[1]Letha Scanzoni and Nancy Hardesty, *All We're Meant to Be: A Biblical Approach to Women's Liberation* (Waco, Tex.: Word, 1974), pp. 26-27.
[2]Gilbert Bilezikian, *Beyond Sex Roles* (Grand Rapids, Mich.: Baker, 1985), p. 32.
[3]Mary J. Evans, *Woman in the Bible* (Downers Grove, Ill.: InterVarsity Press, 1983), p. 17.
[4]Bilezikian, *Beyond Sex Roles,* p. 34.
[5]Evans, *Woman in the Bible,* p. 16.

Chapter 6: Was Eve Responsible for the Fall into Sin?
[1]Tertullian, *On Apparel of Women* 2:1, in *Ante-Nicene Fathers,* eds. Alexander Roberts and James Donaldson, vol. 4 (New York: Scribner's, 1925), p. 18.
[2]Quoted in Jane D. Douglass, "Christian Freedom: What Calvin Learned at the School of Women," *Church History* 53 (June 1984), p. 169.
[3]Quoted in John Winthrop, "Short Story," in *The Antinomian Controversy,* ed. David D. Hall (Middletown, Conn.: Wesleyan University Press, 1968), pp. 205-13.
[4]Martin Luther, *Luther's Commentary on Genesis,* (Grand Rapids, Mich.: Zondervan, 1958), 1:68.
[5]George H. Tavard, *Woman in Christian Tradition* (Notre Dame, Ind.: University of Notre Dame Press, 1973), p. 13.
[6]Gilbert Bilezikian, *Beyond Sex Roles* (Grand Rapids, Mich.: Baker, 1985), p. 48.
[7]Ortlund, "Male-Female Equality," p. 107.
[8]Ibid.
[9]Elisabeth Elliot, "The Essence of Femininity: A Personal Perspective," in *Recovering Biblical Manhood and Womanhood,* eds. John Piper and Wayne Grudem (Wheaton, Ill.: Crossway, 1991), pp. 398-99.
[10]James Hurley, *Man and Woman in Biblical Perspective* (Grand Rapids, Mich.: Zondervan, 1981), p. 215.

Chapter 7: What Is the Significance of the "Curse" on Adam and Eve?
[1]Gilbert Bilezikian, *Beyond Sex Roles* (Grand Rapids, Mich.: Baker, 1985), p. 55-56.
[2]Helen B. Andelin, *Fascinating Womanhood* (Santa Barbara, Calif.: Pacific, 1965), pp. 89-90.
[3]Susan Foh, *Women and the Word of God: A Response to Biblical Feminism,* (Grand Rapids, Mich.: Baker, 1979), p. 68.
[4]Gini Andrews, *Your Half of the Apple: God and the Single Girl* (Grand Rapids, Mich.: Zondervan, 1972), pp. 51-52.
[5]Phyllis Trible, "Depatriarchalizing in Biblical Interpretation," *Journal of the American Academy of Religion* 41 (March 1973): 41.

[6]Patricia Gundry, "Why We're Here," in *Women, Authority and the Bible,* eds. Alvera Mickelsen (Downers Grove, Ill.: InterVarsity Press, 1986), pp. 12-13.

[7]Foh, *Women and the Word,* p. 66.

[8]Phyllis Trible, "Good Tidings of Great Joy: Biblical Faith without Sexism," *Christianity and Crisis* 31 (4 February 1974): 14.

Chapter 8: Is the Old Testament a Patriarchal Book?

[1]Faith Martin, *Call Me Blessed: The Emerging Christian Woman* (Grand Rapids, Mich.: Eerdmans, 1988), p. 34.

[2]Denise Lardner Carmody, *Women and World Religions* (Nashville: Abingdon, 1979), pp. 97-98.

[3]Gretchen Gaebelein Hull, *Equal to Serve: Women and Men in the Church and Home* (Old Tappan, N.J.: Revell, 1987), p. 88.

[4]Martin, *Call Me Blessed,* p. 128.

[5]Joan Morris, *The Lady Was a Bishop: The Hidden History of Women with Clerical Ordination and the Jurisdiction of Bishops* (New York: Macmillan, 1973), pp. 110-11.

[6]Hull, *Equal to Serve,* p. 89.

[7]Ibid., p. 93.

[8]Herbert Lockyer, *All the Women of the Bible* (Grand Rapids, Mich.: Zondervan, 1985), pp. 13-14.

[9]Evelyn Stagg and Frank Stagg, *Woman in the World of Jesus* (Philadelphia: Westminster, 1978), p. 29.

Chapter 9: How Did God Work through Women in the Old Testament?

[1]Herbert Lockyer, *All the Women of the Bible* (Grand Rapids, Mich.: Zondervan, 1985), p. 14.

[2]Mary J. Evans, *Woman in the Bible* (Downers Grove, Ill.: InterVarsity Press, 1983), p. 31.

[3]James Hurley, *Man and Woman in Biblical Perspective* (Grand Rapids, Mich.: Zondervan, 1981), p. 154.

[4]Gilbert Bilezikian, *Beyond Sex Roles* (Grand Rapids, Mich.: Baker, 1985), p. 32.

[5]"Ms. Moses: Did a Woman Write Scripture?" *Time,* 1 October 1990, p. 80.

[6]Faith Martin, *Call Me Blessed: The Emerging Christian Woman* (Grand Rapids, Mich.: Eerdmans, 1988), p. 92.

[7]E. J. Young, "Prophets," in *The New International Dictionary of the Bible,* eds. J. D. Douglas and Merrill C. Tenney (Grand Rapids, Mich.: Zondervan, 1987), p. 824.

[8]John Calvin, *Corpus Reformatorum* 68, quoted in Evans, *Woman in the Bible,* p. 30.

[9]Aida Besançon Spenser, *Beyond the Curse: Women Called to Ministry* (Nashville: Thomas Nelson, 1985), p. 102.

[10]Bilezikian, *Beyond Sex Roles,* p. 70.

[11]John R. Rice, *Bobbed Hair, Bossy Wives and Women Preachers* (Murfreesboro, Tenn.: Sword of the Lord, 1941), p. 68.

[12]Hurley, *Man and Woman,* p. 47.

Chapter 10: What Glimpses of the Modern Woman Can Be Found in the Old Testament?

[1]Herbert Lockyer, *All the Women of the Bible* (Grand Rapids, Mich.: Zondervan, 1985), pp. 165.

[2]Gilbert Bilezikian, *Beyond Sex Roles* (Grand Rapids, Mich.: Baker, 1985), p. 75.

[3]Mary J. Evans, *Woman in the Bible* (Downers Grove, Ill.: InterVarsity Press, 1983), p. 24.

[4]Bilezikian, *Beyond Sex Roles,* p. 74.

Chapter 11: Was Jesus a Feminist?

[1]Leonard Swidler, "Jesus Was a Feminist," *Catholic World,* January 1971, p. 177.

[2]Quoted in Swidler, "Jesus Was a Feminist," p. 178.

[3]Stephen Clark, *Man and Woman in Christ* (Ann Arbor, Mich.: Servant, 1980), p. 242.

[4]Dorothy Sayers, *Are Women Human?* (Grand Rapids, Mich.: Eerdmans, 1971), p. 47.

[5]Abraham Kuyper, *Women of the New Testament* (Grand Rapids, Mich.: Zondervan, 1933), p. 32.

[6]Ruth A. Tucker and Walter L. Liefeld, *Daughters of the Church: Women and Ministry from New Testament Times to the Present* (Grand Rapids, Mich.: Zondervan, 1987), p. 33.

[7]Gilbert Bilezikian, *Beyond Sex Roles* (Grand Rapids, Mich.: Baker, 1985), p. 95.

[8]William E. Phipps, *Was Jesus Married?* (New York: Harper, 1970), p. 186.

[9]Paul K. Jewett, *Man As Male and Female* (Grand Rapids, Mich.: Eerdmans, 1975), p. 102.

[10]Marjorie Holmes, *Three from Galilee* (New York: Harper & Row, 1985), p. 186.

[11]Ibid.

[12]Jewett, *Man As Male and Female,* p. 102.

[13]James Hurley, *Man and Woman in Biblical Perspective* (Grand Rapids, Mich.: Zondervan, 1981), p. 88.

[14]Ibid.

[15]Rachel Conrad Wahlberg, *Jesus According to Women* (New York: Paulist Press, 1975), p. 15.

[16]Hurley, *Man and Woman,* p. 108.

Chapter 12: Did Jesus Offer Public Ministry to Women?

[1]James Hurley, *Man and Woman in Biblical Perspective* (Grand Rapids, Mich.: Zondervan, 1981), p. 91.

[2]Grant Osborne, "Women in Jesus' Ministry," *Westminster Theological Journal* 51 (1989): 280.

[3]Ibid.

[4]Ruth A. Tucker and Walter L. Liefeld, *Daughters of the Church: Women and Ministry from New Testament Times to the Present* (Grand Rapids, Mich.: Zondervan, 1987), p. 28.

[5]Ibid.

[6]Osborne, "Women in Jesus' Ministry," p. 269.

[7]Charles Ryrie, *The Place of Women in the Church* (Chicago: Moody Press, 1968), p. 37.

[8]Dorothy Pape, *In Search of God's Ideal Woman* (Downers Grove, Ill.: InterVarsity Press, 1976), p. 64.

[9]Evelyn Stagg and Frank Stagg, *Woman in the World of Jesus* (Philadelphia: Westminster, 1978), p. 160.

[10]Osborne, "Women in Jesus' Ministry," p. 270.

Chapter 13: What Ministry Roles Did Women Fill in the Infant Church?

[1]Dorothy Pape, *In Search of God's Ideal Woman* (Downers Grove, Ill.: InterVarsity Press, 1976), pp. 89-90.

[2]Abraham Kuyper, *Women of the New Testament* (Grand Rapids, Mich.: Zondervan, 1933), p. 86.

[3]James Hurley, *Man and Woman in Biblical Perspective* (Grand Rapids, Mich.: Zondervan, 1981), p. 120.

[4]Gilbert Bilezikian, *Beyond Sex Roles* (Grand Rapids, Mich.: Baker, 1985), p. 202.

[5]Hurley, *Man and Woman*, pp. 122-24.

[6]Aida Besançon Spencer, *Beyond the Curse: Women Called to Ministry,* (Nashville: Thomas Nelson, 1985), pp. 115-16.

[7]Dorothy Pape, *In Search of God's Ideal Woman* (Downers Grove, Ill.: InterVarsity Press, 1976), p. 216.

[8]Ibid., p. 101.

[9]John Chrysostom, *Homily on the Epistle of St. Paul the Apostle to the Romans,* p. 31, quoted in Spencer, *Beyond the Curse,* p. 101.

[10]Spencer, *Beyond the Curse,* p. 101.

[11]Pape, *In Search,* pp. 215-16.

[12]Herbert Lockyer, *All the Women of the Bible* (Grand Rapids, Mich.: Zondervan, 1985), pp. 257.

[13]Spencer, *Beyond the Curse,* pp. 109-10.

Chapter 14: Was Paul a Chauvinist?

[1]Joan Berends, "Was St. Paul a Woman-Hater?" *Church Herald,* 5 February

1971, p. 9.

[2]Pearl S. Buck, *The Exile* (New York: Reynal & Hitchcock, 1936), p. 283.

[3]Paul K. Jewett, *Man As Male and Female* (Grand Rapids, Mich.: Eerdmans, 1975), p. 112, 117.

[4]Quoted in Willard M. Swartley, *Slavery, Sabbath, War and Women: Case Issues in Biblical Interpretation* (Scottdale, Penn.: Herald, 1983), p. 150.

[5]Evelyn Stagg and Frank Stagg, *Woman in the World of Jesus* (Philadelphia: Westminster, 1978), p. 17.

[6]Sarah B. Pomeroy, *Goddesses, Whores, Wives and Slaves: Women in Classical Antiquity* (New York: Schocken, 1975), pp. 35-38, 74.

[7]Stagg and Stagg, *Woman in the World of Jesus,* pp. 155-57.

[8]Letha Scanzoni and Nancy Hardesty, *All We're Meant to Be: A Biblical Approach to Women's Liberation,* (Waco, Tex.: Word, 1974), p. 64.

[9]Richard Kroeger and Catherine Kroeger, "Sexual Identity in Corinth," *Reformed Journal* 28 (1978): 12.

[10]Patricia Gundry, *Woman Be Free! Free to Be God's Woman* (Grand Rapids, Mich.: Zondervan, 1977), pp. 64-65.

[11]Susan Foh, *Women and the Word of God: A Response to Biblical Feminism* (Grand Rapids, Mich.: Baker, 1979), p. 36.

[12]Walter L. Liefeld, "A Plural Ministry View: Your Sons and Daughters Shall Prophesy," in *Women in Ministry: Four Views,* eds. Bonnidell Clouse and Robert G. Clouse (Downers Grove, Ill.: InterVarsity Press, 1989), p. 143.

Chapter 15: Did Paul, in 1 Timothy 2, Forbid Women to Teach and Have Authority?

[1]Aida Besançon Spencer, *Beyond the Curse: Women Called to Ministry* (Nashville: Thomas Nelson, 1985), p. 75.

[2]Ibid., p. 86.

[3]Alvera Mickelsen, "An Egalitarian View: There Is Neither Male nor Female in Christ," in *Women in Ministry,* eds. Bonnidell Clouse and Robert G. Clouse (Downers Grove, Ill.: InterVarsity Press, 1989), p. 202.

[4]Philip Payne, "Oude in 1 Timothy 2:12," address given at Evangelical Theological Society meeting, Atlanta, November 1986.

[5]Walter Kaiser, "Shared Leadership," *Christianity Today,* 3 October 1986, p. 112.

[6]Robert Culver, "A Traditional View: Let Your Women Keep Silence," in *Women in Ministry,* p. 36.

[7]Walter Martin, *The Kingdom of the Cults* (Minneapolis: Bethany House, 1985), p. 250.

[8]Letha Scanzoni, *Update,* Evangelical Women's Caucus (I have been unable to recover fuller information on this citation).

[9]Spencer, *Beyond the Curse,* p. 94.

[10]D. A. Carson, " 'Silent in the Churches': On the Role of Women in 1 Corin-

thians 14:33b-36," in *Recovering Biblical Manhood and Womanhood,* eds. John Piper and Wayne Grudem (Wheaton, Ill.: Crossway, 1991), pp. 145-53.

[11]David M. Scholer, "Women in Ministry," *The Covenant Companion,* February 1984, pp. 13-14.

[12]Bruce L. Shelley, *Church History in Plain Language* (Waco, Tex.: Word, 1982), p. 55.

[13]Evelyn Stagg and Frank Stagg, *Woman in the World of Jesus* (Philadelphia: Westminster, 1978), p. 163.

[14]Walter L. Liefeld, "A Plural Ministry View: Your Sons and Daughters Shall Prophesy," in *Women in Ministry: Four Views,* eds. Bonnidell Clouse and Robert G. Clouse (Downers Grove, Ill.: InterVarsity Press, 1989), p. 138.

Chapter 16: Did the Apostles Affirm Male Headship and Wifely Submission?

[1]Alvera Mickelsen, "An Egalitarian View: There Is Neither Male nor Female in Christ," in *Women in Ministry,* eds. Bonnidell Clouse and Robert G. Clouse (Downers Grove, Ill.: InterVarsity Press, 1989), p. 193.

[2]Ibid., p. 97.

[3]Quoted in Mary J. Evans, *Woman in the Bible* (Downers Grove, Ill.: InterVarsity Press, 1983), p. 82.

[4]Ibid., p. 88.

[5]Quoted in Walter L. Liefeld, "Women, Submission and Ministry in 1 Corinthians," in *Women, Authority and the Bible,* ed. Alvera Mickelsen (Downers Grove, Ill.: InterVarsity Press, 1986), p. 145.

[6]Ibid., pp. 145-46.

[7]Leon A. Jick, "Jews," in *World Book Encyclopedia,* vol. 11 (Chicago: World Book, 1983), p. 98.

[8]Mark R. Littleton, "Submission Is for Husbands, Too," *Moody Monthly,* February 1987, pp. 34-35.

[9]Mark Twain, "The McWilliamses and the Burglar Alarm," *Harper's,* Christmas 1882 (reprint).

[10]Ruth A. Tucker and Walter L. Liefeld, *Daughters of the Church: Women and Ministry from New Testament Times to the Present* (Grand Rapids, Mich.: Zondervan, 1987), p. 452.

[11]Ibid., p. 459.

[12]James Hurley, *Man and Woman in Biblical Perspective* (Grand Rapids, Mich.: Zondervan, 1981), p. 156.

[13]Gilbert Bilezikian, *Beyond Sex Roles* (Grand Rapids, Mich.: Baker, 1985), p. 192.

[14]Faith Martin, *Call Me Blessed: The Emerging Christian Woman* (Grand Rapids, Mich.: Eerdmans, 1988), p. 46.

[15]Mary J. Evans, *Woman in the Bible* (Downers Grove, Ill.: InterVarsity Press, 1983), p. 120.

[16]Elisabeth Elliot, address to Trinity Wives' Fellowship, Trinity Evangelical Di-

vinity School, Deerfield, Ill., 15 February 1988.

Chapter 17: Did the Influence of Women Decline after the New Testament Era?
[1]F. F. Bruce, *The Spreading Flame* (Grand Rapids, Mich.: Eerdmans, 1979), pp. 160-71.
[2]Eusebius, *Ecclesiastical History* (Grand Rapids, Mich.: Baker, 1955), pp. 157-58.
[3]Ruth A. Tucker, *From Jerusalem to Irian Jaya: A Biographical History of Christian Missions* (Grand Rapids, Mich.: Zondervan, 1989), pp. 33-35.
[4]Kari Torjesen Malcolm, *Women at the Crossroads: A Path beyond Feminism and Traditionalism* (Downers Grove, Ill.: InterVarsity Press, 1982), p. 94.
[5]Ibid., pp. 94-95.
[6]Philip Schaff, *History of the Christian Church* (Grand Rapids, Mich.: Eerdmans, 1979), 2:399.
[7]Ruth A. Tucker and Walter L. Liefeld, *Daughters of the Church: Women and Ministry from New Testament Times to the Present* (Grand Rapids, Mich.: Zondervan, 1987) p. 88-91, 107-9.
[8]Kari Torjesen Malcolm, *Women at the Crossroads: A Path Beyond Feminism and Traditionalism* (Downers Grove: InterVarsity Press), p. 97.
[9]Tertullian, *On the Apparel of Women* 2:1, in *Ante-Nicene Fathers,* eds. Alexander Roberts and James Donaldson, vol. 4 (New York: Scribner's, 1925), p. 18.
[10]Quoted in Patricia Gundry, *Woman Be Free!: Free to be God's Woman* (Grand Rapids, Mich.: Zondervan, 1977), p. 22.
[11]Schaff, *History of the Christian Church,* 2:398.

Chapter 18: Did Women Find Meaningful Ministry in Medieval Catholicism?
[1]Schaff, *History of the Christian Church,* 5:399.
[2]Quoted in author, "article," in *Medieval Women's Visionary Literature,* eds. Elizabeth Alvida Petroff (New York: Oxford University Press, 1986), p. 232.
[3]Schaff, *History of the Christian Church,* 2:402.
[4]Will Durant, *Age of Faith* in History of World Civilization (New York: Simon & Schuster, 1950), p. 806.
[5]*The Letters of Abelard and Heloise,* trans. Betty Radice (New York: Penguin, 1974), pp. 98, 180.
[6]Eleanor McLaughlin, "Women, Power and the Pursuit of Holiness in Medieval Christianity," in *Women of Spirit: Female Leadership in the Jewish and Christian Traditions,* eds. Rosemary Ruether and Eleanor McLaughlin (New York: Simon & Schuster, 1979), p. 102.
[7]Don Sharkey, *The Woman Shall Conquer* (New York: All Saints Press, 1961), pp. 6-8.
[8]Ruth A. Tucker and Walter L. Liefeld, *Daughters of the Church: Women and Ministry from New Testament Times to the Present* (Grand Rapids, Mich.: Zondervan, 1987), pp. 168-69.

⁹Paul Helm, "Aquinas," in *The New International Dictionary of the Christian Church*, eds. J. D. Douglas (Grand Rapids, Mich.: Zondervan, 1974), p. 61.

¹⁰Quoted in Durant, *Age of Faith*, p. 826.

¹¹Quoted in Emma T. Healy, *Woman According to Saint Bonaventure* (New York: Georgian, 1956), p. 46.

¹²Schaff, *History of the Christian Church*, 5:500-504, 5:393.

¹³Caroline W. Bynum, *Jesus As Mother: Studies in the Spirituality of the High Middle Ages* (Berkeley: University of California Press, 1982), p. 184.

¹⁴Henry Osborn Taylor, *The Medieval Mind* (Cambridge, Mass.: Harvard University Press, 1949), pp. 470-71.

Chapter 19: Did the Reformation Open or Close Doors for Women in Ministry?

¹Quoted in Linda Eckenstein, *Woman under Monasticism* (New York: Russell & Russell, 1896), p. 471.

²Arthur F. Glasser, "One-Half the Church—and Mission," in *Women and the Ministries of Christ*, eds. Roberta Hestenes and Lois Curley (Pasadena, Calif.: Fuller Theological Seminary, 1978), p. 91.

³Quoted in Roland H. Bainton, *Women of the Reformation in Germany and Italy* (Minneapolis: Augsburg, 1971), p. 106.

⁴Martin Luther, *Luther's Commentary on Genesis* (Grand Rapids, Mich.: Zondervan, 1958), 1:68.

⁵Quoted in Jane D. Douglass, "Christian Freedom: What Calvin Learned at the School of Women," *Church History* 53 (June 1984): 162.

⁶Ruth A. Tucker and Walter L. Liefeld, *Daughters of the Church: Women and Ministry from New Testament Times to the Present* (Grand Rapids, Mich.: Zondervan, 1987), p. 189.

⁷Quoted in Roland H. Bainton, *Women of the Reformation in Germany and Italy* (Minneapolis: Augsburg, 1971), pp. 66-67, 72.

⁸"Integrating Faith and Partying," *Calvin College Cheers*, 30 March 1990, p. 3.

⁹Quoted in Bainton, *Women of the Reformation*, p. 73.

¹⁰Ibid., pp. 248-49.

Chapter 20: Why Have Women Historically Found Ministry in Sectarian Movements?

¹Joyce I. Irwin, *Womanhood in Radical Protestantism, 1525-1675* (New York: Edwin Mellen, 1979), pp. 202-3.

²Edith Deen, *Great Women of the Christian Faith* (New York: Harper & Row, 1959), pp. 164-71.

³John Wesley, *The Works of John Wesley*, vol. 1 (Grand Rapids, Mich.: Zondervan, 1959), pp. 385-86.

⁴Ruth A. Tucker, *First Ladies of the Parish: Historical Portraits of Pastors' Wives* (Grand Rapids, Mich.: Zondervan, 1988), pp. 67-68.

⁵Earl Kent Brown, *Women of Mr. Wesley's Methodism* (New York: Edwin

Mellen, 1983), pp. 105, 185-98.

[6]Patricia R. Hill, *The World Their Household: The American Woman's Foreign Mission Movement and Cultural Transformation, 1870-1920* (Ann Arbor: University of Michigan, 1985), p. 2.

[7]Flora Larsson, *My Best Men Are Women* (London: Hodder & Stoughton, 1974), pp. 17, 19-22.

[8]I. D. Steward, *The History of the Freewill Baptists,* vol. 1 (Dover, England: Freewill Baptists Printing, 1862), pp. 308-10, 318, 338, 377, 391.

[9]Jerena Lee, *Religious Experiences and Journal* (Philadelphia: Self-published, 1849), pp. 14-17.

[10]Timothy Smith, *Revivalism and Social Reform: American Protestantism on the Eve of the Civil War* (Gloucester, Mass.: Peter Smith, 1976), pp. 67-68.

Chapter 21: What Can We Learn from the Role of Women in the Non-Western Church?

[1]Quoted in Ruth A. Tucker, *Guardians of the Great Commission: The Story of Women in Modern Missions* (Grand Rapids, Mich.: Zondervan, 1988), p. 25.

[2]Ruth A. Tucker, *Stories of Faith* (Grand Rapids, Mich.: Zondervan, 1990), p. 173.

[3]Ruth A. Tucker, "The Role of Bible Women in World Evangelism," *Missiology,* April 1985, pp. 133-46.

[4]Olive Rogers, "The Ministry of Women in the Church," in *In God's Community: Essays on the Church and Its Ministry,* eds. David J. Ellis and W. Ward Gasque (Wheaton, Ill.: Harold Shaw, 1978), p. 62.

Chapter 22: How Have World Missions Affected Women's Ministries?

[1]John R. Rice, *Bobbed Hair, Bossy Wives and Women Preachers* (Murfreesboro, Tenn.: Sword of the Lord, 1941), pp. 63-64.

[2]Ruth A. Tucker, *Guardians of the Great Commission: The Story of Women in Modern Missions* (Grand Rapids, Mich.: Zondervan, 1988), p. 97.

[3]Ruth A. Tucker and Walter L. Liefeld, *Daughters of the Church: Women and Ministry from New Testament Times to the Present* (Grand Rapids, Mich.: Zondervan, 1987), pp. 300-301.

[4]Helen Barrett Montgomery, *Western Women in Eastern Lands* (New York: Macmillan, 1910), pp. 243-44.

[5]R. Pierce Beaver, *American Protestant Women in World Mission: A History of the First Feminist Movement in North America,* rev. ed. (Grand Rapids, Mich.: Eerdmans, 1980), p. 63.

[6]Jane Hunter, *The Gospel of Gentility: American Women Missionaries in Turn-of-the-Century China* (New Haven, Conn.: Yale University Press, 1984), p. 88.

[7]Elisabeth Elliot Leitch, "The Place of Women in World Missions," in *Jesus Christ: Lord of the Universe, Hope of the World,* eds. David M. Howard (Downers Grove, Ill.: InterVarsity Press, 1974), pp. 123-29.

[8]Tucker, *Guardians of the Great Commission,* p. 41.

Chapter 23: Have Women Made Gains in the Church in the Twentieth Century?
[1]Quoted in Ruth A. Tucker and Walter L. Liefeld, *Daughters of the Church: Women and Ministry from New Testament Times to the Present* (Grand Rapids, Mich.: Zondervan, 1987), p. 375.
[2]Norris Magnuson, *Salvation in the Slums: Evangelical Social Work, 1865-1920* (Grand Rapids, Mich.: Baker, 1990), pp. 112-17.
[3]Vinson Synan, *The Holiness-Pentecostal Movement in the United States* (Grand Rapids, Mich.: Eerdmans, 1971), p. 101.
[4]Tony Campolo, *Twenty Hot Potatoes Christians Are Afraid to Touch* (Waco, Tex.: Word, 1988), p. 41.
[5]Elisabeth Schüssler Fiorenza, *In Memory of Her: A Feminist Theological Reconstruction of Christian Origins* (New York: Crossroad, 1983), p. 30.

Chapter 24: Is the Bible a Sexist Volume?
[1]Quoted in Ari L. Goldman, "Catholic, Episcopal Bishops at Odds over Role of Women in Church," *Grand Rapids Press,* 2 February 1911, p. B5.
[2]Dana L. Robert, Review of *Guardians of the Great Commission,* in *International Bulletin of Missionary Research,* July 1989, pp. 135-36.
[3]F. F. Bruce, "Can the Text Be Trusted?" in *Eerdmans Handbook to the History of Christianity,* ed. Timothy Dowley (Grand Rapids, Mich.: Eerdmans, 1977), p. 93.
[4]F. F. Bruce, *Commentary on the Greek Text of Acts* (Grand Rapids, Mich.: Eerdmans, 1990), p. 374.
[5]Gordon O. Fee, *The First Epistle to the Corinthians* (Grand Rapids, Mich.: Eerdmans, 1987), pp. 700-702.
[6]Fath Martin, *Call Me Blessed: The Emerging Christian Woman* (Grand Rapids, Mich.: Eerdmans, 1988), p. 94.
[7]Richard Ostling, "Unmanning the Holy Bible," *Time,* 3 December 1980, p. 128.
[8]Ed Golder, "New Revised Bible Is Becoming a 'Best Seller,'" *Grand Rapids Press,* 19 January 1991, p. B1.
[9]Donald A. Carson, "A Review of the New Revised Standard Version," paper presented at the Annual Meeting of the Society of Biblical Literature, New Orleans, 19 November 1990.
[10]Quoted in Dorothy Pape, *In Search of God's Ideal Woman* (Downers Grove, Ill.: InterVarsity Press, 1976), p. 53.
[11]Ibid.
[12]Susan Foh, *Women and the Word of God: A Response to Biblical Feminism* (Grand Rapids, Mich.: Baker, 1979), pp. 17, 19.

Chapter 25: On What Basis Do Churches Today Deny Women Ordination?
[1]Susan Foh, *Women and the Word of God: A Response to Biblical Feminism*

(Grand Rapids, Mich.: Baker, 1979), p. 159.

2Ibid., p. 238.

3Mary Stewart Van Leeuwen, "Does God Listen to Girls?" *Reformed Journal,* June 1986, p. 7.

4Carma Van Liere in "Letters to the Editor," *Church Herald,* 19 April 1985, p. 18.

5Marjorie Warkentin, *Ordination: A Biblical-Historical View* (Grand Rapids, Mich.: Eerdmans, 1982), p. 41.

6Ibid., pp. 52, 75-76.

7Douglas Frank, *Less Than Conquerors: How Evangelicals Entered the Twentieth Century* (Grand Rapids, Mich.: Eerdmans, 1986), p. 181.

8Quoted in Philip Schaff, *History of the Christian Church* (Grand Rapids, Mich.: Eerdmans, 1979), 3:260-61.

9Nancy A. Hardesty, *Women Called to Witness: Evangelical Feminism in the Nineteenth Century* (Nashville: Abingdon, 1984), pp. 96-97.

10Van Liere, "Letters," p. 18.

11Quoted in Marlys Taege, *And God Gave Women Talents!* (St. Louis: Concordia, 1978), p. 90.

Chapter 26: Has Modern Feminism Influenced the Church?

1Patricia Gundry, "Point, Counterpoint," *Grand Rapids Press,* 23 February 1985, p. D2.

2Ibid.

3Sylvia Ann Hewlett, *A Lesser Life: The Myth of Women's Liberation in America* (New York: Morrow, 1986), pp. 142, 147.

4Rosemary Tong, *Feminist Thought: A Comprehensive Introduction* (San Francisco: Westview, 1989), pp. 2-3.

5Ibid., p. 219.

6Beverly LaHaye, *The Restless Woman* (Grand Rapids, Mich.: Zondervan, 1984), p. 33.

7Raymond C. Ortlund, "Male-Female Equality and Male Headship," in *Recovering Biblical Manhood and Womanhood,* eds. John Piper and Wayne Grudem (Wheaton, Ill.: Crossway, 1991), p. 102.

8Dale A. Johnson, *Women in English Religion, 1700-1925* (New York: Edwin Mellen, 1983), p. 122.

9Ibid., pp. 129-30.

10Quoted in Alan Graebner, "Birth Control and the Lutherans," in *Women in American Religion,* ed. Janet Wilson James (Philadelphia: University of Pennsylvania Press, 1980), p. 231.

Chapter 27: Does Women's Equality in the Church Negatively Affect Men?

1John R. Rice, *Bobbed Hair, Bossy Wives and Women Preachers* (Murfreesboro, Tenn.: Sword of the Lord, 1941), pp. 59, 65.

2Ruth A. Tucker and Walter L. Liefeld, *Daughters of the Church: Women and*

Ministry from New Testament Times to the Present (Grand Rapids, Mich.: Zondervan, 1987), p. 368.

[3]Tim Stafford, "Single Women: Doing the Job in Missions," *Leadership,* Fall 1982, p. 86.

[4]Emily Mitchell, "The Long and Short of It," *Time,* 10 December 1990, p. 74.

Chapter 28: How Do Women Fare in Today's Church?
[1]June Salstrom, letter to Ruth A. Tucker, 24 February 1983.

[2]Rural Home Mission Association, "Statement Regarding the Status and Relationship of the R.H.M.A. and Its Lady Workers," adopted by the board of directors in January 1961.

[3]Faith Martin, *Call Me Blessed: The Emerging Christian Woman* (Grand Rapids, Mich.: Eerdmans, 1988), p. 13.

[4]"Danvers Statement," in *Recovering Biblical Manhood and Womanhood,* eds. John Piper and Wayne Grudem (Wheaton, Ill.: Crossway, 1991), pp. 469-70.

[5]Stuart Briscoe, "The Biblical Woman: We've Buried a Treasure," *Moody Monthly,* February 1983, p. 6.

[6]Tony Campolo, *Twenty Hot Potatoes Christians Are Afraid to Touch* (Waco, Tex.: Word, 1988), p. 35.

[7]Ibid., p. 42.

[8]Alvera Mickelsen, "An Egalitarian View: There Is Neither Male nor Female in Christ," in *Women in Ministry,* eds. Bonnidell Clouse and Robert G. Clouse (Downers Grove, Ill.: InterVarsity Press, 1989), p. 176.

[9]Ibid.

[10]Quoted in Tim Stafford, "Roberta Hestenes: Taking Charge," *Christianity Today,* 3 March 1989, pp. 17-22.

[11]Kristine Veldheer, "Finding Affirmation," *Church Herald,* June 1989, p. 29.

[12]Dee Jepson, *Women Beyond Equal Rights* (Waco, Tex.: Word, 1984), pp. 52-53.

Chapter 29: How Does the Women's Issue Affect Contemporary Family Life?
[1]Rodney Clapp, "Is the 'Traditional' Family Biblical?" *Christianity Today,* 16 September 1988, p. 24.

[2]Ibid., p. 26.

[3]Beverly LaHaye, *The Restless Woman* (Grand Rapids, Mich.: Zondervan, 1984), p. 89.

[4]Mary Stewart Van Leeuwen, *Gender and Grace: Love, Work and Parenting in a Changing World* (Downers Grove, Ill.: InterVarsity Press, 1989), pp. 119, 170.

[5]James Reapsome, "What's Holding Up World Evangelization? The Church Itself," *Evangelical Missions Quarterly,* April 1988, p. 119.

[6]Ruth A. Tucker, "Working Mothers," *Christianity Today,* 15 July 1988, pp. 17-21.

Chapter 30: How Can Gender Reconciliation Best Be Attained?

[1]John Piper and Wayne Grudem, "An Overview of Central Concerns: Questions and Answers," in *Recovering Biblical Manhood and Womanhood,* eds. John Piper and Wayne Grudem (Wheaton, Ill.: Crossway, 1991), p. 77.

[2]Susan Foh, *Women and the Word of God: A Response to Biblical Feminism* (Grand Rapids, Mich.: Baker, 1979), p. 69.

[3]Rosemarie Tong, *Feminist Thought: A Comprehensive Introduction* (San Francisco: Westview Press, 1989.), pp. 123, 134.

[4]Ibid., p. 111.

[5]Raymond C. Ortlund, Jr., "Male-Female Equality and Male Headship," in *RecoveringBiblical Manhood and Womanhood,* eds. John Piper and Wayne Grudem (Wheaton, Ill.: Crossway, 1991), pp. 111-12.

Bibliography

Andelin, Helen B. *Fascinating Womanhood*. Santa Barbara, Calif.: Pacific Press, 1965.

Andrews, Gini. *Your Half of the Apple: God and the Single Girl*. Grand Rapids, Mich.: Zondervan, 1972.

Bainton, Roland H. *Women of the Reformation in Germany and Italy*. Minneapolis: Augsburg, 1971.

Beaver, R. Pierce. *American Protestant Women in World Mission: A History of the First Feminist Movement in North America,* revised edition. Grand Rapids, Mich.: Eerdmans, 1980.

Bilezikian, Gilbert. *Beyond Sex Roles: What the Bible Says About a Woman's Place in Church and Family*. Grand Rapids, Mich.: Baker, 1985

Bristow, John Temple. *What Paul Really Said About Women: An Apostle's Liberating Views on Equality in Marriage, Leadership, and Love*. San Francisco: HarperCollins, 1988.

Brown, Earl Kent. *Women of Mr. Wesley's Methodism*. New York: Edwin Mellen, 1983.

Bynum, Caroline W. *Jesus as Mother: Studies in the Spirituality of the High Middle Ages*. Berkeley: University of California Press, 1982.

Carmody, Denise Lardner. *Women and World Religions*. Nashville: Abingdon, 1979.

Clouse, Bonnidell, and Clouse, Robert G., eds. *Women in Ministry: Four Views*. Downers Grove, Ill.: InterVarsity, 1989.

Dean, Edith. *Great Women of the Christian Faith*. New York: Harper & Row, 1959.

Eckenstein, Lina. *Woman Under Monasticism*. New York: Russell and Russell, 1896.

Evans, Mary J. *Woman in the Bible*. Downers Grove, Ill.: InterVarsity, 1983.

Fiorenza, Elisabeth Schüssler. *In Memory of Her: A Feminist Theological Reconstruction of Christian Origins*. New York: Crossroad, 1983.

Foh, Susan. *Women and the Word of God: A Response to Biblical Feminism*. Grand Rapids, Mich.: Baker, 1979.

_____ . *Heirs Together: Mutual Submission in Marriage*. Grand Rapids, Mich.: Zondervan, 1980.

Gundry, Patricia. *Woman Be Free!: Free to be God's Woman*. Grand Rapids, Mich.: Zondervan, 1977.

Hardesty, Nancy A. *Women Called to Witness: Evangelical Feminism in the 19th Century*. Nashville: Abingdon, 1984.

Hassey, Janette. *No Time For Silence: Evangelical Women in Public Ministry Around the Turn of the Century*. Grand Rapids, Mich.: Zondervan, 1986.

Hayter, Mary. *The New Eve in Christ: The Use and Abuse of the Bible in the Debate about Women in Christ*. Grand Rapids, Mich.: Eerdmans, 1987.

Healy, Emma T. *Woman According to Saint Bonaventure*. New York: Georgian, 1956.

Hestenes, Roberta, and Curley, Lois, eds. *Women and the Ministries of Christ*. Pasadena,

Calif.: Fuller Theological Seminary, 1978.

Hewlett, Sylvia Ann. *A Lesser Life: The Myth of Women's Liberation in America.* New York: Morrow, 1986.

Hill, Patricia R. *The World Their Household: The American Woman's Foreign Mission Movement and Cultural Transformation, 1870-1920.* Ann Arbor, Mich.: University of Michigan, 1985.

Hull, Gretchen Gaebelein. *Equal to Serve: Women and Men in the Church and Home.* Old Tappan, N.J.: Fleming H. Revell, 1987.

Hunter, Jane. *The Gospel of Gentility: American Women Missionaries in Turn-of-the-Century China.* New Haven, Conn.: Yale, 1984.

Hurley, James B. *Man and Woman in Biblical Perspective.* Grand Rapids, Mich.: Zondervan, 1981.

Irwin, Joyce I. *Womanhood in Radical Protestantism, 1525-1675.* New York: Edwin Mellen, 1979.

James, Janet Wilson, ed. *Women in American Religion.* Philadelphia: University of Pennsylvania Press, 1980.

Jepson, Dee. *Women Beyond Equal Rights.* Waco, Tex.: Word Books, 1984.

Jewett, Paul K. *Man as Male and Female.* Grand Rapids, Mich.: Eerdmans, 1975.

Johnson, Dale A. *Women in English Religion, 1700-1925.* New York: Edwin Mellen Press, 1983.

Kuyper, Abraham. *Women of the New Testament.* Grand Rapids, Mich.: Zondervan, 1933.

LaHaye, Beverly. *The Restless Woman.* Grand Rapids, Mich.: Zondervan, 1984.

Larsson, Flora. *My Best Men Are Women.* London: Hodder and Stoughton, 1974.

Lockyer, Herbert. *All the Women of the Bible.* Grand Rapids, Mich.: Zondervan, 1985.

Magnuson, Norris. *Salvation in the Slums: Evangelical Social Work, 1865-1920.* Grand Rapids, Mich.: Baker, 1990.

Malcolm, Kari Torjesen. *Women at the Crossroads: A Path Beyond Feminism and Traditionalism.* Downers Grove: InterVarsity, 1982.

Martin, Faith. *Call Me Blessed: The Emerging Christian Woman.* Grand Rapids, Mich.: Eerdmans, 1988.

Mickelsen, Alvera, ed. *Women, Authority and the Bible.* Downers Grove, Ill.: InterVarsity, 1986.

Montgomery, Helen Barrett. *Western Women in Eastern Lands.* New York: Macmillan, 1910.

Morris, Joan. *The Lady Was a Bishop: The Hidden History of Women with Clerical Ordination and the Jurisdiction of Bishops.* New York: Macmillan, 1973.

Pape, Dorothy. *In Search of God's Ideal Woman.* Downers Grove, Ill.: InterVarsity, 1976.

Petroff, Elizabeth Alvida, ed. *Medieval Women's Visionary Literature.* New York: Oxford University, 1986.

Phipps, William E. *Was Jesus Married?* New York: Harper, 1970.

Piper, John, and Grudem, Wayne, eds., *Recovering Biblical Manhood and Womanhood.* Wheaton, Ill.: Crossway Books, 1991.

Pomeroy, Sarah B. *Goddesses, Whores, Wives, and Slaves: Women in Classical Antiquity.* New York: Schocken, 1975.

Rice, John R. *Bobbed Hair, Bossy Wives, and Women Preachers.* Murfreesboro, Tenn.: Sword of the Lord Publishers, 1941.

Ruether, Rosemary Radford, and Keller, Rosemary Skinner, eds. *Women and Religion in*

America. San Francisco: Harper & Row, 1981.

Ruether, Rosemary, and McLaughlin, Eleanor, eds. *Women of Spirit: Female Leadership in the Jewish and Christian Traditions*. 3 vols. New York: Simon and Schuster, 1979.

Ryrie, Charles. *The Place of Women in the Church*. Chicago: Moody, 1968.

Sayers, Dorothy. *Are Women Human?* Grand Rapids, Mich.: Eerdmans, 1971.

Scanzoni, Letha, and Hardesty, Nancy. *All We're Meant to Be: A Biblical Approach to Women's Liberation*. Waco, Tex.: Word, 1974.

Schaef, Anne Wilson. *Women's Reality: An Emerging Female System in a White Male Society*. San Francisco: Harper & Row, 1981.

Sharkey, Don. *The Woman Shall Conquer*. New York: All Saints Press, 1961.

Spencer, Aida Besançon. *Beyond the Curse: Women Called to Ministry*. Nashville: Thomas Nelson, 1985.

Stagg, Evelyn and Frank. *Woman in the World of Jesus*. Philadelphia: Westminster Press, 1978.

Swartley, Willard M. *Slavery, Sabbath, War, and Women: Case Issues in Biblical Interpretation*. Scottdale, Penn.: Herald Press, 1983.

Tavard, George H. *Woman in Christian Tradition*. Notre Dame: University of Notre Dame Press, 1973.

Tong, Rosemarie. *Feminist Thought: A Comprehensive Introduction*. San Francisco: Westview Press, 1989.

Trible, Phyllis. *Texts of Terror: Literary-Feminist Readings of Biblical Narratives*. Philadelphia: Fortress, 1984.

Tucker, Ruth A., and Liefeld, Walter L. *Daughters of the Church: Women and Ministry from New Testament Times to the Present*. Grand Rapids, Mich.: Zondervan, 1987.

Tucker, Ruth A. *First Ladies of the Parish: Historical Portraits of Pastors' Wives*. Grand Rapids, Mich.: Zondervan, 1988.

_____. *Guardians of the Great Commission: The Story of Women in Modern Missions*. Grand Rapids, Mich.: Zondervan, 1988.

Van Leeuwen, Mary Stewart. *Gender and Grace: Love, Work & Parenting in a Changing World*. Downers Grove, Ill.: InterVarsity Press, 1989.

Wahlberg, Rachel Conrad. *Jesus According to a Woman*. New York: Paulist Press, 1975.

Subject and Name Index